# The Gadianton Robbers

# The Gadianton Robbers

The second great challenge to the
Christian Nephite Nation 52BC—AD34

Troy J. Smith

CFI
An imprint of Cedar Fort, Inc.
Springville, Utah

ISBN 13: 978-1-4621-3705-3

Published by CFI, an imprint of Cedar Fort, Inc.
2373 W. 700 S., Springville, UT, 84663
Distributed by Cedar Fort, Inc., www.cedarfort.com

Library of Congress Control Number: 2020937945

Cover design by Wesley Wheeler


Printed in the United States of America

10 9 8 7 6 5 4 3 2 1

Printed on acid-free paper

# CONTENTS

## Part 3: The Second Period of the Robbers (12 BC–AD 25)



## Part 4: The People of the Lord—A New Period of Persecution (AD 25–AD 34)

# PREFACE

LIKE THE FIRST BOOK by this author, this book focuses upon Nephite history during the pre-Christ period in the land of Zarahemla. Whereas the first book, *The War Against Christianity* contains an in-depth study of the Amalickiah and Ammoron War, the first great challenge to Christian Nephites, this book looks closely at the rise and fall of the Gadianton robbers, the second great challenge. The robbers were first established in 52 BC and were completely destroyed in the Great Storm of AD 34. The account of the robbers of Gadianton begins in Helaman 1 and ends in 3 Nephi 10.

In Mormon's perspective, the eighty-sixth year of the Gadianton robbers ended almost 300 years before he was born. His account, which he took from the large plates of Nephi, has been carefully organized into a chronological and geographical narrative. Like *The War Against Christianity*, this book contains frequent references to previous times and events throughout the pre-Christ period, which provide a deeper understanding of the larger pagan conspiracy that continually afflicted the Nephites throughout the entire Zarahemla period.

By placing the Book of Mormon under such close scrutiny, it becomes more and more apparent that it is a true history of the inhabitants of the Western Hemisphere. Its scriptural form, internal complexity, and factual consistency eliminate even the possibility that it could have been conceived and written by an uneducated boy from upstate New York in the early 1800s.

The Book of Mormon speaks eloquently for its own authenticity and emphatically confirms the veracity of the final dispensation of the gospel in the fulness of times. It is the one thing that anyone on earth today can hold in their hands, which firmly supports our belief that Joseph Smith was a true prophet of God. It is a testament to the visitation of the Angel Moroni as a true event, for it was Moroni who delivered the plates of Mormon into Joseph's hands.

# INTRODUCTION

THIS BOOK CONCERNS THE second great challenge to the Nephites—the Gadianton robbers. It is divided into five parts. Part 1 looks briefly at the growth and development of the Nephite culture through time as their lands began to spread across the Western Hemisphere. Various topics are considered, which lead into and parallel the time of the robbers. Though they are peripheral to the primary subject of this book, they provide the cultural and geographical setting of the world in which the robbers lived.

Part 2 considers the rise of the Gadianton robbers in 52 BC and the first period of their insidious attack against Christianity and against the freedom enjoyed by the Nephites. It ends with their complete disbandment in 17 BC as a result of Nephi's drought.[1] Part 3 concerns the re-establishment of the robbers five years later in 12 BC—the resumption of their criminal activities, and the resulting war which ended with their second defeat and termination in AD 25. Part 4 then addresses a third period of rebellion, which began in AD 29. In effect, this third period was simply another period of the robbers, though it is not identified as such in the Book of Mormon. It ended with the Great Storm of AD 34, which took place immediately before the Savior's appearance to the Nephites. Part 5 presents the author's perspective of Nephite geography during the period of the robbers (52 BC to AD 34).

# PART 1

# THE EXPANDING WORLD OF THE NEPHITES

CHAPTER 1.1

# THE NEPHITE FRONTIER

SIMILAR TO THE UNITED States of America between AD 1600 and 1900, the Nephites had a frontier of wilderness that bordered the lands of their habitation for much of their history. In the history of the United States, the frontier was an entirely positive experience that has been theorized by some to be the primary reason for the phenomenal success in becoming one of the greatest nations of all time.[2]

For the Nephites, the frontier was a multifaceted experience that affected them differently at various times, as they slowly moved outward from the land of Nephi—their first region of habitation. In some periods, the frontier impeded growth. In other periods, it was the primary stimulus for geographical expansion through migration.

Throughout the approximately 390 years in the land of Nephi (589 to *ca.* 200 BC), the Nephites were hemmed in on the north by an extensive wilderness that prevented them from moving outward and expanding their settlement areas. During that period, they did not see the wilderness as desirable land for habitation. Though it was a frontier, it did not invite them to inhabit or even to fully explore its hidden recesses, so forbidding it was to the potential Nephite explorer. Perhaps Nephite hunters frequently slipped quietly into the outer margins of its deep forests in search of game,[3] but for habitation, it was not considered prime real estate. Thus, it was a barrier to growth and development, rather than a magnet that stimulated expansion.

In about 200 BC, the prophet-king Mosiah I, heeding the voice of God, led as many as would follow out of the land of Nephi into the heart of the wilderness. Ultimately they reached the Sidon River, where they discovered the people of Zarahemla. Whereas they had previously lived at the edge of the wilderness, the settlement on the banks of the Sidon was located in its very center. Thereafter, this natural impediment, which for a time would pose a barrier to Lamanite aggression, would also, for more than a hundred years, prevent the Nephites from moving outward from the new heartland region along the Sidon River to neighboring regions.

## SETTLEMENT OF ZARAHEMLA FROM SEA TO SEA

Shortly before 92 BC, the outlying wilderness regions, which surrounded the core region, finally became a viable frontier—largely a result of religious contention in Zarahemla[4] but also a consequence of population growth.[5] At that time, the Nephites began settling outlying regions, both westward and eastward from the Sidon River.[6] Some of the cities established at that time are described in Alma's missionary journey throughout the land of Zarahemla, as found in Alma 5–15.

By 83 BC, the city of Gideon was established to the east of the Sidon.[7] On the west, several cities were founded by 82 BC, including Melek, Ammonihah, Aaron, Sidom, and Noah.[8] The exact time of their establishment is not given, though it occurred sometime between 92 BC to 82 BC—a rather small window of time. Establishment of cities is not a primary subject in the Book of Mormon, and cities are referenced only as they played a role in the Book of Mormon account.

At some time prior to 81 BC, the Nephites established the city of Manti by the headwaters of the Sidon, at the southern border of the heartland region.[9] Between 72 and 68 BC, walls were built around existing perimeter cities,[10] and many additional walled cities were established along the southern and eastern borders of Nephite lands[11] under the direction of Chief Captain Moroni.[12] Under the protection of the fortified cities, the southern border was extended all the way from the east sea to the west sea.

Most of the cities placed at or along the periphery of Nephite lands were established by Moroni's army to defend Nephite lands against Lamanite invasion. However, some were established by dissenters to plan the overthrow of the Nephite government in secret and to more easily take advantage of Lamanite military resources. Actually, only two perimeter cities are identified in the Book of Mormon text as being established by dissenters—the cities of Ammonihah[13] and Antionum.[14]

Ammonihah was a city of the Nehors,[15] and Antionum was a city of the Zoramites.[16] The two groups represent the two pagan religions that waged war against the Christian Nephites throughout the pre-Christ period. The Order of the Nehors and the Zoramites were initially considered in *The War Against Christianity*.[17]

Because cities are mentioned only as they affected the Book of Mormon account, the reference in Mosiah 27:6 to "large cities and villages in all quarters of the land" likely refers primarily to unknown cities in what later came to be known as "the most capital parts of the land."[18] That is the specific region being settled during the period immediately following 92 BC, which extended outward in all four compass directions from the city of Zarahemla.[19] It likely refers to cities on all sides of the city of Zarahemla, which are never mentioned in the Book of Mormon, some within less than a day's travel.

As an example, in the account of Coriantumr's march, cities lying northward of the city of Zarahemla are referenced, though not by name.[20] Those cities would otherwise be completely unknown to the reader. Through time and population growth, such cities would eventually expand outward to border directly upon one another. Accordingly, by the time of the prophet Mormon almost 500 years later, the "whole face of the land [of Zarahemla] had become covered with buildings."[21]

## THE PIVOTAL EFFECT OF THE AMALICKIAH AND AMMORON WAR

The Amalickiah and Ammoron conflict, which continued without pause in one form or another from 73 through 61 BC, had a profound effect on the Nephite frontier.[22] Through the establishment of fortified Nephite cities around the entire perimeter of Zarahemla to defend against the Lamanite attack, the frontier within the land southward in effect disappeared. At the same time, the new frontier—the land northward—began to loom larger than life. Both phenomena were direct outcomes of the war, as described below:

1. Moroni's line of peripheral defensive cities encouraged the settlement of outlying regions. Ultimately, these fortified cities completely surrounded Nephite lands. Lamanites were driven southward from all Nephite lands into the land of Nephi, and Nephites were invited to move into those lands.[23] Because of the security provided, the people were enabled to freely move outward. The immediate result was the dispersion of the people of Nephi throughout the greater land of Zarahemla. Furthermore, extensive military operations were conducted throughout the seemingly endless war. As a result, the Nephites became thoroughly familiar with the land southward.

2. By defending the narrow neck of land—which prevented Amalickiah from taking control of the land northward—the Nephites would always "have a country whither they might flee, according to their desires."[24] The high priority placed upon protecting the narrow neck throughout the war brought the land northward to the direct attention of the Nephites. It was only natural that many would become captivated and drawn toward the uninhabited land.

Thus, it can be said that as a direct consequence of the Amalickiah and Ammoron war, the frontier in the land southward was eliminated, and the new frontier in the land northward was brought into sharp focus.

CHAPTER 1.2

# MULEKITES: NO INTEREST IN RETURNING TO THE LAND NORTHWARD

Throughout the period of the kings in Zarahemla (*ca.* 200–92 BC), there seems to have been no inclination by the Mulekites (people of Zarahemla) to deliberately strike out in a northward direction. This is in sharp contrast to the reaction of a small number of the Nephites who came with Mosiah into the wilderness. Immediately, and in spite of obvious danger, the people of Zeniff returned to the land of Nephi, where the Nephites had lived for almost 400 years. The Lamanite king deceptively allowed them to occupy the lands of Lehi-Nephi and Shilom.[25] There, they struggled continually against Lamanite oppression for three generations before fleeing once more to the land of Zarahemla.[26]

Similar to the Nephites, the Mulekites had lived in the land northward for more than 350 years. They did not voice any desire, however, to return to their former homeland during that first period in Zarahemla. Their lack of interest in the land northward is considered as follows:

It is apparent that the people of Zarahemla had migrated into the land southward only shortly before they were encountered by the Nephites. Such a limited timeframe becomes quite obvious when the following information is considered:

1. When discovered by the Nephites, the extent of Mulekite habitation was limited exclusively to their settlement on the Sidon River.
2. Many Mulekites bore Jaredite names and practiced Jaredite idolatry. According to the book of Ether, Jaredite lands of habitation were limited exclusively to the land northward. Whereas "the whole face of the land northward was covered

with inhabitants," the Jaredites "did preserve the land southward for a wilderness, to get game."[27]

3. The people of Zarahemla did not depart from the land northward until the death of Coriantumr, the only survivor of the Jaredite wars.[28] Apparently, they encountered him when he wandered back from the Hill Ramah to his home in the land of Moron, for it was near the Mulekite land of Desolation.[29] They remained with Coriantumr until the time of his death nine months later.[30]

## THE JAREDITE WAR OF EXTINCTION

The Mulekite departure into the land southward had come on the heels of the final Jaredite War. Therefore, there were no other inhabitants across the entire face of the land northward to affect their decision. Of course, there was the stench of millions of Jaredites, whose bodies littered the entire landscape.[31]

Looking even more closely, the reason for the Mulekite disinterest in the land northward becomes abundantly clear. Unlike the land of Nephi, the land northward was completely uninhabitable at that time in more ways than one. Not only were the Jaredite lands uninhabitable, but also the Mulekite lands, which neighbored on the south. In this vein, specific references are made to other environmental conditions, which made it impossible for them to return to their previous homeland. In fact, such conditions are blatantly obvious, simply in the names they gave to their former homeland and the adjacent region to the south—Desolation and Bountiful.[32]

A couple of scriptures seem to indicate the land northward was ravaged by drought from *ca.* 200 BC, when the Mulekites fled southward, until 55 BC, when the Nephite northward migrations began. They are considered as follows:

1. Alma 22:31 refers to the land of Bountiful as a wilderness "filled with all manner of wild animals of every kind, a part of which had come from the land northward for food."[33]

   This is not a reference to the Heth disaster[34]—a drought that had taken place more than a thousand years earlier. In all likelihood, the people of Zarahemla knew nothing about a purely Jaredite event that occurred a half a millennium before they arrived in the Western Hemisphere. They were, however, personally aware of similar conditions, which had caused the wild animals to flee into the land southward shortly before they found it necessary to do the same.

2. Helaman 3:6 contains a reference to the land northward, the former land of the Jaredites, as a land without timber in 55 BC "because of the many inhabitants who had before inherited the land."[35] Verses 10 and 11 of the same chapter inform us that due to the scarcity of timber, the Nephites "did send forth much by the way of shipping" from the land southward to assist the Nephite emigrants in building their cities, "both of wood and of cement."

   Such a lack of trees would not have resulted purely from the great number of Jaredites who had inhabited the land. When the Nephites first journeyed forth into the land northward, approximately 150 years had passed since the Jaredite destruction—enough time in a climate conducive to the growth of vegetation for a new generation of forest to have sprung forth and grown to maximum maturity, completely enshrouding the former cities in a sea of vegetation—as observed by the Spaniards in the sixteenth century.

It is concluded that the above scriptures refer to a long and decimating drought following the Jaredite destruction. Apparently, it began in the days of Shiblom, at the beginning of the terminal civil war and continued throughout the war.[36] Following the war, it drove the Mulekites from the land northward, and then continued largely throughout the following 150–year period.

Without doubt, the great drought had been exacerbated by the pestilence associated with millions of unburied bodies, as well as the related stench that drifted into the neighboring land of the Mulekites. Likely, the combined effect of all of these factors required the people of Zarahemla to migrate in mass into the land southward, following Coriantumr's death.[37]

While the Book of Mormon does not provide a definite exclusionary statement concerning Nephite travel into the land northward during the first 150–year period in Zarahemla, no migrations are recorded until 55 BC.[38] The only reference to habitation within the land northward prior to 55 BC concerns the Jaredites and the Mulekites prior to their migration into the land southward.[39]

Such conditions would not eliminate the possibility of Nephite northward explorations on a small scale prior to 55 BC. A number of Nephites inhabited the land of Bountiful between 77 and 55 BC.[40] Some settled next to the land of Desolation and were therefore poised at the gateway to a completely uninhabited land. Certainly they had the opportunity to explore at least the southern reaches of the land northward. Perhaps there was an occasional excursion to observe current conditions within the land northward.

The immediate purpose of habitation in Bountiful at that time was to prevent the Lamanites from moving into the land northward. There is no doubt, however, that the lure of the unknown would have enticed them to venture further. Through time, the Nephites became more and more intrigued to inhabit the land beyond the narrow neck, as word of the captivating land northward filtered across the land of Zarahemla.

CHAPTER 1.3

# THE LAND NORTHWARD—A MAGNET FOR DISSENTERS

In 68 BC, Morianton became the first dissenter to consider the land northward as a potential refuge from Nephite justice—instead of the usual option of fleeing to the land of Nephi. He thus attempted to flee with his followers from the city of Morianton into the land northward. Due to the volatile atmosphere generated by the current war, it was very bad timing on his part. The establishment of the fortified city of Morianton was a part of Moroni's defensive preparations for Amalickiah's next attack.[41]

In Moroni's perspective, Morianton's departure into the land northward would weaken Nephite defenses in two ways. First, an important defensive location along the east coast would be lost. Second, it could potentially enable Amalickiah to take control of the narrow neck of land—especially if he should receive assistance from Morianton. Throughout the remainder of the war, Moroni's standard with respect to the narrow neck would remain the exclusion of dissenters as well as Lamanites.[42]

Such blanket exclusion was indeed a direct result of the war. With Amalickiah threatening to invade from the south, Moroni was sensitive to keeping the narrow neck open. Should the tide of the ensuing war turn against them, the Nephites must be able to flee into the land northward.

## MORIANTON'S PURPOSES

Prior to Morianton, Nephite dissenters had always been content to direct their discontent through Lamanite channels in the land of Nephi. Lamanite support always provided an immediate opportunity to attempt the overthrow of the Nephite government. Morianton's northward flight may have been chosen, simply because the Lamanites were currently involved in Amalickiah's war against Zarahemla, with whom Morianton was not affiliated. It is also possible that he was not interested in warring against Zarahemla, but had simply fled from Moroni's justice to a safe, remote location, not currently engaged in warfare.[43]

## THE IMPORTANCE OF CONTROLLING THE NARROW NECK OF LAND

If one should have any reservations that perhaps Moroni's high priority of guarding the narrow neck[44] was self-imposed, or resulted purely from Morianton's attempted flight, then Amalickiah's first objective in the war should be considered. In 67 BC, he attacked along the eastern seaboard with the ultimate goal of taking control of the narrow neck. It was only after his death that the Lamanites "abandoned their design in marching into the land northward."[45]

Looking further, it can be seen in all of the various moves and countermoves surrounding the war along the eastern seaboard that the narrow neck was the center of attention. Indeed, it appears that even before Amalickiah began his campaign along the east coast, Moroni knew of his intentions with respect to the land northward. The related events, which both preceded and followed the Lamanite attack on the city of Moroni at the southeastern border of Jershon, are listed as follows:

1. In preparation for the impending war, Moroni sent a Nephite army in 72 BC to drive all Lamanites scattered along the east coast southward across the southern border of Jershon into the land of Nephi.[46]
2. Between 72 and 67 BC, Moroni established a line of six cities along the coast of Jershon, extending from Moroni on the south to Mulek on the north.
3. In 68 BC, Morianton led his people from their city on Jershon's east coast toward the land northward.[47]
4. Moroni sent Teancum with an army to pursue them and prevent them from going into the land northward. The people of Morianton were overtaken at the narrow neck. Morianton was slain, and his people were brought back to their city in Jershon.[48]
5. In 67 BC, Amalickiah attacked and took control of the city of Moroni. He continued northward, capturing all six coastal

cities in Jershon. His ultimate goal was to "take possession of the land Bountiful, and also the land northward."[49]

6. As the year 67 BC came to a close, Amalickiah's assault was halted by Teancum's army at the city of Bountiful, which bordered the land of Jershon on the north.

In retrospect, it seems that for each of the above actions, whether by Nephites, Lamanites, or dissenters, a primary focus was the narrow neck of land and the land northward. This underlying scenario would not be so apparent if the Lamanites did not drive the Nephites entirely from the land southward only thirty-two years later. In the offensive of 35 BC,[50] it was only at the narrow neck of land that the Nephites were able to halt the advancing Lamanite army and begin to retake the four regional lands of Zarahemla, from which they had been driven.[51]

It is thus concluded that throughout the Amalickiah and Ammoron War, and for the first time ever, the narrow neck of land at Desolation was considered by Nephite military leaders as being critical to their survival, and by Lamanites and Nephite dissenters as being critical to their success.

It would then be a focal point of the war of 35 BC. The same is true of the final series of wars that took place during Mormon's day, in which the narrow neck served as a crucial element in the Nephite defense of the land northward.[52] It drives home the point that the narrow pass was the only land route between the land southward and the land northward.

CHAPTER 1.4

# NEPHITE MIGRATIONS INTO THE LAND NORTHWARD

THE YEAR 55 BC was a pivotal year in Nephite history. With the single exception of the party of forty-three men sent in 121 BC by King Limhi in search of Zarahemla,[53] there is no record in the Book of Mormon of any Nephite traveling into the land northward prior to that year. Even that lone venture was purely accidental—or rather providential, considering the importance of their discovery to the Book of Mormon account.[54]

After departing from highland Nephi, Limhi's party had become lost in the wilderness. Their wanderings carried them through the narrow neck of land,[55] past the former land of the Mulekites (Desolation), and into the land of the Jaredites. The fact that they traveled in the wrong direction attests to a complete lack of geographical understanding of the great wilderness and of the location of Zarahemla, in relation to Nephi. The great distance they traveled before finding the ruins of the Jaredite culture within the land northward attests to the sheer desperation of the people of Limhi.[56]

## LET THE MIGRATIONS BEGIN!

Following the conclusion of the Amalickiah and Ammoron War, in the atmosphere of peace and spiritual revival[57] that settled upon the Nephites between 60 and 55 BC, an unprecedented permissiveness developed with respect to northward migration that had not existed during the war. At the same time, the obsession to migrate into the uninhabited land northward continued to grow. As a result, the northward migrations began in 55 BC with a flurry. In that year alone, many thousands of Nephites journeyed northward, both by land and by sea.

The first expedition was by land, consisting of 5,400 men who departed from the land of Zarahemla with their wives and children.[58]

The total number of people, therefore, which made up the first party, was likely 15,000–20,000, a very large number to kick off the new era. In the same year, additional immigrants boarded an "exceedingly large ship" built by a man named Hagoth and sailed northward.[59]

During the following year, Hagoth built other ships, which also set sail with many additional people and supplies. The first ship returned for another load of passengers, then again departed for the land northward. Throughout 54 BC, the migrations continued, and "many people . . . went forth into the land northward."[60] Long-range commerce quickly developed between the two regions as provisions, lumber, and other products were shipped into the land northward.[61] The Nephite migrations likely continued from year to year. In 46 BC, however, "there were an exceedingly great many," most if not all of which were dissenters, "who departed out of the land of Zarahemla, and went forth unto the land northward to inherit the land."[62]

In some cases, the Nephites remaining in Zarahemla had no idea where the colonists had gone, for they never heard of them again.[63] It might therefore be concluded that a very large scale movement had begun into a relatively vast region. The account of these immigrants into the land northward is not included in the Book of Mormon, and with the exception of the city of Jacobugath[64] near the end of the pre-Christ period, no specific information is given concerning their cities or activities in the land northward.[65] Some general information is provided, such as the manner of their building construction.[66] For the most part, however, the land northward is treated as another world, far removed from Nephite awareness in the land of Zarahemla where the Book of Mormon account was being written at that time.

In 55 BC, and for the first time in the Nephite era, the land northward became a part of the Nephite world. In the context of the northward migrations, Helaman 3:8 refers to ocean on all sides of Nephite lands. The passage likely reflects Mormon's understanding of the fully expanded Nephite geography after the Nephite migrations began, not the understanding of the Nephites at the time of the first migrations. The Nephites thus became actively engaged in migrations that would carry them northward to the full extent and the far reaches of Nephite geography.

At that point in time (with respect to both Nephite and Lamanite habitation), the cultures that emanated from Lehi were no longer restricted by wilderness or by the narrow neck of land. Following the extensive and widespread settlement of the land northward, as outlined in Helaman 3:3–8, there were no more frontiers.

## TRAVEL RESTRAINTS INTO THE LAND NORTHWARD—IMPOSED BY THE WAR

Considering Moroni's rigid control of the narrow neck, it is surprising to see that in 55 BC—only five years after the conclusion of the Amalickiah and Ammoron War—such control was nonexistent. At that time, all Nephites were suddenly allowed to migrate into the land northward, without restriction. The only logical conclusion is that the restrictions had been dictated exclusively by the war. When it ended, normal peacetime freedoms were restored to Nephite citizens, including the freedom to migrate into the land northward.

## OPEN BORDERS—NEGATIVE CONSEQUENCES FOR THE NEPHITES

The unrestricted migrations of 55 BC would have negative consequences for the Nephites. During the war of 35 BC, when they were driven to the narrow neck of land, they seemingly had no idea that they were surrounded by enemies—Lamanites and robbers on the south and dissenters on the north who had previously migrated from Zarahemla into the land northward. The full extent of pagan power and control within the land northward does not become evident in the Book of Mormon, however, until twelve years later in 23 BC.

During the period from 29 to 23 BC, Nephi had served a six-year mission in the land northward with his brother, Lehi.[67] He then returned to his home in the city of Zarahemla: "For he had been forth among the people who were in the land northward, and did preach the word of God unto them, and did prophesy many things unto them; And they did reject all his words, insomuch that he could not stay among them, but returned again unto the land of his nativity."[68] Thus, in 23 BC, there was no place of safety within the land northward for the servants of Jesus Christ, notwithstanding the missions of Nephi, Lehi, and "many of the Lamanites."[69]

## THE LORD'S INTERVENTION

As a result of letting dissenters freely pass through the narrow neck of land, the very situation developed that the Nephites had tried to avoid. In a short period of time, they would become surrounded by their enemies—Lamanites and robbers on the south and robbers on the north. As will be seen, this ominous situation would be significantly reduced by the Lord through the miraculous conversion of the entire Lamanite nation to the gospel of Jesus Christ in 30 BC.[70] Then, only eighty-eight years later, such wickedness and evil would come to a sudden and violent end when the wicked were all destroyed in the Great Storm of AD 34.

# PART 2

## THE FIRST PERIOD OF THE GADIANTON ROBBERS (52 BC–17 BC)

# INTRODUCTION

As addressed in *The War Against Christianity* in considerable detail, the Amalickiah and Ammoron War, which took place from 73 through 61 BC, was the first of three great challenges to the Christian Nephite nation. A subsequent attack took place ten years later under the direction of Tubaloth,[71] the son of Ammoron, who had ascended to the Lamanite throne following his father's death.[72] In 51 BC, Tubaloth sent an army headed by a man named Coriantumr[73] into the Nephite heartland to attack the capital city of Zarahemla. After taking control of the city, Coriantumr continued his march "through the most capital parts of the land . . . taking possession of many cities and of many strongholds."[74]

Ultimately, Coriantumr's army was surrounded by multiple Nephite armies.[75] In the battle that followed, Coriantumr was slain, and his army was defeated. Afterward, the Lamanite warriors were allowed to "depart out of the land in peace."[76]

## CORIANTUMR'S ATTACK—THE END OF THE FIRST GREAT CHALLENGE, OR THE BEGINNING OF THE SECOND?

Looking at Coriantumr's attack in connection with the Amalickiah and Ammoron War, it might be considered in some ways to have represented the final battle of the previous war. Indeed, it may seem apparent that Tubaloth was simply trying to accomplish what his father had tried unsuccessfully to do, using a different mode of attack.

However, as concluded in *The War Against Christianity*, Chapter 2.6, Coriantumr's foray into the Nephite heartland was not a resumption of the Amalickiah and Ammoron War. Rather, it was the beginning of the Gadianton Robber Conspiracy—the second great challenge to the existence of the Christian Nephite nation. Accordingly, Part 2 begins with Kishkumen's assassination of Pahoran II in 52 BC. It then incorporates Coriantumr's attack during 51 BC, as part of the developing sequence of events engineered by the robbers. It continues in 50 BC with the rise of Gadianton to the preeminent position of leadership in Kishkumen's band, followed by Kishkumen's attempt to assassinate Helaman.

## PAGAN CULTS WITHIN THE GADIANTON ROBBERS

As first considered in the Introduction to Part 2 of *The War Against Christianity*, it seems that pagan cults did not become established among the Nephites while they occupied the highlands of Nephi, but appeared only after the people of Mosiah arrived in the land of Zarahemla.[77] It was further noted in Chapter 2.1 of the previous book[78] that the people of Zarahemla (the Mulekites) were an idolatrous people when they were discovered by the people of Mosiah.[79] At that time, the people of Zarahemla "denied the being of their Creator,"[80] Jesus Christ,[81] which implies much more than simply having no knowledge of the Savior. Instead, it implies a hostility toward the gospel as taught by the people of Mosiah—one of the effects of idolatry.

The conclusion that idolatry was first introduced to the Nephites by the Mulekites is based upon the specific pagan source of contention[82] within the lands of both Zarahemla[83] and Nephi during the initial period following the *ca.* 200 BC arrival of the Nephites in Zarahemla. The Jaredite Order of Nehor[84] was the first of only two pagan religions ever identified in the Lamanite land of Nephi, the Zoramite religion[85] being the second. Both came to the Lamanites from the land of Zarahemla. In succession, the two religions would plague the Nephites throughout the remainder of the pre-Christ era, leading to the Savior's appearance in Bountiful.[86] Their influence would end suddenly and emphatically, however, in the Great Storm of AD 34.[87]

In the Book of Mormon, idolatry and secret combinations always go hand in hand. It was no different with respect to the Gadianton robbers, who first arose during the period from 52 to 50 BC.[88] Without doubt, idolatry was a primary element of the robber organization from the beginning, though it is not revealed until 25 BC.[89] As will be shown, the robbers were simply a new phase of the pagan conspiracy to destroy the Christian Nephite culture.

## MODERN-DAY GADIANTON ROBBERS

Throughout Nephite history in the land of Zarahemla, the ultimate goal of Gadianton robbers, and of Nephite dissenters in general, was the elimination of Christianity. Today, the same forces are coming into alignment throughout the world. Christians familiar with the Book of Mormon and the Bible believe that we are in the last days prior to the coming of Christ. They are fully aware that, as prophesied, the war against Christianity is being waged today and has recently begun to escalate rapidly.

In reading the account of the Gadianton robbers, which ended suddenly with the Great Storm of AD 34, readers will frequently see many parallels in the events currently taking place. They will see similarities in the glaring duplicity that can be observed today in the actions of those who openly and unashamedly are enemies of Christ, His followers, and the nation of Israel. As with the Gadianton robbers, the current conspiracy to destroy Christianity is likely much more well developed than what can be seen on the surface.

The parties involved in this present-day conspiracy are many, all of which adhere to one indulgence or another. They can frequently be identified by their disdain for biblical principles of righteousness. At the same time, they profess to hold the high ground of morality, accepting everyone on their own merits, and allowing everyone the freedom to engage in any perversion that is desired. There is no acknowledgment of the laws of God and no apparent expectation of the judgment that awaits the incorrigible and unrepentant sinner when life comes to an end.

The conspirators seek to destroy the Christian underpinnings of the United States of America. The conspiracy extends throughout the Western Hemisphere, however, and throughout the world. This explains the current obsession for one world government, which conceivably would enable the worldwide elimination of Christianity.

By faith, Christians understand that God will not be mocked and that "the wages of sin is death."[90] Though we do not always rise to the high standard of our Savior, Jesus Christ, we must constantly be striving to improve. We must seek the guidance of the Holy Spirit in everything we do. We trust that God will protect His people and that all of the designs of the enemies of God will end suddenly when the Savior returns in great power.

The subject of conspiratorial dissent in the present day, as it compares with the Gadianton robbers, is a subject in and of itself. It cannot be adequately presented in this book. It will be left to the reader to make comparisons between the Book of Mormon account and the present day.

# CHAPTER 2.1

# THE SECOND GENERATION OF DISSENT—THE RISE OF THE GADIANTON ROBBERS

IN *THE WAR AGAINST Christianity*, no mention was made of separating dissent into two periods. However, upon the death of the third chief judge, Pahoran I,[91] two distinctly new tactics of deceit were put into practice by the dissenters, which drastically raised the bar and began to produce alarming results among the Nephites:

1. The pretended acceptance of the political system of judges. Previously, the dissenters had openly sought to return to monarchy. It was a relatively subtle approach that would create a facade of civility and adherence to existing laws.
2. The establishment of the Gadianton robbers, whose most basic and rigid tenet was secrecy.

The Christians, in their openness and forthrightness, would immediately be set at a much greater disadvantage, for pagan deception and secrecy would rise to a new standard.

## POLITICAL CONTENTION FOLLOWING THE DEATH OF CHIEF JUDGE PAHORAN

Unlike all previous instances of dissent after 91 BC, Nephite dissidents took advantage of Pahoran's death in 52 BC to seek political control within the system of judges. When Pahoran had first ascended to the judgment seat in 68 BC, they were still obsessed with the abolishment of the free government and the establishment of a king.[92] This they tried to accomplish, first with Pahoran's support,[93] and when that failed,[94] by the voice of the people.[95]

In 52 BC, having supposedly accepted the system of judges, they placed their support behind one of the legitimate candidates, a man who apparently shared their political goals, and likely their religion as well. Any of Pahoran's sons was a rightful heir to the judgment seat, and three of them—Pahoran II, Pacumeni, and Paanchi—commenced political campaigns, seeking the support of the people. When the election was held, Pahoran II "was appointed by the voice of the people to be chief judge and a governor over the people of Nephi."[96]

## PAANCHI INCITES A REBELLION

Following the election, Pacumeni graciously accepted the results and acknowledged his brother Pahoran as the winner—obviously the correct ethical reaction, showing respect for the electoral process. Paanchi, however, was angry over the results. He began to incite his supporters to rise up and overthrow the free government, as Amlici had done in 87 BC,[97] and as Amalickiah had done in 73 BC.[98]

Paanchi's reaction reflected the spirit of the political faction that supported him. Need one wonder concerning the identity of this party? Without doubt, it was comprised of king-men, who had supported Amalickiah when he dissented from the Church.[99] Later, they had supported him when he came down against the Nephites.[100] Near the end of the war, they had supported Pachus in his unholy alliance with Ammoron.[101] The last attempted coup had taken place only ten years prior to 52 BC. The philosophy of this faction, or party, was to seek power by any means, and if all else failed, to overthrow the government through violence.

## A NEW POLITICAL PLAN OF ATTACK FOR THE PAGAN DISSIDENTS

As considered in *The War Against Christianity*,[102] during the period of the judges, political ambition in the land of Zarahemla was not illegal when it was channeled within the framework of the law. Several times throughout the period, pagan dissenters tried to take advantage of the new democratic process to leapfrog into power. Their compliance with the rule of law was not a reflection of their new respect for it. It merely afforded them a legitimate avenue to the control of government.

In every case between 91 and 51 BC, pagan attempts to seize power through the political process were frustrated. In each case, when they failed to gain the support of the people, they resorted to warfare, rising up in an attempt to overthrow the government and eliminate the law that initially in each instance they pretended to respect and uphold.

For a number of years, their obsession was to return to monarchy.[103] Amalickiah's quest for power was a slight variation from the others, in that he first sought leadership within the Church, rather than in the political arena. But when that failed, the focus of his animosity was directed at the government as he tried to violently rise to power. From the very beginning, however, his goal was to be the king of the Nephites.[104] That he would first seek status within the Church in his attempt to achieve power alludes to the great influence of Christianity among the Nephites at that time.

Following the utter failure of the king-men during the Amalickiah and Ammoron War, and the severe consequences they suffered,[105] the dissenters were likely looking for a way to rise to power within the system of judges. At that time, Paanchi provided them with a more acceptable approach. Through Paanchi, a rightful heir to the judgment seat,[106] they were given an avenue of opportunity to achieve power without returning to monarchy.

## THE TEMPORARY ABANDONMENT OF OPENLY ANARCHIST GOALS

As a result, the king-men obsession to violently overthrow the Nephite government and establish a king was abandoned in 30 BC. For the next sixty years, the dissenters would focus their efforts upon working politically within the system of judges.[107] On the surface, their sudden penchant for working within the present form of government may appear to have been a matter of necessity.

At the end of the Amalickiah and Ammoron War, it had been considered a treasonable offense to openly petition for the abolishment of the free government and return to monarchy.[108] Likely, the king-men support of Amalickiah and Ammoron[109] was the final straw for the Nephites with respect to any attempt to return to monarchy. Thereafter, any talk of reestablishing a king would have been viewed as an assault against Nephite freedom, as provided by the democratic system of judges Mosiah II had established in 91 BC.[110]

On the other hand, the dissenters had never considered the consequences of their subversive actions throughout the entire period of dissent prior to 30 BC. In their lust for power, they were always willing to quickly resort to warfare. Furthermore, more than thirty years had passed, and a new generation of Nephites had arisen, which had not witnessed the previous atrocities. It is thus concluded that the new mode of attack was not undertaken as a matter of necessity. Rather, the dissenters simply took advantage of their first opportunity through

Paanchi, a rightful heir, to achieve power without eliminating the system of judges.

## DISCRIMINATION—A NEW PAGAN RATIONALE

Though their attempt with Paanchi failed, the new mindset would thereafter form the conceptual foundation for a political attack on current laws that apparently prohibited anyone but descendants of Nephi from having rights to the highest judgment seat.[111] In keeping with the new age of secrecy, the new mode of attack would be much more subtle than attempting to return to monarchy, for the system of government would remain the same.

For the Nephites, this was uncharted territory. The danger of an unrighteous king had been fully defined by Mosiah II.[122] It had been further accentuated in the turmoil instigated by Amlici, Amalickiah, Ammoron, and the king-men. In the political world of the Nephites during the period of the judges, there were likely three distinct voting blocks: 1) Christians, 2) pagans, and 3) the undecided. Whereas the majority of the undecided had always voted with the Christians over the issue of returning to kings, it had now become a more complicated matter.

The choice was no longer government by kings versus government by the people, but now revolved around seemingly discriminatory issues. If it was truly a free society, shouldn't anyone, regardless of lineage or religion, be given an opportunity for high political status based purely on popularity with the people?

The undecided, likely consisting of Christians who did not take their religion seriously, as well as others who ascribed to no religion, looked at everything at face value, whereas the devout Christian block could see beyond to the not so long-range ramifications of this change. Christians who held their religion sacred and precious were vividly aware of the pagan assault over the past forty years. If the pagans should ever attain power, freedom would very quickly be lost, and the land of Zarahemla would cease to be a haven for Christianity.

## PUNCTUATED EQUILIBRIUM—THE SUDDEN FORWARD SURGE IN THE ART OF DECEPTION

When it was discovered that Paanchi was attempting to start a revolution, he was apprehended, tried for treason, and "condemned to death" by "the voice of the people."[113] His supporters, having seen him as a ticket to their first control of the government, immediately began plotting the assassination of the new chief judge Pahoran II, who by the nature of his position and the magnitude of the crime had likely pronounced the death sentence upon his brother Paanchi.[114] Of course, the principle reason for their plot was not revenge, but quite simply the fact that he stood between them and the judgment seat.

They sent a man named Kishkumen in disguise to the judgment seat, where he assassinated Pahoran. The assassin then fled with such swiftness of foot that he was able to elude Pahoran's servants. He returned to his accomplices, and they entered into a pact to keep his identity a secret from the investigators of the crime.

It is not difficult to visualize the thoroughness of the investigation into the murder of the chief judge over all the land, especially at that time before the people became thoroughly polarized into separate factions. Given the chain of events that had led to Pahoran's murder, as outlined in the book of Helaman, it is likely the assumption was automatic that the crime had been committed by Paanchi's supporters. In that case, no stone would have been left unturned as the investigators interrogated everyone known to be involved in the previous political campaign for Paanchi's election, as well as all witnesses who had any knowledge of the crime. Some of the co-conspirators were identified, which were tried and condemned to death.[115] However, the identity of Kishkumen remained a secret.

## CORIANTUMR'S ATTACK—SIMPLY ANOTHER STEP IN THE ATTEMPTED COUP

Kishkumen's assassination of Pahoran was the first response of Paanchi's supporters to his execution. Upon reflection, it becomes apparent that in addition to sending Kishkumen to the judgment seat,[116] they petitioned Tubaloth for support. He responded by sending Coriantumr directly to the city of Zarahemla to assist them in their revolution. If Coriantumr had not slain Pacumeni,[117] his assassination would surely have been Kishkumen's next objective. As it was, Helaman became the next target.[118]

Collusion between dissenters in Zarahemla and Nephi occurred frequently throughout the Zarahemla pre-Christ period. Such cooperation demonstrates their singular identity as enemies of the people of Christ. Truly, all were accomplices in a perpetual, revolutionary pagan movement, dedicated entirely to the destruction of Nephite Christianity and the establishment of pagan religion.

During the following year, a man named Gadianton would become "the leader of the band of Kishkumen."[119] Thereafter, they would be known as the Gadianton robbers. Accordingly, Coriantumr's attack was the second assault of the Gadianton robber offensive, whereas the assassination of Pahoran II was the first. Kishkumen's attempt to assassinate Helaman would be the third.[120]

## GADIANTON ROBBERS

Helaman 1 thus describes the rise of the Gadianton robbers, a criminal organization that utilized murder and secrecy in the pursuit of political power in the land of Zarahemla. The Gadianton Society was born naturally as a result of the events surrounding the assassination of Pahoran II, through the suppression of evidence concerning the identity of Kishkumen, the perpetrator of the crime.[121] Subsequently, the art of secrecy was fully implemented by Gadianton, who because of his great expertise in such clandestine activities, became the leader of Kishkumen's band.[122]

Gadianton, with guidance from the evil one,[123] had already developed his art of deception to perfection. In his devious mind, the principles of secrecy were much more refined than the haphazard plan conceived on the spur of the moment[124] to conceal Kishkumen's crime. Perhaps he had been waiting for the right moment and situation to introduce the secret oaths and covenants to the dissenters.

## PASSING DOWN THE SECRET COMBINATIONS

The sixth chapter of Helaman traces the history of secret combinations in the Western Hemisphere.[125] It was a meandering path that began with Cain and afterward led across the ages and around the world. It led past the Flood and the destruction of all human life on earth, with the exception of Noah and his family, who were transported by the ark to the Eastern Hemisphere. The path then led past Nimrod and the Tower of Babel, where a new rebellion against God culminated in the confusion of tongues, which dispersed the Jaredites and other post-Flood descendants of Noah and his sons into distant parts of the earth.[126] After the Jaredites arrived in the Western Hemisphere, the path continued on, across the 2,000 years of Jaredite history and into the Nephite nation.

According to the book of Moses and the Book of Mormon, secret combinations in the Western Hemisphere had been the source of the violence, murder, and mayhem, which ultimately had caused the termination of both the pre-Flood[127] and Jaredite cultures.[128] In Zarahemla, secret combinations would resume their work of destruction, finding fertile ground in the thoughts and schemes of Gadianton. The principles of darkness would quickly take root within the Nephite culture.

## TRANSFERRING THE TORCH OF EVIL

Nothing happens in a vacuum. Prior to receiving the First Vision, Joseph Smith was never a member of any Christian denomination. Nevertheless, he was well aware of the basic tenets of Christianity, having attended church meetings with his mother, and having read from the pages of the Bible. His parents taught him to believe in God and to strive to keep the commandments, as recorded in the Bible. By placing Joseph in a time and place where the people were actively seeking truth, and in a righteous Christian family, the Lord had thus laid in the young boy a foundation of righteousness and a knowledge of Jesus Christ, preparatory to the restoration of the gospel in its fulness upon the earth.

As with principles of righteousness, it seems that for every person in the Book of Mormon in which Satan instilled the ideas of the secret combinations, at least a cursory knowledge of the former cults was held. The daughter of Jared possessed knowledge of the pre-Flood cults. She said to her father, "Whereby hath my father so much sorrow? Hath he not read the record which our fathers brought across the great deep? Behold, is there not an account concerning them of old that they by their secret plans did obtain kingdoms and great glory?"[129] She "put it into [the heart of Jared] to search up these things of old; and Jared put it into the heart of Akish."[130]

The secret combination thus inspired by Jared's daughter and put into action by Akish resulted in King Omer having to flee out of the land to avoid destruction, whereupon his son Jared seized the throne. Subsequently, Akish (most likely in league with his wife—Jared's daughter) slew Jared and acquired the throne. Ultimately, war between Akish and his own sons caused the near extinction of the entire Jaredite culture, with the exception of thirty souls, who reunited with Omer and his family and friends. Omer was restored to the throne.

Four generations after the Akish tragedy, Heth, the son of Com "began to embrace the secret plans again of old, to destroy his father."[131] Once again, the result was the near extinction of the Jaredite culture. Following Heth, nothing is written of secret combinations in the Jaredite culture until the reign of the righteous Jaredite king Com. At that time, "Com did fight against them much; nevertheless he did not prevail against them."[132] Seven generations of kings then passed before the secret works of darkness caused the extinction of the entire Jaredite culture through civil war. In every case, knowledge of secret combinations was available from an earlier time.

Detailed instructions concerning the secret plans and oaths of the Jaredite secret combinations were held by the Nephites in the twenty-four gold plates of Ether. Independent of the twenty-four gold plates, at least a cursory knowledge of the oaths and covenants of darkness was held by the Mulekites, who had a direct knowledge of the Jaredites through almost 400 years of interaction. Furthermore, it is apparent that the entire Mulekite nation had succumbed to the enticements of Jaredite pagan religion, for they knew little or nothing about Christ and denied His existence.[133]

The Mulekite homeland of Desolation—"the place of their first landing"[134]— had bordered on the Jaredite capital city of Moron,[135] the place where the last Jaredite king (Coriantumr) lived.[136] From Desolation, they had witnessed the Jaredite destruction, which was brought about by secret combinations. The violence had engulfed the entire Jaredite culture, as the people became obsessed with a lust for human carnage.

Alma the Younger took measures to keep the oaths and covenants of the Jaredite secret combinations, as contained within the twenty-four gold plates of Ether,[137] from the knowledge of the Nephite populace.[138] However, the information was obtained by Gadianton directly from Satan. Likely, his mind was already fertile with an inherent knowledge of such things, having been passed down in the Mulekite practice of pagan religion and preserved in their oral traditions. In reality, a devious mind and evil intent were the only things actually required of Gadianton to enable him to implement the explicit instructions of Satan. Still, a large following among the people would be greatly facilitated by a pagan mindset, which was already present in the Mulekite traditions.

## A NEW STANDARD OF DECEPTION

The second generation of deception was characterized most noticeably by a sudden change in the political perspective of the dissenters. No longer did they openly disdain the free government and seek to eliminate it in favor of kings. Instead, they focused their efforts in a much more subtle fashion toward changing the law to facilitate their rise to power within the system of judges.

This clever new tactic was apparently a very difficult step for the king-men due to their overwhelming obsession to convince the people of their rights of nobility.[139] However, it blended very well with the calculated secrecy of the Gadianton robbers. It became perhaps the most important technique of the robbers who infiltrated the Nephite government, and of many lesser judges and lawyers who would soon be recruited into the ranks of Gadianton's secret society.

The secrecy of the robbers, which constituted the second defining aspect of the second generation of dissent was by far the more devious of the two aspects. The robbers did not merely keep their plans a secret. Their very existence was a secret.[140] Affiliates could not reveal the existence of the secret combination, or admit their involvement to anyone outside the organization, upon penalty of death.[141] Through these rigid principles of secrecy, the Gadianton robbers would quickly rise to the pinnacle of power in Nephite government. As in the pre-Flood and Jaredite cultures, they would soon threaten the very existence of the Christian Nephite culture.

# CHAPTER 2.2

# ALMA'S LINEAGE RETURNS TO THE JUDGMENT SEAT

## *50 BC (42ND YEAR OF THE JUDGES)*

### HELAMAN IS ELECTED CHIEF JUDGE

FOLLOWING THE DEATH OF Pacumeni, all three sons of Pahoran I who had sought the judgment seat were deceased. Though Pahoran had other sons,[143] they did not contend for the office.[144] Perhaps they were not of legal age to hold such a position. Perhaps they were not interested in, or possibly they were not well-suited for, political office.

Hence, a new election was held in which Helaman II, the son of Helaman I and grandson of Alma the Younger, was chosen "to fill the judgment seat, by the voice of the people."[145] It was not an enviable position. In a period of less than two years, all three of the recent candidates, which had either sought or were elected to the office, had been assassinated or put to death.

Little information is provided concerning Helaman II during the period that preceded his election. Apparently he had not been a public figure, at least not in a political sense. Alma's son Shiblon (Helaman's uncle) had chosen him to assume the responsibility of maintaining the large plates of Nephi, which had passed from Alma to Helaman I and subsequently to Shiblon. In keeping with the sacred duty of protecting and maintaining the plates,[146] Helaman "was a just man, and he did walk uprightly before God; and he did observe to do good continually, to keep the commandments of the Lord his God."[147]

Helaman's ascent to the judgment seat was the return of Alma's lineage to Nephite politics.[148] On his part, it was an act of great faith and courage, considering the turmoil that engulfed the land of Zarahemla at that time. Politically, it was a move made out of necessity and indicated that even at that time (forty-two years into the reign of the judges) the

Church remained a powerful influence in the affairs of the government. It further revealed the great respect the people had for Alma's posterity, as well as confidence that they could restore peace to the land.

Helaman's lineage was a who's who in terms of church leadership. His father, grandfather, and great-grandfather were all previous heads of the Church (the only leaders up to that point in church history). It is apparent that he was an important part of the hierarchy of the Church, and likely was the head of the Church. His election was a statement of trust and hope that his calming spiritual and moral influence would bring an end to the hostilities. As in the earlier election of Pahoran II, it reflected the fact that the Christian segment of the population was significant, and still held the majority vote.

Nevertheless, the dissenters were relentless. In their perspective, the latest action of the people called for another reaction on the scale of the previous reactions. By this time, they were following the direction of Gadianton, who had assumed leadership of Kishkumen's band.[149] Gadianton promised his followers power if they would support him in a bid to take control of the government. He sent Kishkumen to stir the political pot one more time by assassinating Chief Judge Helaman.

At this point in the book of Helaman, a glimpse is given of government activities that are not seen elsewhere in the Book of Mormon. One of Helaman's servants, either calculatedly or opportunistically, had ventured into the clandestine world of the robbers.[150] He had gained knowledge of their secret signs, by which on this fateful night he was able to learn of Kishkumen's intention to murder Helaman.[151] Feigning support for the cause, he led Kishkumen in the direction of the judgment seat. Waiting for the right moment, however, he caught Kishkumen off guard and stabbed him to death, ending the conspiracy attempt. He then went and informed Helaman of what had transpired.

Helaman immediately sent agents to apprehend Gadianton and his gang. When they arrived at the robbers' hideout, however, they were nowhere to be found. Gadianton had become alarmed when Kishkumen did not immediately return[152] and fearing "lest that he should be destroyed,"[153] he had fled with his band into the wilderness by a secret way. Unfortunately, this was not the end of the Gadianton robbers. Having a remote secret location would suit them well. Gadianton secret operatives would soon be sent among the Nephite and Lamanite peoples to sow the seeds of discord, and to recruit both dissenters and Lamanites to their evil cause.

## *50–39 BC*

## HELAMAN RULES AND THE CHURCH PROSPERS WHILE SECRETLY A CANCER GROWS

After the departure of Gadianton's band from Zarahemla, the intense period of political violence came to an abrupt end. The tension within the city of Zarahemla lessened, and the political leaders returned to normal peacetime activities. Helaman settled into his new role at the head of government. He became known for his "justness and equity" to all. He governed his own life according to the commandments of God and "did walk after the ways of his father, insomuch that he did prosper in the land."[154]

Helaman's reign was characterized by both positive and negative developments within the Nephite culture:

1. From the time of the departure of the robbers in the first year of his reign through the fourth year (50–47 BC), there was little or no contention in the land.
2. The peace would not continue, for in the fifth year (46 BC), violence suddenly erupted to the point of internal warfare and "there were many dissensions; [in which] there were an exceedingly great many who departed out of the land of Zarahemla, and went forth unto the land northward to inherit the land."[155]
3. The intense "contentions, and disturbances, and wars, and dissensions"[156] continued for almost three years (46–44 BC) before they began to lessen near the end of Helaman's seventh year in office.
4. In the eighth year of his reign (43 BC), there was peace throughout the land. Unbeknownst to the Nephite government, however, the Gadianton robbers had surreptitiously re-entered the land and were secretly establishing their craft among the dissenters and cultivating their insidious influence across the face of the land.[157]

The robbers may have been at the root of the contention that occurred during the fifth through seventh years of Helaman's reign. If so, the northward migrations in 46 BC marked the first incursion of robbers into the land northward. This is a reasonable assumption, since by AD 15 (sixty-one years later) they would gain complete control of the land northward[158] and bring down a great curse upon that land.[159]

The Gadianton robbers were merely a new organization of dissent, comprised of many individuals who for many years had sought to overthrow the Christian Nephite government. Most of the robbers' recruits came from the ranks of pagans and apostates who already were sworn enemies of the Church of God and the Christian Nephite government. The only difference was that they now utilized secrecy as an art to achieve the overthrow of the Nephite government. Therefore, though the techniques were new, the goals and purposes of the robbers were identical to those of dissenters throughout the previous sixty years.

Gadianton agents also recruited disgruntled members of the Church. A prime focus was the youth of the Nephites and the Lamanites, who were, as is characteristic of youth, highly impressionable and who in general had little or no knowledge of the dark history of dissent.[160] The Gadianton Society was a shadowy organization, and therefore, its involvement in any particular occurrence or movement could seldom be firmly identified, particularly in the earlier stages before they attained power and openly challenged the Nephite and Lamanite armies.[161]

Beginning in 43 BC (the eighth year of Nephi's reign), there was a great influx of converts into the Church, to the number of "thousands"[162] and "tens of thousands."[163] This phenomenal growth continued throughout the remainder of Helaman's reign. Almost immediately, there began to be contention within the Church, primarily because the new members, many of which came from pagan backgrounds, would not conform to the principles of the gospel. As the tremendous growth continued, "pride began to enter into the church—not into the church of God, but into the hearts of the people who professed to belong to the church of God."[164]

Oh, the innocence and vulnerability of the dedicated and obedient children of God in the face of an evil, sinister, secretive enemy! While church members were rejoicing over the sudden extraordinary growth of the Church, the Gadianton robbers were secretly infiltrating the land and sowing seeds of discord among the people, even within the Church. While the people of the Church were expecting good and honest seekers of truth in the new members, the reality was that frequently the new members were intent from the start upon the destruction of the Church and the free government that protected it. They searched for ways to cause dissension, while appearing to be honest and forthright in their convictions.

## HELAMAN'S SONS

Helaman had two sons whom he named after the first Nephite fathers. "He gave unto the eldest the name of Nephi, and unto the youngest, the name of Lehi."[165] His purpose in so doing rested upon his hope that they would emulate the righteous lives of the earliest prophets of the Nephite culture. It was his desire that they would declare the Word of God to the Nephites—that they would teach the people the sacred truth that salvation comes only through Jesus Christ, who would come to redeem the people "from their sins," not "in their sins."[166] He taught them that salvation comes only through repentance and turning away from sin.

## *39 BC*

## NEPHI ASCENDS TO THE JUDGMENT SEAT

In the fifty-third year of the judges, after a reign of eleven years, Helaman died. At his death, his eldest son Nephi was appointed (likely by Helaman himself according to the rights of lineage) to "reign in his stead."[167] Following the example of his father, Nephi "did keep the commandments of God" and "did fill the judgment-seat with justice and equity."[168] However, notwithstanding his dedication to truth and righteousness, the period of his reign was a time of great contention, as the Gadianton robbers continued to sow discord and make great headway among the Nephites. In the second year of his reign (38 BC), "there were many dissensions in the church, and there was also a contention among the people, insomuch that there was much bloodshed."[169]

## THE MECHANISMS OF DISSENT

The process by which the voice of dissent developed in the land of Zarahemla during the period of the judges was generally the same in every case and is laid out in Helaman, as well as many other places in the Book of Mormon. Dissenters would frequently become disenchanted over a particular government issue, which initially was an obsession to eliminate the system of judges and reestablish a king over all the land. Following the Amalickiah and Ammoron War, the issue changed to an obsession to alter the system of judges to enable anyone, regardless of religion or lineage to seek office, including the office of chief judge.

At other times, dissensions would first surface within the Church. Such disagreements were seldom private or low-key affairs in which church members responded civilly to differences of opinion over a point of doctrine or a matter of discipline. In some cases the disagreements would grow until they reverberated throughout the land of Zarahemla, ultimately resulting in violence among the people.

Apparently, there was an apostate/pagan faction standing by, ready for reprisal at the drop of a hat. At times, they used the problems within the Church as a platform for their discontent over the free government. The first such incident, the Amlicite War of 87 BC, had revealed the political nature of the contention, for it did not begin within the Church but resulted simply from the desire of Amlici's followers to establish him as king.[170] It was further characterized as a political movement by the king-men in 67 BC, who "were desirous that the law should be altered in a manner to overthrow the free government and to establish a king over the land."[171] They voiced their contentions in the political arena against Chief Judge Pahoran I.[172]

In the case of Amalickiah in 73 BC, the dissension began within the Church, though it quickly expanded into the political arena.[173] The expansion of Amalickiah's dissension from the Church to a conflict that extended across the entire land of Zarahemla points to the vital relationship between the free government and the Church of Christ. As in Amlici's 87 BC attempt to become the king of Zarahemla, the freedom to practice the Christian religion was always at stake.[174] Thus, when Amalickiah apostatized and immediately began to rally the advocates of monarchy,[175] it is quite apparent that his ultimate purpose was to destroy the Church and eliminate Christianity.

In 38 BC, while Nephi was the chief judge, the dissenting church members, though apparently no longer seeking a return to monarchy, immediately stirred up dissenting factions across the land of Zarahemla.[176] The tragic bloodshed which then followed only heightened their anger, ensuring that it would soon be repeated again. Many of the dissenters were slain and many fled to the land of Nephi, where they attempted without success to incite the Lamanites to go to war against the Nephites.

They laid their case before the Lamanite king.[177] Though the text is unclear, it is possible that the king may have been inclined to go against the Nephites, but unlike the results Amalickiah had achieved,[178] none of the Lamanites would join their cause.[179] Two years later, however, in 36 BC, other dissenters "went up from the Nephites unto the Lamanites."[180] Joining with the previous dissenters, they succeeded in stirring up the Lamanites. In 35 BC, "they did come down against the Nephites to battle."[181]

## CHAPTER 2.3

# THE FIRST NEPHITE MILITARY DEFEAT

UNTIL THE LAMANITE OFFENSIVE of 35 BC,[182] the Nephites had always found a way to repel each Lamanite attack against the land of Zarahemla. Following Coriantumr's defeat in 51 BC, the Nephite war record was eight victories against no defeats. Table 1.0 in this chapter lists each previous attack and describes the final results.

Notwithstanding the unblemished record, a dangerous trend can be seen, which had begun to develop during the reign of Mosiah II, the last Nephite king.[183] With every dissension "among the brethren" they became more numerous. As their numbers grew over the course of his reign, the dissenters became more and more aggressive. Shortly before 92 BC, it became necessary for Mosiah to issue a proclamation forbidding persecution of the Church by unbelievers.[184]

As outlined in *The War Against Christianity*, Lamanite attacks against the Nephites generally began as dissenter revolts within the land of Zarahemla. Two exceptions to this are the attacks of 81 BC[185] and 77 BC,[186] which originated within the land of Nephi, rather than Zarahemla. Even those incidents, however, were caused by pagan dissenters who had originally come to the land of Nephi from the land of Zarahemla.[187]

Therefore, the frequent warfare that took place between 87 and 35 BC, as well as the war that had previously taken place during the reign of King Benjamin, was a reflection of an internal problem of dissent within the land of Zarahemla, rather than an external problem of spontaneous Lamanite aggression. It might also be projected that the growing potential for Nephite defeat during the period of the judges was specifically related to the number of dissidents within the Nephite nation. They had become much more outspoken and influential under a democratic form of government. As their numbers grew, it became more and more difficult to put down each Lamanite attack.

## *CA. 155 BC*

## THE WAR DURING THE REIGN OF KING BENJAMIN

The first recorded war in the land of Zarahemla took place during the reign of King Benjamin. At that time, as concluded from Words of Mormon 1:12–16, an unidentified party dissented away to the land of Nephi and brought back a Lamanite army to attack Zarahemla.[188] It was postulated in *The War Against Christianity*[189] that the Amalekites were the unidentified dissenters. The account of their dissension is likely recorded in the 116 lost pages of Mormon's abridgment.

## *87 BC*

## THE AMLICITE WAR

Amlici acquired a large following of pagan Nephites during the five-year period which followed the execution of Nehor.[190] The Amlicites were united through their religion (the Order of Nehor),[191] and their ultimate goal was the destruction of the Church of Christ.[192] Their numbers were large enough to seriously threaten the Nephite system of judges with an early extinction by "the voice of the people."[193]

Though they comprised a large and significant portion of the Nephites, however, they were still in the minority, and they lost the election. In the war that soon followed they were large enough to vastly outnumber the Christian Nephites, when combined with a large Lamanite army. The Nephites prevailed, however, through faith in God. Because of their faith and righteousness, they were strengthened by the Lord.[194]

## SUBSEQUENT WARS

The same factors brought a similar outcome to the Zoramite War of 74 BC. In that war, Moroni's armor innovations[195] and a resolute effort by the Nephite army turned back the Lamanite attack. In 73 BC, similar results were achieved in the defense of Ammonihah against Amalickiah's first attack, due primarily to Moroni's fortifications.[196]

The episode surrounding Amalickiah's second attack—the invasion of 67 BC—appears to have reflected a significant increase in the relative size of the dissent faction. Though Moroni apparently was able to recruit a larger than normal portion of the Nephite population,[197] they were countered by a large number of dissenters (king-men), which rose up within the land of Zarahemla in support of Amalickiah. It required a great military effort and the death of 4,000 king-men to put down the insurrection.[198] Only then could Moroni turn his full attention to the Lamanite attack.

The king-men revolt during Amalickiah's second attack revealed that in large part, dissent was an ethnic phenomenon. The king-men were identified as people of high birth or nobility.[199] They occupied entire cities, which can be ascertained by the statement: "those dissenters . . . were compelled to hoist the title of liberty . . . in their cities."[200]

After being smitten at the beginning of the war, they rose up again during the latter part of the war under the leadership of Pachus.[201] In 62 BC, Moroni's armies were in the final stages of expelling the Lamanites from the eastern and southern perimeter regions of Nephite lands.[202] At that time, the king-men deposed Chief Judge Pahoran in the capital city of Zarahemla.

The Amalickiah and Ammoron War marked the first time in the history of Zarahemla when the Christian Nephites teetered on the precipice of destruction. Nephite righteous leadership was an extremely important factor in the defeat of Amalickiah and Ammoron. It was only through the courageous awe-inspiring efforts of righteous leaders such as Moroni, Lehi, Teancum, Helaman, Antipas, Pahoran, and patriots of faith like the freemen[203] and the Stripling Warriors[204] that the king-men uprising was put down, and the Lamanites were defeated and driven out of the land.

### *TABLE 1.0*

### EIGHT NEPHITE VICTORIES IN ZARAHEMLA FROM THEIR ARRIVAL CIRCA 200 BC THROUGH 51 BC

| Year BC | Nephite Military Leader(s) | Dissent Group | Results |
|---|---|---|---|
| ~ 155 | King Benjamin (Omni 1:24; Words of Mormon 1:13) | Not Identified—Likely the Order of Nehor (Amalekites) | The Lamanites were defeated and driven out of the land. After the war ended, many of the dissenters, who had incited the Lamanites to violence, fled to the land of Nephi to avoid Benjamin's justice. Others were punished according to the law. |

| | | | |
|---|---|---|---|
| 87 | Alma the Younger (Alma 2:16) | Order of Nehor—Amlicites | The Lamanites joined with the Amlicites and attacked Zarahemla. Though vastly outnumbering the Nephites, they were overpowered and driven into the wilderness of Hermounts. |
| 81 | Zoram, Lehi, and Aha (Alma 16:5) | Order of Nehor | Nehor-influenced Lamanites attacked the western border of Zarahemla and unwittingly destroyed the Nehor-controlled city of Ammonihah. Afterward, they were pursued by the Nephite armies. In a subsequent series of battles, the Nephites drove them deep into the east wilderness. |
| 77 | Unknown—Possibly Zoram, Lehi, and Aha (Alma 28:1–3) | Order of Nehor | The Lamanites pursued the people of Anti-Nephi-Lehi to the land of Zarahemla. There, they were met by the Nephite armies and a great battle ensued. Tens of thousands of Lamanites "were slain and scattered abroad." |
| 74 | Moroni and Lehi (Alma 43:16–17, 35) | Order of Nehor (Amalekites) and Zoramites (Alma 43:6, 44) | The Lamanites attacked the Nephites at Manti. Though they far outnumbered the Nephites, they were defeated due in part to Moroni's innovative armor (Alma 43:21). Moroni required that they give an oath not to return and then allowed them to depart in peace. |
| 73 | Moroni and Lehi (Alma 49:16) | Amalickiah, Zoramites | Amalickiah sent a large Lamanite army to attack the rebuilt city of Ammonihah. The army was intimidated by Moroni's fortifications at Ammonihah and attacked the city of Noah instead. They failed to defeat the city, primarily because of similar fortifications, and returned to the land of Nephi. |

| | | | |
|---|---|---|---|
| 67–61 | Moroni, Lehi, Teancum, and Helaman (Alma 51–62) | Amalickiah and Ammoron | Amalickiah and Ammoron invaded the land of Zarahemla with an innumerable host of Lamanite warriors. Dissenters (king-men) within the land of Zarahemla joined forces with the Lamanites. Together, they almost succeeded in defeating the Nephites. They were driven from the land of Zarahemla only after a long and deadly conflict. |
| 51 | Moronihah (Helaman 1:25–34) | Gadianton Robbers and Tubaloth | Tubaloth (the son of Ammoron) sent Coriantumr with a Lamanite army to attack the city of Zarahemla during a time of internal turmoil. After taking control of the city of Zarahemla, the army headed northward through the capital parts of the land, slaying many Nephites along the way. Ultimately, they became entrapped between Nephite armies led by Moronihah and Lehi, and Coriantumr was slain. His army surrendered and was allowed by Moronihah to "depart out of the land in peace" (Helaman 1:33). |

## CHIEF CAPTAIN LEHI

In the last event of the above table, Chief Captain Lehi joined with Moronihah in the 51 BC Nephite military operation, a pincer movement to contain the army of Coriantumr. At that time,[205] Moronihah set up the operation by first sending "Lehi with an army round about to head the Lamanite army before they should come to the land Bountiful."[206] He then followed them from the south, while apparently sending other divisions to the east and to the west (verse 31). By this means, the Lamanite army became completely entrapped with no place to flee.

This is the last time Lehi is referenced in the Book of Mormon, following a thirty-year career, which was exceeded only by Mormon's forty-three years.[207] However, Mormon's long tenure was purely a consequence of necessity. Due to his great calling and purpose of preparing and preserving the Nephite record for the restoration of the gospel in the fulness of times, he was protected and sustained by the hand of the Lord until his work was completed.

Though it is not clearly stated in Mormon's account, it seems apparent that Lehi was the son of Zoram. If correct, then his first military experience occurred in 81 BC, when he took part in a military operation under his father's command which carried them into the wilderness located to the south of the land of Manti.[208] There, a Lamanite army was intercepted as they journeyed toward the east wilderness, after destroying the city of Ammonihah. The Lamanites carried hostages with them, which had been taken from the city of Noah. The hostages were all rescued, and the Lamanites were "scattered and driven into the wilderness."

Seven years later, in the Zoramite war of 74 BC, Lehi led one of the Nephite armies, which defeated the Zoramite/Lamanite army at the city of Manti. In that battle, the armies of Moroni and Lehi staged the first recorded pincer movement, which was previously described in the previous book by this author, *The War Against Christianity*.[209] In the battle at the city of Noah in 72 BC, he is described as being feared by the Lamanites, who knew him well, even at that relatively early stage of his career.[210] Subsequently, between 67 and 61 BC during the war with Amalickiah and Ammoron, the military triumvirate which led the Nephites was comprised of Moroni, Lehi, and Teancum. Throughout the long and intense struggle—the difficulty of which is revealed in Pahoran's epistle to Moroni in 62 BC[211]—their leadership was crucial to the Nephite victory. Lehi thus played an important role in the cause of freedom between 81 and 51 BC, and for that reason, he is acknowledged at this time.

## THE STRENGTH OF THE LORD

Frequently in the Book of Mormon, a powerful factor is identified (in addition to righteous leadership) that contributed greatly to the eight Nephite victories against overwhelming odds. It was the blessing of strength bestowed by Deity upon the righteous. So important is this phenomenon that it is touched upon without fail in the account of each and every conflict,[212] including the War of 35 BC. Helaman 4 identifies the War of 35 BC as the first war in which the Nephites went into battle without the strength of the Lord.[213] This was a principle reason they were unable to stand before the Lamanite attack and were compelled to flee to the narrow neck of land.[214] Previously, they had prevailed even when greatly outnumbered.[215]

The decline in Nephite morality and spiritual purity thus had a two-fold effect upon the Nephites. First, it was directly related to the number of apostate and pagan dissenters, which turned against the Nephite government. Second, it affected the personal physical strength of Nephite warriors who did not defect over to the Lamanites. The two factors would align in a powerful way to adversely affect the outcome of the War of 35 BC.

### *35 BC*

### THE NEPHITES ARE DRIVEN FROM THE LAND SOUTHWARD

In the fifty-seventh year of the judges and the fifth year of Nephi's reign, the dissenters and Lamanites came down into the land of Zarahemla with great force.[216] It was a tragic time for the Nephites. Over the following three years, they were driven from their homes and their cities. It was the first time after 175 years in the land of Zarahemla in which they were forced to abandon their capital city. Yet, it was only the beginning of their sorrow. Ultimately, they were driven entirely from the land southward, being compelled to abandon all of the lands in their possession, including 1) the land of Zarahemla, 2) the land of Hermounts,[217] 3) the land of Jershon, and 4) the land of Bountiful.

They fled into the borders of Desolation on the narrow neck of land. Only there, they were able to halt the invasion.[218] The successful utilization of the narrow pass, which led into the land northward as a place of last resort immediately validated the high priority the Nephites had placed upon controlling the narrow neck of land after 68 BC.[219]

### THE NARROW NECK OF LAND

It is at this point in the Book of Mormon, in reference to the Lamanite invasion of 35 BC, that the narrow neck of land, which connected the land northward to the land southward, is described for the third time. The Nephites constructed fortifications across the narrow neck "from the west sea, even to the east; it being a day's journey for a Nephite, on the line which they had fortified and stationed their armies to defend their north country."[220]

The innumerable hordes of Lamanites and dissenters had been able to overwhelm the Nephites by attacking at multiple locations across the land southward and drive them to the border of Desolation. However, the choke point at Desolation made it possible to focus all Nephite forces at that one location, which equalized the playing field. The Lamanites could involve only a portion of their warriors, while the majority was forced to stand idle behind the line of attack. They could not mobilize their forces to the east or west because they were hemmed in by ocean on both sides.[221]

## CAUSES OF THE COLLAPSE

As the year 33 BC came to an end, the forward thrust of the Lamanite invasion was finally halted at Desolation. Mormon then pauses to reflect on the causes of the terrible predicament in which the Nephites found themselves. The great destruction they had experienced had resulted from their own wickedness, as stated in the following verses:

> Now this great loss of the Nephites and the great slaughter which was among them, would not have happened had it not been for their wickedness and their abomination which was among them; yea, and it was among those also who professed to belong to the church of God.
>
> And it was because of the pride of their hearts, because of their exceeding riches, yea, it was because of their oppression to the poor, withholding their food from the hungry, withholding their clothing from the naked, and smiting their humble brethren upon the cheek, making a mock of that which was sacred, denying the spirit of prophecy and of revelation, murdering, plundering, lying, stealing, committing adultery, rising up in great contentions, and deserting away into the land of Nephi, among the Lamanites.[222]

The two verses describe the specific nature of the wickedness that had begun to creep into the Church eight years previously (43 BC).[223] Many of the new members could not abide the standards of the gospel. Many were on their way out of the Church almost as soon as they came up out of the waters of baptism. Large numbers of former members became bitter and vicious enemies of the Church, joining the ranks of the unbelievers and frequently dissenting away to the Lamanites. One of the principle factors that contributed greatly to the defeat is found at the end of verse 12: "rising up in great contentions, and deserting away into the land of Nephi among the Lamanites."

With each event of apostasy, there was a reduction of Nephite numbers and a corresponding increase in the forces of evil gathering in the land of Nephi. Many others became secretly involved with Gadianton robbers within the land of Zarahemla. The problem was further intensified by the departure of a great many more Nephites into the land northward[224]—though the negative effect may have been lessened somewhat by the fact that many of them were dissenters, as revealed in Helaman 7:1–3.

Additionally, as considered above, many believers became complacent in their faith and obedience to God, and transgressed against the commandments. As a result, they lost the gift of strength, which had blessed the previous generations.[225] This was perhaps the principle reason they were unable to repel the Lamanite attack and were compelled to flee to the narrow neck of land.[226] Previously they had always prevailed, even when greatly outnumbered.

## TWO PREVIOUS CAPTURES OF THE CITY OF ZARAHEMLA

On two previous occasions, the city of Zarahemla had fallen briefly into the hands of the enemy—once to the king-men during the Amalickiah and Ammoron War, and once to the Lamanite army led by the dissenter Coriantumr. However, those were localized and temporary incidents in which the following occurred:

1. Pahoran and the freemen were driven out of the city by the king-men faction within the land of Zarahemla, while Moroni defended the perimeter of the land against Ammoron's attack.[227] The uprising was put down as soon as Moroni came to Pahoran's aid.[228]
2. Coriantumr's Lamanite army entered the land of Zarahemla by marching between the fortified cities lining the southern perimeter, surprising the Nephites in the city of Zarahemla. The Nephites could not flee and were captured within the walls of the city. Subsequently, Coriantumr's army was defeated in their first encounter with Moronihah's armies.[229]

In contrast, the War of 35 BC marked the first time in which the Lamanite armies were able to sweep across the entirety of the land of Zarahemla. The Nephites were forced to abandon every city and land within the land southward. Only at the narrow pass leading into the land northward were they finally able to halt the Lamanite invasion.

According to Mormon's account, the War of 35 BC took place in three phases:

Phase 1: The three-year Lamanite offensive (35–33 BC).[230]
Phase 2: The two-year Nephite counteroffensive (32–31 BC).[231]
Phase 3: The one-year mission of Nephi and Lehi among both Nephites and Lamanites in 30 BC. Their mission is further divided into the following three stages:

- They first preached the gospel to the Nephites in Bountiful and Jershon.
- Then, they preached to the Lamanites and dissenters in the heartland region.
- Finally, they went up to the land of Nephi and preached to the Lamanites. Their mission will be considered in Chapters 2.4 and 2.5.

## THE INVASION OF 35 BC—A DUPLICATE OF AMALICKIAH'S INVASION

Having failed so miserably in Coriantumr's Nephite heartland attack in 51 BC,[232] the invasion of 35 BC was a return to the two-pronged battle plan first utilized by Amalickiah in 67 BC, in which two separate and independent campaigns were coordinated with a king-men uprising within the land of Zarahemla.[233] Amalickiah conducted a campaign along the eastern seaboard of Jershon, the ultimate purpose being to take control of the entire coast from the city of Moroni on the south to the narrow neck of land on the north. A second campaign, which took place simultaneously with the first, was conducted against the heartland region of Nephite lands. The objective of the heartland campaign was to capture the core region extending northward from the cities of Manti, Zeezrom, and Cumeni to the coastal city of Bountiful. See Map 11.0: The Lamanite Invasion of 35 BC—Nephites Driven from the Land Southward in Part 5, Chapter 5.3.

In 35 BC, no doubt the perimeter fortifications established by Chief Captain Moroni between 72 and 67 BC remained in place, yet all fell very quickly to the Lamanites. Not until they were driven to the narrow neck of land at Desolation were the Nephites finally able to halt the Lamanite offensive.

## A LOOK BACK AT THE AMALICKIAH AND AMMORON WAR

As considered in *The War Against Christianity*,[234] a total of four separate campaigns were conducted by the Lamanites over the course of the Amalickiah and Ammoron War. However, the western perimeter campaign and the king-men rebellion within the land of Zarahemla were not designed components of the original battle plan. The western campaign was purely an ad hoc phase, which materialized only as the war proceeded. In fact, it was launched by Ammoron as an act of desperation after his brother Amalickiah was slain and the two primary campaigns came to a complete standstill.

Apparently, the western seaboard was never involved in the War of 35 BC, though the Nephites were driven entirely from the land southward. It is not mentioned during any of the war's three phases. This further supports the premise that Ammoron's attack at the unnamed city[235] in 66 BC was a purely diversionary tactic unique to that war.[236]

The dissenter (king-men) uprising within the heartland region—so detrimental in the Amalickiah and Ammoron War—apparently did not materialize in the War of 35 BC. Though the latter war was the direct result of Lamanite provocation by dissenters from the land of Zarahemla, many had been expelled well in advance of the war.[237] Other dissenters had later journeyed up to the land of Nephi, joining with the first in persuading the Lamanites to go to war against the Nephites.[238] Furthermore, the 35 BC war was of such short duration that dissenters within Zarahemla perhaps did not find it necessary or timely to participate. Hence, instead of rising up within the land of Zarahemla during the war, most of the dissenters which remained in Zarahemla may have either fled with the Nephites, or remained behind to welcome the Lamanites.

## THE NEPHITES REPENT AND MORONIHAH LEADS AN OFFENSIVE

Through transgression, the Nephites had lost the gift of strength to enable them to repel the Lamanite invasion. Therefore, Moronihah, displaying the same righteous leadership that had set his father apart within the Nephite culture, joined with Nephi and Lehi to preach repentance to the people.[239] The message was simple and basic—repent and have faith so that the Lord would begin to bless them once again. Only when they showed signs of repentance did

Moronihah lead them against the Lamanites to take back the lands and cities that had been lost.[240]

In the sixtieth year of the judges (32 BC), Moronihah's armies began to drive the Lamanites from Nephite lands. Over the following two years (32–31 BC), they had some success and were able to take back half of their cities. However, the number of Lamanites and dissenters within the heartland region was so great that it was impossible to drive them out.[241] Moronihah made the decision to halt the offensive and concentrate on defending the lands they had retaken.

## CONSIDERING THE THREE PHASES OF THE WAR OF 35 BC

Combining the information from all three phases of the War of 35 BC, it becomes apparent that the sectioning of Nephite lands into discrete geographic regions took place with respect to both the Lamanite attack and the Nephite counterattack. Such a scenario is not even suggested in the account of the Lamanite invasion. It first begins to become evident in the account of Moronihah's counteroffensive.

To that end, it is stated that after the Nephites repented, "Moronihah . . . did venture to lead them forth from place to place, and from city to city, even until they had regained the one-half of their property and the one-half of all their lands." However, "they did abandon their design to obtain the remainder of their lands, for so numerous were the Lamanites that it became impossible for the Nephites to obtain more power over them; therefore Moronihah did employ all his armies in maintaining those parts which he had taken."[242]

Not until the third phase of the conflict is enough specific information supplied to enable understanding of that which was supplied ambiguously for the second phase. In the account of Phase 3 (Nephi and Lehi's mission), the specific regions recaptured by Moronihah in Phase 2 are clearly identified for the first time. Helaman Chapter 5 reveals that Nephi and Lehi preached first among the Nephites in the re-captured lands, and then among Lamanites and dissenters in the lands still under Lamanite control. Even then, the crucial geographic information is given through the identification of individual cities, rather than regional lands:

> And therefore [Nephi and Lehi] went forth, keeping the commandments of God, to teach the word of God among all the people of Nephi, beginning at the city Bountiful;

> And from thenceforth to the city of Gid; and from the city of Gid to the city of Mulek;[243]
>
> And even from one city to another, until they had gone forth among all the people of Nephi who were in the land southward; and from thence into the land of Zarahemla, among the Lamanites.[244]

Based on these three verses, it becomes evident that Moronihah's armies had retaken the city of Bountiful and the cities along the east coast of Jershon prior to Nephi and Lehi's mission, and "the people of Nephi" had returned to those lands. It can also be determined that the land of Zarahemla and the land of Hermounts,[245] remained in Lamanite hands. Moronihah had opted to focus entirely on defending the retaken lands, rather than conducting an offensive against the heartland region, where greater numbers of Lamanites and dissenters were congregated,[246] many of which had fled there after being expelled from Jershon.

In agreement with the statement in Helaman 4:16 that they "had regained the one-half of their property and the one-half of all their lands," the coastal region of Bountiful and Jershon together lined the entire east coast and numerically speaking, constituted one half of Nephite regional lands. The other half would have included Zarahemla and Hermounts. See Map 12.0: "Moronihah Leads the Nephites to Retake Half of Their Lands" in Part 5, Chapter 5.3.

## LAMANITE ENTRY POINTS INTO THE LAND OF ZARAHEMLA

On the basis of the above considerations, it is projected that the Lamanite invasion of 35 BC was conducted in the same manner as the Amalickiah and Ammoron War. That is to say they simultaneously attacked the heartland region and the land of Jershon. Such projections are based upon the meager information supplied for the second and third phases of the latter war. They are in no way considered as absolute, but are merely offered as logical extensions of the brief descriptions presented in Helaman 4:9–19 and 5:14–16.

Such projections could not be attempted without the information contained in Alma 50–62. Those thirteen chapters present in great detail the events of the Amalickiah and Ammoron War and the related geography of the land southward. The Amalickiah and Ammoron War was previously addressed in *The War Against Christianity*.[247]

In 35 BC, the Lamanites are described as coming "down against the Nephites to battle,"[248] implying they came down from highland Nephi. Additionally, the third leg of Nephi and Lehi's mission carried them to highland Nephi, for they were immediately incarcerated in the same prison "Ammon and his brethren" were placed by the people of King Limhi.[249] It is therefore assumed that they went directly to the source of the Lamanite attack and that the war had been initiated from region surrounding the city of Nephi. However, given the expanded scope of the war, it is reasonable to further assume that, as in the Amalickiah and Ammoron War, Lamanite forces were deployed from the eastern region for the attack on Jershon.

## CONTINUING INTERNAL DISSENT

By this time in Nephite history, the dissenter track record was a lengthy rap sheet of treasonous crimes against their own nation, all attached to their obsession for power. Yet, notwithstanding their long history of rebellion and violence, dissenters boldly maintained a pretense of respectability, transparent though it was to the victims of their crimes—the Christian Nephites. They could not be firmly tied to previous atrocities, because they did not represent a single organization or entity like the Church of Christ. If they belonged to the recently organized band of Gadianton robbers, no one knew, for "they did mingle themselves among the people."[250]

When dissenters departed in the two separate instances during Nephi's tenure as chief judge, and then jointly returned with a Lamanite army,[251] they may very well have been greeted in Zarahemla by other dissenters who were closely allied with them. Then, as the Nephites fled in the direction of the narrow neck of land, it is likely that other dissenters fled with them, not necessarily associated with the ones who came with the Lamanite army.

Notwithstanding the recent establishment of the Gadianton robbers, there was no specific unified movement of dissent at that time. Many dissent groups do not seem to have been associates, other than through the fact that they were pagan and shared a common hatred for Christianity, as well as a similar lust for power. To the extent recorded in the Book of Mormon, they did not contend against one another but considered themselves allies in the war against the Christian Nephites. Any animosity they had for each other could be set aside until the

Christians were destroyed. Only then would they openly become mortal enemies in their personal quests for supremacy.[252]

Even as Moronihah's army struggled to expel the Lamanites from Nephite lands, the political struggle inside the Nephite nation continued without abatement. While the war raged nearby, the internal dissenting factions, among whom the Gadianton robbers had become entrenched, became even more active in taking control of the government. Similar to the king-men in the account of the Amalickiah and Ammoron war, they took advantage of the war to further their political cause, as will be seen in the following chapter.

While the very existence of Christianity and the free government lay in the balance, dissenters within the land of Zarahemla pretended as though the greater threat came from the Christian leaders at the head of the Nephite government. It was this internal instability caused by a constantly growing number of dissenters, which cast an ominous pall upon the first Nephite military defeat in Zarahemla as a preview of things to come.

No scenario can be ruled out as to the extent of dissent and the various alliances, because in the new era of secrecy, nothing could be ascertained with any degree of confidence. Consequentially, the Book of Mormon is unclear on the subject. It can be stated with certainty, however, that dissenters within Zarahemla took political advantage of the turmoil and instability caused by the war to further their cause, and it would not be surprising to learn one day that the internal dissent faction did indeed coordinate efforts with the 35 BC Lamanite attack, as in the case of Tubaloth, who had sent Coriantumr to assist the Gadianton robbers sixteen years earlier.[253]

If indeed that was the case, secrecy would have been highly necessary, for they would have learned the vital lesson from the Amalickiah and Ammoron War, that if they joined the military struggle against the Nephite government as the king-men had done, the Nephite military leaders would rightly see them as the enemy and quickly engage them in battle,[254] or cast them into prison and execute them.[255] This may very well have been the reason they remained neutral in the war, but stepped up their political attack. Soon their attention became focused entirely upon the chief judge, Nephi.

## CHAPTER 2.4

# NEPHI RELINQUISHES THE JUDGMENT SEAT

### *30 BC*

THE FIFTH CHAPTER OF Helaman signals a new era in Nephi's life. In 30 BC, after nine years in office, he stepped down from his position at the head of government. He did not resign from office to enjoy a leisurely retirement dedicated to gardening and writing his memoirs, though he did have a garden,[256] and he did take the time to keep a record of the things that transpired during his life.[257] Rather, his retirement from government enabled him to concentrate entirely on the work of the Lord. He and his brother Lehi dedicated the remainder of their lives to preaching the gospel.

The account of Nephi appears to be largely the same as Alma's story, where Alma, seeing great problems in the Church in which wickedness was making enormous strides over righteousness and church doctrine was being corrupted by pagan influences, decided to step down from his position as chief judge. Alma's purpose was to focus exclusively on spiritual matters, to "[bear] down in pure testimony"[258] against such wickedness within the Church, and to set the affairs of the Church in order. Upon closer examination, however, it seems that whereas Alma resigned purely because of his concern for the Church and chose his own successor, Nephi was removed from office and did not choose his successor.

One must be aware of the previous two chapters of Helaman to fully comprehend the events that led to Nephi's departure from office and the critical nature of the problems facing the Christian Nephites at that time. In 30 BC, the seat of Nephite government had not returned to the city of Zarahemla. Though the Nephites had recovered many of their lands and cities in the land southward, the Nephite heartland remained in the hands of the Lamanites and dissenters.[259] After four years of warfare, the Nephite campaign to drive them from Nephite lands was in stalemate. The city of Zarahemla, the traditional center of government and politics, was still under enemy control. It is apparent that Nephi was functioning as chief judge in temporary quarters within the city of Bountiful, for that is where he and Lehi began their mission.[260]

Nephi's popularity may have fallen sharply as the war continued, particularly as the dissenters placed his leadership of the Nephite government under the microscope. Perhaps he was accused of unjustly causing the dissident unrest that had led to the war, or of improperly directing the war. If indeed there was an overall loss of popularity in the general Nephite population, perhaps it was nothing more than the effect of the people directing the brunt of their displeasure over the war and the loss of the heartland region toward the head of the government.

According to Nephi, however, the Nephites "had altered and trampled under their feet the laws of Mosiah . . . their laws had become corrupted, and . . . they had become a wicked people, insomuch that they were wicked even like unto the Lamanites."[261] The hostility surrounding the campaign to alter the law would have become a tremendous burden to the chief judge. Within this line of reasoning, it might be envisioned by some that Nephi resigned of his own volition after becoming "weary because of their iniquity"[262] and their disrespect[263] for laws that he knew were ordained of God.[264]

Based upon Helaman 5:1–4, however, it is concluded that an election had been held and that Nephi was defeated. For that reason, he "delivered up the judgment seat" to Cezoram. In this perspective, it is obvious that the statement, "they who chose evil were more numerous than they who chose good,"[265] refers to the fact that Cezoram received the majority of the votes. Though the specific events leading to Nephi's departure from office are not clearly described in the above passage, they can be deduced with reasonable confidence on the basis of two similar events in the past:

1. In 87 BC, the first political attack on the free government was perpetrated only five years after Mosiah established the system of judges. In that instance, Amlici had acquired a following, which was sufficient to require a vote of the people.[266] The free government would have been automatically abolished if he had been chosen as king. Amlici lost the election, but it

was demonstrated at that early time that the free government established by Mosiah could be eliminated at any time, if a majority of the people should vote against it in favor of another form of government.

2. In 67 BC, the second political attack was raised against Pahoran, the son of Nephihah, at the beginning of his reign.[267] The king-men "had sent in their voices by way of petitions that advocated the altering of the law,"[268] which would eliminate the free government and restore monarchy. When Pahoran would not allow the law to be altered, they—likely a group of lower judges—sought through additional petitions to remove him from office.

The matter was brought to a vote. When the results were tabulated, the king-men were overruled and grudgingly submitted to the voice of the people. Therefore, the government was not reverted back to monarchy, and Chief Judge Pahoran retained his position at the head of Nephite government. Again, the majority ruled, but as before, it was painfully evident that the free government could disappear overnight.

## A Constitutional Crisis

The events leading to Nephi's departure from office were similar to those engineered by Amlici and the king-men, but the end result was entirely different. The attempts to remove Alma and Pahoran I from office had failed. With Nephi, however, the dissenters achieved their goal, and as a result, he "yielded up the judgment-seat"[269] according to "the voice of the people."[270]

As considered above, it is likely that the results of the election in 30 BC were at least partially due to the frustration of the people over the war. There was, however, another contributing factor, which was much less disruptive than before. Whereas the Amlicites and the king-men had both advocated the elimination of the system of judges and the return to monarchy, the dissenters in 30 BC sought power within the system of judges. Therefore, resulting changes would not alter the form of government, and ostensibly, the freedom of the people would not be destroyed.

Considering the final result of the election, it seems that the changes revolved around an expansion of the legitimate candidates for chief judge, that is, the relaxation of the ethnic and religious requirements.

Any person regardless of lineage or religion could thereafter seek the highest office in the land. Before the law was changed, only Christians of direct descent from Nephi, the son of Lehi, had held the office.[271] In 30 BC, the new chief judge likely descended from Zoram, considering his name—Cezoram, and he may very well have been a pagan.

Like Pahoran I,[272] Chief Judge Nephi may have resisted the dissenters' petitions to make changes to Mosiah's laws.[273] It was, however, a legal battle he had already lost, for the account states, "their laws had become corrupted."[274] It is projected that two votes were cast at that time: the first to change the law, and the second to elect Cezoram as the new chief judge.

## CULTURAL AND RELIGIOUS FACTORS

The alarm felt by many Nephites surrounding the above events thus emanated from both cultural and religious principles, which are further considered as follows:

1. **CULTURAL:** The kingdom established by Mosiah I in the land of Zarahemla was a Nephite kingdom. The people of Zarahemla were made Nephites during the reign of Mosiah II, it was because they lived within the boundaries of Mosiah's kingdom. "And now all the people of Zarahemla were numbered with the Nephites, and this because the kingdom had been conferred upon none but those who were descendants of Nephi." [275] The right to rule was therefore limited to Mosiah's descendants, a tradition that was natural and compatible with monarchy.

   The system of judges, as established by Mosiah in 91 BC, perpetuated the right to rule by Nephites of pure descent from Nephi, though it became a continual source of contention in the new democratic government. Still, many Nephites supported rule by descendants of Nephi simply because it was an established cultural tradition.
2. **RELIGIOUS:** The descendants of Nephi were for the most part Christian, and the dissenters were pagans, who were predominantly descendants of Mulek. As more and more Nephites were drawn into the pagan cults, however, the cry for government reform became louder.

   On the other side of the issue, the Christians vigorously defended the laws of Mosiah as instituted, due to their fear of the pagan mindset. The fact that only Christians believed in freedom of religion cemented in the minds of the Christian Nephites the absolute necessity of limiting the office of chief judge to Christian Nephites of pure descent. It thus began as a cultural tradition and ultimately became a matter of life and death for the Christians.

# CHAPTER 2.5

# NEPHI AND LEHI SERVE A 1-YEAR MISSION—THE MIRACULOUS CONVERSION OF THE LAMANITES

## *30 BC*

SOME MEN ARE BORN to be leaders and are preordained to accomplish the purposes of God in powerful ways. Through our knowledge of the premortal life, we know that it is a law of destiny and foreordination.[276] Jesus Christ is the supreme example of this very important law, as we have learned from our understanding of the Great Council in heaven.[277] Other leaders in the spirit world, such as Adam, Noah, Abraham, Jeremiah,[278] and Joseph Smith were set apart during the pre-earth life for very important and critical roles to be accomplished during their mortal lives.[279]

Within the Nephite culture, Nephi and Lehi (the sons of Helaman), were set apart for a most delicate and difficult task at an extremely wicked time in Nephite history. It was one that would require tremendous courage, unwavering faith in God, and total commitment to the cause of Christ. Their roles would be crucial in the preservation of Christianity at that pivotal and formidable time when the forces of evil were joining together for its destruction. Their work would truly set the stage for the appearance of Christ in the Western Hemisphere.

After he yielded the judgment seat to Cezoram, Nephi was deeply troubled about the wickedness that had settled upon the land of Zarahemla. He knew the word of God was the only solution to the problem. The dilemma could not be resolved by military force, but required a change in the hearts of the people. He also knew that if unchecked, the pagan faction would destroy the Church of God.

Like his great-grandfather Alma the Younger, he knew that the influence of God's word was much more potent than the power of the scepter or the sword. Given the great power of Deity that rested upon

Nephi and his brother Lehi during the events that followed, it cannot be denied that they were explicitly following the direction of the Holy Ghost when they united in a great and marvelous missionary effort.

## NEPHI AND LEHI BEGIN THEIR MISSION IN BOUNTIFUL AND JERSHON

Nephi and Lehi began their mission in the Nephite city of Bountiful[280] and thereafter went from city to city within the Nephite lands that had been reclaimed by Moronihah's armies. (See Map 13.0 at the end of Chapter 5.3.) Their journey carried them southward along the eastern seaboard of Jershon, likely all the way to the coastal city of Moroni, which lay at the southeast corner of Nephite lands. Moroni bordered upon the narrow strip of wilderness, which marked Jershon's southern border. They may have also visited the cities of Nephihah and Aaron, which were located eastward of Moroni along the narrow strip of wilderness. Then, they turned their attention to the heartland of Zarahemla, which remained in Lamanite hands.[281]

## NEPHI AND LEHI PREACH WITH GREAT POWER IN ZARAHEMLA

It seems that in times of great wickedness and peril for the people of God, the Lord intervenes on behalf of His people in miraculous ways, much more than in less wicked times. Being empowered by the Holy Ghost and given the words that they should speak, "they did preach with great power" among the Lamanites and dissenters, "insomuch that they did confound many of those dissenters who had gone over from the Nephites, insomuch that they came forth and did confess their sins and were baptized unto repentance, and immediately returned to the Nephites to endeavor to repair unto them the wrongs which they had done."[282] In addition to the dissenters, 8,000 of the occupying Lamanites were brought to the knowledge of Christ, and were "baptized unto repentance" and "convinced of the wickedness of the traditions of their fathers."[283]

## THE SONS OF HELAMAN JOURNEY TO THE CITY OF NEPHI

The two men of God then went up by the grace of the Lord into the hostile land of Nephi to preach in the Lamanite center of power. When they reached the vicinity of the cities of Nephi and Shilom,[284] they were captured by a Lamanite army and placed in a holding cell, the same one where Ammon and his brethren were jailed by Limhi's guards in 121 BC.[285] After holding them for several days without food, a company of warriors comprised of Lamanites and Nephite dissenters came to the prison for the purpose of putting them to death. However, as they reached forth to take them, Nephi and Lehi were suddenly surrounded by "a pillar of fire."[286] The guards were afraid to touch them, believing they would be burned.

When the two missionaries realized they were standing in the midst of fire and were not burned, "their hearts did take courage," for when they saw the Lamanites were fearful and dumbfounded, they knew the protective hands of God surrounded them.[287] They told the soldiers that it was God who had performed this great miracle, which prevented them from laying their hands on them. As they spoke, the earth began to quake and the walls of the prison shook violently around them. Simultaneously, a cloud of darkness enveloped the Lamanites, and "an awful solemn fear" came over them.

In the midst of this horrifying scene, "a still voice of perfect mildness, as if it had been a whisper," spoke suddenly from above the cloud of darkness saying, "Repent ye, repent ye, and seek no more to destroy my servants whom I have sent unto you to declare good tidings."[288] Notwithstanding its mildness, the voice "did pierce even to the very soul," while the earth and the prison walls continued to shake violently. The "cloud of darkness, which had overshadowed them, did not disperse."[289]

The voice came again, saying, "Repent ye, repent ye, for the kingdom of heaven is at hand, and seek no more to destroy my servants," while the earth trembled again as before. A third time "the voice came, and did speak unto them marvelous words which cannot be uttered by man." Again, the prison walls trembled "and the earth shook as if it were about to divide asunder."[290] The men were frightened beyond measure—too frightened to move, and unable to move because of the darkness which engulfed them.

There was a man among them, a Nephite by birth, who had once been a member of the Church of God, but had apostatized and dissented away to the Lamanites:

> And it came to pass that he turned him about, and behold, he saw through the cloud of darkness the faces of Nephi and Lehi, and behold, they did shine exceedingly, even as the faces of angels. And he beheld that they did lift their eyes to heaven; and they were in

the attitude as if talking or lifting their voices to some being whom they beheld.

And it came to pass that this man did cry unto the multitude, that they might turn and look. And there was power given unto them that they did turn and look; and they did behold the faces of Nephi and Lehi.

And they said unto the man: Behold, what do all these things mean, and who is it with whom these men do converse?

Now the man's name was Aminadab. And Aminadab said unto them: They do converse with the angels of God.

And it came to pass that the Lamanites said unto him: What shall we do, that this cloud of darkness may be removed from overshadowing us?

And Aminadab said unto them; You must repent, and cry unto the voice, even until ye shall have faith in Christ, who was taught unto you by Alma, and Amulek, and Zeezrom; and when ye shall do this, the cloud of darkness shall be removed from overshadowing you.

And it came to pass that they all did begin to cry unto the voice of him who had shaken the earth; yea, they did cry even until the cloud of darkness was dispersed.

And it came to pass that when they cast their eyes about, and saw that the cloud of darkness was dispersed from overshadowing them, behold, they saw that they were encircled about, yea every soul, by a pillar of fire.

And Nephi and Lehi were in the midst of them; yea they were encircled about; yea, they were as if in the midst of a flaming fire, yet it did harm them not, neither did it take hold upon the walls of the prison; and they were filled with that joy which is unspeakable and full of glory.

And behold, the Holy Spirit of God did come down from heaven, and did enter into their hearts, and they were filled as if with fire, and they could speak forth marvelous words.

And it came to pass that there came a voice unto them, yea, a pleasant voice, as if it were a whisper, saying:

Peace, peace be unto you, because of your faith in my Well Beloved, who was from the foundation of the world.

And now, when they heard this they cast up their eyes as if to behold from whence the voice came; and behold, they saw the heavens open; and angels came down out of heaven and ministered unto them.

> And there were about three hundred souls who saw and heard these things; and they were bidden to go forth and marvel not, neither should they doubt.
>
> And it came to pass that they did go forth, and did minister unto people, declaring throughout all the regions round about all the things which they had heard and seen, insomuch that the more part of the Lamanites were convinced of them, because of the greatness of the evidences which they had received.
>
> And as many as were convinced did lay down their weapons of war, and also their hatred and the traditions of their fathers.
>
> And it came to pass that they did yield up unto the Nephites the lands of their possession. [291]

The cloud of darkness, which overshadowed the Lamanites in this marvelous heavenly manifestation, provided perfect symbolism for the spiritual darkness that engulfed them prior to the experience. The dispersal of the cloud was followed immediately by the dispersal of their spiritual darkness. Their conversion to the gospel of Jesus Christ was sudden and complete, similar to the experience of the people of Ammon sixty years previously.[292] Truly, the love and compassion of God, and His magnificent power to influence the lives of His children are beyond our understanding.

It is noted that the dissenters and Lamanites, which had taken control of the land of Zarahemla, did not have the power to give back the Nephite lands to them, even after 8,000 Lamanites were converted and baptized. It was required that Nephi and Lehi must go into the land of Nephi to the source of Lamanite political power. Only after the conversion of Lamanites at the center of Lamanite government were the Nephite lands returned to them.[293]

Through this miraculous series of events, Nephi and Lehi became mighty instruments in the hands of God to bring about the conversion of the majority of the Lamanite nation during a period of only a few months. By means of the great work accomplished by God through their mission, the Lamanites within the land of Nephi entered their first period of righteousness. The gospel spread throughout the land of Nephi, and they became an enlightened and choice people.

Surely it was part of the Lord's preparation for His appearance in the New World. It would allow righteous Lamanites to fully comprehend the significance of the Atonement of Christ and to experience true joy at the time of His appearance. It would enable them to take an active role in the golden age of love and peace that would then follow.

## A NEW ERA OF PEACE AND PROSPERITY?

In the months that followed the great Lamanite conversion, a new atmosphere of peace settled upon the land southward.[294] The borders between Nephite and Lamanite lands became transparent, as both Lamanites and Nephites could thereafter pass freely between the two countries. In the great flurry of commercial activity which followed, both nations prospered and many merchants in both lands became rich. Goods of every kind flowed between the two nations, including gold and silver, and products of every kind. Previously, there had never been an era of peace and unfettered trade across the entirety of the land southward.

Moreover, there was a continuation of growth in the long-range commercial relations between the land southward and the land northward. The scope of commercial enterprise expanded rapidly. Merchant activities and the distances involved quickly exceeded anything that could have been imagined before the colonization of the land northward. This description of commercial activity and general prosperity throughout an expanded Nephite world seemed to paint an extremely positive picture of the cultural well-being of the Nephite and Lamanite peoples. It appeared that with the conversion of the Lamanites to Christ, an unprecedented and enduring age of peace and harmony had finally arrived, which would thereafter fill the entire Nephite/Lamanite world. However, it was not to be.

## CHAPTER 2.6

# A MAJOR SHIFT IN THE DYNAMICS OF DISSENT

When Laman, Lemuel, and the sons of Ishmael plunged their descendants into spiritual darkness in their rebellion against God, it drastically affected the Lamanite culture for hundreds of years. The resulting state of extreme Lamanite depravity is graphically portrayed by Enos, the son of Jacob, who described them as "a wild, and ferocious, and a blood-thirsty people, full of idolatry and filthiness; feeding upon beasts of prey; dwelling in tents, and wandering about in the wilderness with a short skin girdle about their loins and their heads shaven; and their skill was in the bow, and in the cimeter, and the ax. And many of them did eat nothing save it was raw meat; and they were continually seeking to destroy us."[295]

A few centuries after the days of Enos, changes began to occur among the Lamanites, which could be classified as cultural improvements. This was at least in part through the influence of Nephite dissenters—the priests of Amulon—who in 121 BC were embraced by the Lamanites because of their shared hatred for the Nephites. The Amulonites brought with them the cultural learning of the Nephites. Soon they taught the Lamanites across the land of Nephi how to read and write.[296]

Despite the cultural development that took place under the direction of the Amulonites, the cloud of Lamanite spiritual darkness would remain fully in place for another thirty years. Upon the arrival of the sons of Mosiah in 91 BC, the darkness began to dissipate. Between 91 and 77 BC, thousands of Lamanites were converted to Christianity through the efforts of Mosiah's sons and their associates.[297]

Within the land of Nephi, however, there was no lasting effect from the Lamanite conversions. The people of Anti-Nephi-Lehi, or the people of Ammon as the Lamanite converts would become known to the Nephites, were attacked by other Lamanites under the influence of Amalekites and Amulonites, who practiced the pagan religion of

Nehor.[298] In 77 BC, it became necessary for them to flee with Ammon and his brethren to the land of Zarahemla to preserve their own lives. Their departure left the land of Nephi as before, fully immersed in spiritual darkness, which would remain firmly in place for still another forty-seven years.

### *30 BC*

### THE NECESSITY OF THE LAMANITE CONVERSION

The mission of Nephi and Lehi to the Lamanites (Chapter 2.5) was a crucial event in the endless struggle between the Christians and the pagan dissenters. During the period immediately preceding their mission, the pagan conspiracy had come dangerously close to achieving its primary purpose of eradicating Christianity—both in the land southward, and in the land northward. In 35 BC, when the Lamanites and dissenters succeeded in driving the Nephites all the way to the border of Desolation, the Nephites were in even greater danger than they realized. As they fled into the constriction of the narrow neck, they were confident that it would provide a sanctuary from the Lamanite attack.

However, they were unaware of the fact that at that very moment in 33 BC,[299] as they fortified the narrow neck of land and "stationed their armies to defend their north country,"[300] additional forces of evil had already gathered behind them in the land northward. By 33 BC (only twenty-two years after the first northward migrations), the pagans had essentially taken control of the land northward. It was a situation that would not become fully evident to the Nephites until the mission of Nephi and Lehi to that region four years later.[301]

Prior to the 55 BC northward migrations, the Nephites had expended great efforts—especially during the Amalickiah and Ammoron War—to prevent the Lamanites, as well as dissenters within the land of Zarahemla, from migrating into the land northward. They had been quite successful in sealing off the land northward from both groups.

Their efforts were completely nullified after 55 BC, however, as wave after wave of dissenters flowed into the north countries.[302] The situation feared by the Nephites[303] would be personally witnessed by Nephi and Lehi in 29 BC.[304] The Nephites would have nowhere to go, should another Lamanite invasion drive them past the narrow neck of land into the land northward, where likely they would find it necessary to contend with dissenters there as well.

Therefore, the conversion of the Lamanites at that precise moment was essential to the survival of Christianity in the New World, especially as the number of dissenters grew rapidly within the land southward. In the sense that great and miraculous heavenly manifestations were required to achieve the Lamanite conversion, it was a powerful demonstration of the intervention of God in defense of the righteous Nephites—and for the sake of many choice Lamanites, who were engulfed in spiritual darkness, through no fault of their own.

## CONVERTED LAMANITES EXPAND THE WORK INITIATED BY NEPHI AND LEHI

Following the conversion of the 300 Lamanites at the prison in the land of Nephi,[305] the entire Lamanite culture soon became for the most part a righteous people.[306] The work begun by Nephi and Lehi was perpetuated and magnified by the Lamanites themselves, who traveled throughout the land of Nephi and taught the gospel of Jesus Christ to their own people. Many traveled to the land of Zarahemla to share with the Nephites the manner of their conversion and their new-found love for the gospel. Their stories brought great joy to the members of the Church in Zarahemla. Many preached to the Nephites with great power and authority.

## A FUNDAMENTAL ASPECT OF THE LAMANITE CONVERSION

A significant contributing factor to the Lamanite conversion was the age of certain of the Lamanites who came to the prison to slay Nephi and Lehi,[307] and the prominence they apparently held within the Lamanite culture. The approximate age of some, who had previously dissented from the Nephites,[308] can be determined simply by the factor of time—that which had passed following the mission of Alma, Amulek, and Zeezrom to the Zoramites in 74 BC.[309] Apparently, that is the event to which Aminadab referred in Helaman 5:41, whereby the gospel of Jesus Christ had been taught unto them by Alma, Amulek, and Zeezrom, as concluded from the following:

1. The previous mission to the Zoramites is the only instance recorded in the Book of Mormon in which all three men of

God went on a joint mission to teach the gospel. It is possible that an earlier mission was conducted sometime between Zeezrom's baptism in 81 BC[310] and 74 BC, but in that case, Aminadab and those to whom he spoke in the fifth chapter of Helaman would have been even older.

2. Alma was taken up unto the Lord at the beginning of the following year (73 BC).[311] Therefore, any subsequent mission involving all three missionaries to any location in Zarahemla would not significantly change the age of the dissenters.

The Zoramites became Lamanites immediately following the Zoramite mission[312] and departed from the land of Zarahemla. In 30 BC, when the Lamanite conversion took place, at least forty-three years, and more likely forty-five years, had passed since the gospel had been taught to them in the city of Antionum. This is quite significant, for these men were, to some extent, older than fifty years of age and were likely considered wise statesmen among the Lamanites—well-known and well-respected.

Furthermore, they had displayed a rigid and unchanging hatred for the Nephites throughout the entire period since their arrival in the land of Nephi, and in fact had come to the prison to slay Nephi and Lehi. Both of these factors imparted great power to their testimony following the great heavenly manifestation at the prison, which without doubt contributed significantly to the magnitude of the Lamanite conversion.[313]

## *29 BC*

## MANY NEPHITES IN ZARAHEMLA REJECT THE GOSPEL MESSAGE

The joyful experience of the Lamanites was not celebrated by all Nephites throughout the land of Zarahemla. While the Lamanites were drawing close to the Lord and finding delight in what to them were new principles of righteousness, many Nephites were moving in the opposite direction. They had become hardened and were hostile to the principles of the gospel, which had long been taught among them. For that reason, as well as for ethnic considerations, the Gadianton robbers were making great headway among them. Hence, the conversion of the Lamanites was largely countered by the spiritual plummet of the Nephites.

## THE GADIANTON ROBBERS ADVANCE THE CAUSE OF EVIL

As the Lamanites entered an age of gospel light, love, peace, and prosperity, many Nephites continued their descent into the abyss of moral depravity. The Gadianton robbers continued to advance their agenda in Zarahemla, finding fertile ground among many Nephites, who embraced their perverse pagan religion and secret works of darkness, which were centered upon murder for gain.

The robbers introduced a completely new mode of attack against the Christian Nephite culture. Whereas previous political rebellions had been well-defined and apparent, even to the casual observer, the robbers worked under a garb of secrecy. Their world was a shadowy abode, in which nothing was as it appeared. Working in this advanced level of deception, they were able to entice a majority of the people to join in their cause,[314] while the people of the Church in many cases were completely unaware of the cancer growing among them.

## NEW ALLIANCES IN THE NEPHITE RELIGIOUS WARS

The record of Zeniff describes in detail the Lamanite state of mind—the direct result of the traditions that had emanated from their first fathers:

> They were a wild, and ferocious, and a blood-thirsty people, believing in the tradition of their fathers, which is this—Believing that they were driven out of the land of Jerusalem because of the iniquities of their fathers, and that they were wronged in the wilderness by their brethren, and they were also wronged while crossing the sea;
>
> And again, that they were wronged while in the land of their first inheritance, after they had crossed the sea, and all this because that Nephi was more faithful in keeping the commandments of the Lord—therefore he was favored of the Lord, for the Lord heard his prayers and answered them, and he took the lead of their journey in the wilderness.
>
> And his brethren were wroth with him because they understood not the dealings of the Lord; they were also wroth with him upon the waters because they hardened their hearts against the Lord.
>
> And again, they were wroth with him when they had arrived in the promised land, because they said that he had taken the ruling of the people out of their hands; and they sought to kill him.

> And again, they were wroth with him because he departed into the wilderness as the Lord had commanded him, and took the records which were engraven on the plates of brass, for they said that he robbed them.
>
> And thus they have taught their children that they should hate them, and that they should murder them, and that they should rob and plunder them, and do all they could to destroy them; therefore they have an eternal hatred towards the children of Nephi.[315]

Dissenters had always taken advantage of the Lamanite traditions of hatred to stir them up to anger against the Nephites, and as long as the Lamanites remained in spiritual darkness, they were the resource of choice. With the loss of the Lamanite pawns, however, the dissenters began to focus their efforts of recruitment within the land of Zarahemla. During the twenty-two years between the 52 BC establishment of the robbers and the Lamanite 30 BC conversion, they had already begun to make great headway among the Nephites.

Their success within the Nephite nation, however, did not replace their campaign among the Lamanites in the land of Nephi, which was the very center of their power. Even after the Lamanite conversion, they continued for a time to sow seeds among those Lamanites which had not been converted to the gospel in 30 BC.[316] In 25 BC, five years after the Lamanite conversion, the robbers "were more numerous among the more wicked part of the Lamanites," than among the Nephites.[317]

## ROBBERS ARE ELIMINATED FROM AMONG THE LAMANITES

In 24 BC, when the Lamanites discovered the robbers were still operating within the land of Nephi, they "did hunt the band of robbers of Gadianton; and they did preach the word of God among the more wicked part of them, insomuch that this band of robbers was utterly destroyed from among the Lamanites."[318]

It thus becomes evident that the wholesale conversion of the Lamanites had entirely altered the dynamics of dissent.[319]

Prior to their conversion, Lamanite support had been taken for granted by the dissenters. The Lamanites could always be counted on for military assistance, except for a couple of occasions when they were too fearful to go against the Nephites.[320] Throughout the period between the establishment of the robbers[321] and the conversion of the Lamanites, the Lamanite threat did not diminish. At the same time, the number of dissenters in the land of Zarahemla grew. The combined numbers of Lamanites and dissenters became so great that in company with the Nephite loss of physical strength through transgression, they completely overwhelmed the Nephites when they invaded Zarahemla in 35 BC.

Following their conversion, however, the Lamanites were no longer a resource for the pagan dissenters. In fact, they became completely off-limits to the robbers. Conversely, they became a vital source of spiritual and military strength for the Christian Nephites. As a result, the mortal threat posed by the robbers was substantially reduced.

# CHAPTER 2.7

# THE ROBBERS TAKE CONTROL OF THE NEPHITE GOVERNMENT

### *30 BC*

THE SAME PAGAN INFLUENCES, which contributed to Cezoram's election to the office of chief judge, also ushered in a period of greater vulnerability for Christian Nephites within the land of Zarahemla. After Cezoram's election, every new development brought the Christians closer to destruction. Though Cezoram's religious preference is not revealed, it is likely that he was an unbeliever, or his election would not have been considered in the book of Helaman to be an act of evil.[322] Regardless of his religious orientation, however, the new law, which allowed him—a descendant of Zoram—to ascend to the judgment seat, opened the door to the Gadianton robbers, which are directly linked to idolatry.[323]

## A NEW AGE OF ELECTORAL FREEDOM

As with Cezoram, Seezoram's name seems to imply descent from the original Zoram, who came with the people of Lehi from Jerusalem in 600 BC. In that vein, at least seven men—Zoram of Antionum, Amalickiah, Ammoron,[324] Tubaloth, Cezoram, the son of Cezoram, Seezoram, and Seantum—are either directly or implicitly identified as descending from the original Zoram. However, they are never referred to as Zoramites. The word "Zoramite" is never used to identify descendants of the original Zoram, except in a general sense when identifying the major ethnic divisions with the Nephite culture.[325]

Otherwise, the word "Zoramite" is used exclusively to refer to the followers of Zoram, the cult leader in the city of Antionum in 75 BC. They dissented away to the Lamanites in 74 BC and inhabited the land of Nephi for many years thereafter. Obviously, some of them, like their leader, descended from the original Zoram, but that is not why they were called Zoramites. The name Zoramite refers to their affiliation with the pagan religious cult of the same name that Zoram established in 75 BC.

With the election of Cezoram in 30 BC, it is apparent that a descendant of the original Zoram ascended to the judgment seat for the first time in Nephite history. For that to happen, it would have required two changes to the law prior to the election, which greatly expanded the list of rightful candidates for the highest office in the land of Zarahemla. No longer must they be a descendant of Nephi, or belong to the Christian faith. Afterward, anyone, regardless of lineage or religion, could be elected to the highest office in the land of Zarahemla.

## RULES OF SUCCESSION REMAIN UNCHANGED

In the series of events involving the election of Cezoram and his son, important information is provided with respect to the rules of succession, which apparently were not changed with the altering of the law. Once a man attained the position of chief judge, barring a substantial political challenge, rights of lineage were still in force. This was exemplified in 26 BC, when Cezoram's son became the chief judge following his father's assassination,[326] as the first in line according to rights of succession—similar to Pacumeni in 52 BC.[327]

It might seem that the same familial rights of lineage were at play in the assassination of Seezoram by his own brother. In 23 BC, Seantum appears to have expected to become the chief judge (by rights of kinship) at Seezoram's death.[328] However, this is not necessarily the case, unless their father had preceded Seezoram in the judgment seat. There is no mention of Seezoram having a father. It is therefore possible that Seantum was not in line for the judgment seat. Rather, he may have expected to rise to the office purely on grounds of popularity, upon his brother's death.

## *29 BC*

## NEPHI, LEHI, AND MANY LAMANITES JOURNEY TO THE LAND NORTHWARD

Following their conversion to Christ, many Lamanites went into the land northward to preach the gospel.[329] Nephi and Lehi also journeyed into the land northward on a mission that lasted for six years. No specific information is given of their mission, though they had no success. While they were gone, the land of Zarahemla languished both spiritually and politically. Upon Nephi's return "to the land of his nativity in 23 BC," he would be shocked at the conditions he found there.[330]

## *26 BC*

## THE ROBBERS OBTAIN THE JUDGMENT SEAT

Four years after Cezoram was elected as chief judge, while Nephi and Lehi were in the land northward, the Gadianton robbers took advantage of the new laws that had enabled his election. To initiate their rise to power, they assassinated both Cezoram and his son during 26 BC, which opened the door to the top position in Nephite government. It is apparent that, following the second assassination, there were no other blood relatives of Cezoram in line for the judgment seat. At that time, a new election was held, and the vote went to a man named Seezoram, a Gadianton robber. This sequence was similar to the chain of events leading to Helaman's election in 50 BC.[331]

In both instances, the robbers laid the groundwork for obtaining the judgment seat by way of assassination. In the first attempt (52 BC), they had failed when the plot was discovered by Helaman's servant and Kishkumen was slain. The identity of the robbers was exposed, and they were compelled to flee from the land of Zarahemla.[332] In the latter attempt, however, the robbers were not apprehended for the murder of Cezoram and his son. In fact, it was not known that they had returned to Zarahemla around 43 BC,[333] and had worked secretly thereafter among the people.

It does not appear that Cezoram and his son belonged to the Gadianton robbers. In that line of reasoning, Helaman 6:17–19 refers to the assassination of Cezoram and his son as having been perpetrated by the robbers. In those verses, it is implied that the two chief judges were victims of the robbers, not associates.

Upon finding their identity was still a secret, the robbers entered a candidate of their own in the following election.[334] As a result, they were able to achieve total victory when Seezoram was elected.[335] They maintained complete secrecy for a period of three years until Seezoram was assassinated by his brother, Seantum in 23 BC.[336] Even then, the robbers would have remained unidentified, if not for revelations given by the Lord to the prophet Nephi.

### *23 BC*

### NEPHI RETURNS FROM THE LAND NORTHWARD

The Nephites had inhabited the land northward for thirty-two years when Nephi and Lehi traveled there to preach the gospel. As considered previously, it is apparent that pagan dissenters had taken control of the various regions of habitation. Through their power and influence, the people throughout the land northward were hostile to the gospel and "did reject all [their] words."[337] Considering the great and marvelous miracles associated with Nephi and Lehi in the conversion of the Lamanite nation, their inability to achieve success in the land northward truly reflects the rigid control maintained by the pagans, and the complete lack of faith of everyone under their influence.

Consequently, after spending six years in the land northward, the two missionaries were forced to depart out of the land. They returned in great sorrow to the land of their nativity. Helaman 7 contains the account of Nephi's arrival in the city of Zarahemla.

Nephi became even more distressed when he found the Gadianton robbers had obtained control of the Nephite government.[338] The circumstances in Zarahemla, in combination with his painful experience in the land northward, presented a bleak picture for the future of the Nephites. The great Lamanite conversion suddenly seemed insignificant, and no doubt he wondered if Christianity could survive in the face of such iniquity.

He climbed to the top of his garden tower and kneeled in prayer to express his deep sorrow to God for the wickedness that was destroying his homeland. He prayed:

> Oh, that I could have had my days in the days when my father Nephi first came out of the land of Jerusalem, that I could have joyed with him in the promised land; then were his people easy to be entreated, firm to keep the commandments of God, and slow to be led to do iniquity; and they were quick to hearken unto the words of the Lord.
>
> Yea, if my days could have been in those days, then would my soul have had joy in the righteousness of my brethren.

> But behold, I am consigned that these are my days, and that my soul shall be filled with sorrow because of this the wickedness of my brethren.[339]

Unbeknownst to Nephi, his prayer would soon set in motion a chain of events, which like his mission with Lehi to the Lamanites, would be miraculous indeed.

## THE REVELATIONS OF NEPHI

Nephi's home was situated by a major thoroughfare within the city of Zarahemla. It could have been called Market Street, for it was the primary route leading from the entrance of the city to the central market—the commercial hub and the heartbeat of the city.[340] No doubt it was filled with farmers and merchants hauling products of every kind to be sold, and buyers moving to and from the marketplace. The tower upon which Nephi prayed was located next to his garden gate, which opened onto the highway. A few who passed by and heard Nephi's prayer "ran and told the people what they had seen. And the people came together in multitudes."[341] Therefore, as Nephi prayed loudly from his tower with no thought for his surroundings, a large crowd soon congregated below to learn the reason for his anguish of soul. He was, after all, a well-known and well-respected man, and formerly their chief judge.

When he arose from his prayer, Nephi quickly realized that he was not alone. Hearing the commotion below, he looked down and discovered the crowd that peered up at him. He said, "Behold, why have ye gathered yourselves together? That I may tell you of your iniquities?"[342]

He continued:

> And because of my mourning and lamentation ye have gathered yourselves together, and do marvel; yea, and ye have great need to marvel; yea, ye ought to marvel because ye are given away that the devil has got so great hold upon your hearts.
>
> Yea, how could you have given way to the enticing of him who is seeking to hurl away your souls down to everlasting misery and endless wo?
>
> O repent ye, repent ye! Why will ye die? Turn ye, turn ye unto the Lord your God. Why has he forsaken you?
>
> It is because you have hardened your hearts; yea, ye will not hearken unto the voice of the good shepherd; yea, ye have provoked him to anger against you.

> And behold, instead of gathering you, except ye will repent, behold, he shall scatter you forth that ye shall become meat for dogs and wild beasts.[343]

Only seven years earlier, the Lamanites had returned the city of Zarahemla to the Nephites, after occupying it for four or five years. Their departure from the city had resulted purely from the Lord's great and miraculous work through Nephi and his brother, Lehi. The Lamanite conversion to the gospel had completely eliminated the Lamanite threat, but subsequently the city had fallen under the control of the Gadianton robbers. Nephi continued:

> O, how could you have forgotten your God in the very day that he has delivered you?
>
> But behold, it is to get gain, to be praised of men, yea, and that ye might get gold and silver. And ye have set your hearts upon the riches and the vain things of this world, for the which ye do murder, and plunder, and steal, and bear false witness against your neighbor, and do all manner of iniquity.
>
> And for this cause wo shall come unto you except ye shall repent. For if ye will not repent, behold, this great city, and also all those great cities which are round about, which are in the land of our possession, shall be taken away that ye shall have no place in them; for behold, the Lord will not grant unto you strength, as he has hitherto done, to withstand against your enemies.
>
> For behold, thus saith the Lord: I will not show unto the wicked of my strength, to one more than the other, save it be unto those that repent of their sins, and hearken unto my words. Now therefore, I would that ye should behold, my brethren, that it shall be better for the Lamanites than for you except ye shall repent.
>
> For behold, they are more righteous than you, for they have not sinned against that great knowledge which ye have received; therefore the Lord will be merciful unto them; yea, he will lengthen out their days and increase their seed, even when thou shalt be utterly destroyed except thou shalt repent.
>
> Yea, wo be unto you because of that great abomination which has come among you; and ye have united yourselves unto it, yea, to that secret band which was established by Gadianton!
>
> Yea, wo shall come unto you because of that pride which ye have suffered to enter your hearts, which has lifted you up beyond that which is good because of your exceedingly great riches!

> Yea, wo be unto you because of your wickedness and abominations!
>
> And except ye repent ye shall perish; yea, even your lands shall be taken from you, and ye shall be destroyed from off the face of the earth."[344]

There were judges among the crowd who belonged to the Gadianton robbers. They "were angry with [Nephi] because he spake plainly to them concerning their secret works of darkness."[345] They did not lay their hands upon him, because they feared the people, but they called upon the people to bring Nephi to justice that he might be condemned for reviling against the law[346] "For behold, Nephi had spoken unto them concerning the corruptness of their law."[347] He also prophesied of the destruction of the people and their cities,[348] to which they responded, "We are powerful, and our cities great, therefore our enemies can have no power over us."[349] Others defended Nephi, saying, "Let this man alone, for he is a good man, and those things which he saith will surely come to pass except we repent."[350]

When Nephi saw that "he had gained favor in the eyes of some," he began to preach to them concerning the power given to prophets of old, including Moses at the shores of the Red Sea.[351] "And now behold, if God gave unto this man such power, then why should ye dispute among yourselves, and say that he hath given unto me no power whereby I may know concerning the judgments that shall come upon you except ye repent?"[352]

He said that Moses had testified of the "coming of the Messiah,"[353] and that Abraham also saw the coming of the Lord, and "was filled with gladness and did rejoice."[354] He referred to other prophets who had seen the coming of Christ in vision, including the prophet Jeremiah, a contemporary of Father Lehi in Jerusalem. He said, "Jeremiah [was] the same prophet who testified of the destruction of Jerusalem . . . and we know that Jerusalem was destroyed according to the words of Jeremiah. O then why not the son of God come, according to his prophecy?"[355] He told them that they could not deny that Jerusalem was destroyed according to the words of Jeremiah, unless they lied. "But behold, ye have rejected the truth"[356] and "because of your murders and your fornication and wickedness," "except ye repent," the judgment of God "will come unto you soon."[357]

It was at this time that Nephi dropped a bombshell. He said,

> Yea, behold it is now even at your doors; yea, go ye in unto the judgment-seat, and search; and behold, your judge is murdered, and he lieth in his blood; and he hath been murdered by his brother, who seeketh to sit in the judgment-seat.
>
> And behold, they both belong to your secret band, whose author is Gadianton and the evil one who seeketh to destroy the souls of men.[358]

Five men were immediately dispatched to the judgment seat to see if the chief judge was dead. They ran in their might, saying, "Behold, now we will know of a surety whether this man be a prophet and God hath commanded him to prophesy such marvelous things unto us. Behold, we do not believe that he hath; yea, we do not believe that he is a prophet; nevertheless, if this thing which he has said concerning the chief judge be true, that he be dead, then will we believe that the other words which he has spoken are true."[359]

At the judgment seat, they did indeed find the chief judge lying in his own blood. They were "astonished exceedingly" at the sight and fell to the earth in great fear, "lest all the judgments which Nephi had spoken should come upon the people."[360] Soon they were discovered lying where they had fallen. It was automatically assumed that they had perpetrated the crime and were stricken by God before they could escape. They were immediately seized and cast into prison.

On the following day, the people gathered to attend the funeral of the chief judge. At the funeral, the judges who were at the garden of Nephi inquired "among the people" concerning the five who had been sent to the judgment seat. They were told that five men had been arrested for the murder of the chief judge, but "concerning this five whom ye say ye have sent, we know not."[361]

The five men were immediately brought from the jail and interrogated publicly. They told of the revelation that had been announced by Nephi concerning the death of the chief judge. The judges then sent to have Nephi brought before them. When he stood in front of them, they accused him of plotting with someone to assassinate the chief judge.

In response to their accusation, and for the third time, Nephi proclaimed a revelation, and this time it was one they could not deny. He told the judges to go to Seantum, the brother of the chief judge and ask him if he had plotted with Nephi to murder his brother. He said that Seantum would deny any relationship with Nephi and would emphatically deny that he had killed his brother. He prophesied that they would then examine the skirt of Seantum's garment and discover blood. They would ask him if it was the blood of his brother, whereupon he would break down and confess that he had committed the crime. Seantum would then tell them that Nephi could not have known of his crime unless God told him. They went as Nephi instructed, and the scene unfolded before their eyes exactly as he had prophesied. When news of this development reached the assembly hall, Nephi and the five were set free.[362]

## THE POWER OF NEPHI'S WORDS

Helaman 5:17–19 describes the miraculous spiritual power with which Nephi and Lehi were endowed. In 30 BC, they had preached the word of the Lord in the land of Zarahemla with such power that they confounded many of the dissenters and greatly astonished the Lamanites who had expelled the Nephites and taken possession of the heartland region.[363] Now, seven years later, Mormon provides an explicit example of Nephi's gift of discernment—first through his discourse from his garden tower, and then by what followed at the judgment seat. He told the people things he could not have known unless they were given to him by God.

Several times during the verbal exchange, he used undeniable and traditionally accepted revelation as a foundation for his own prophecies of coming judgment for their sins. When he quoted other prophets, he qualified their authority by recounting the miracles they had performed and the prophecies given by them that had already been fulfilled. Nephi was a veritable fountain of knowledge. When the people were seemingly unaffected by a revelation, he would simply provide them with yet another revelation. The revelations are listed as follows:

1. **KNOWLEDGE OF SECRET WORKS**—Nephi informed the judges that he knew of their involvement in the Secret Society of Gadianton, which generally was not known by anyone outside the Gadianton organization. It was a secret that was rigidly concealed upon penalty of death.[364] The fact that the chief judge and many of the lesser judges were Gadianton robbers[365] could only be known to Nephi through revelation from God. Thus it was his knowledge of their great secret, which lent credence to his pronouncement of the Lord's impending judgments against them. However, the real impact was on the

robbers themselves, not on other people who were for the most part unaware of their dark secrets.

2. **THE POWER GIVEN TO MOSES**—Nephi made reference to the great miracle performed by Moses, first, in parting the Red Sea, which allowed the Israelites to cross over on dry ground, and then, in closing the waters upon the Egyptian army. In so doing, he appealed to Nephites who still believed in that great and pivotal event of Jewish history, without which they would not have escaped from Egypt. The great power given to Moses then became the foundation for belief in further prophecies concerning the coming birth of the Savior of mankind,[366] which had also been taught by Moses, as well as other prophets of old, including Abraham, Melchizedek, Isaiah, and Jeremiah.
3. **JEREMIAH'S PROPHECY OF JERUSALEM'S DESTRUCTION**—Nephi said that Jeremiah was the same prophet who had testified of the destruction of Jerusalem. "And we know," said he, "that Jerusalem was destroyed according to the words of Jeremiah."[367] Jeremiah's prophecy had been proven true beyond refutation by the delayed presence of the Mulekites among the Nephites.[368] Therefore, if his first revelation be true, then why should Christ not also come according to Jeremiah's prophecy?
4. **FOREKNOWLEDGE OF SEEZORAM'S ASSASSINATION**—The wicked judges with which Nephi contended refused to admit any guilt for sin. They denied the first revelation concerning the fact that Gadianton robbers had infiltrated the government. They refused to believe the prophecies of the coming of Christ, even though they were validated by the power given by God to Moses and by the fulfillment of Jeremiah's prophecy of the destruction of Jerusalem which they could not deny.

Nephi then moved to the present, even to that very moment in time, presenting them with a revelation, which immediately seized everyone's attention, and which was verified within moments. He told them that the chief judge, Seezoram had been assassinated by his brother, Seantum and was at that moment lying in his own blood. He also said that both Seezoram and Seantum belonged to the Gadianton robbers.

Their secret works had thus become an open book to Nephi through the power of God.

5. **FOREKNOWLEDGE OF SEANTUM'S CONFESSION**—The following day, as developments surrounding the death of the chief judge unfolded, Nephi was brought in to be questioned about the murder, for the judges declared that if he knew of the murder before it occurred, then he must have been in league with the murderers. Nephi then provided another revelation—a prophecy of something that would immediately be fulfilled. In like manner to his previous prophecies, by association it would prove the truthfulness of all of his previous declarations. He presented them with a detailed preview of Seantum's confession and declaration that Nephi could not have known of his murderous deed unless he was told by God. This final prophecy came to pass while the judges served as witnesses and participants in a developing scenario.

After all these things had occurred, there was no doubt to the honest of heart that a true prophet of God had spoken to them in the city of Zarahemla. As a spokesman for God, Nephi's words were:

1. Revelation which exposed their secret works of darkness.
2. Condemnation for their gross wickedness.
3. Prophecy of coming judgment if they did not repent.

In revealing the identity of the murderer of the chief judge, he had shown that by the power of God, nothing could be hidden from him. The people were insensitive to the voice of the Spirit, however, having given themselves over to the desires of the flesh. For that reason, the power of his words and the miraculous turn of events had little effect upon them.

## CHAPTER 2.8

# A GREAT DROUGHT—THE 17 BC EXTINCTION OF THE ROBBERS

### *23 BC*

After Nephi's great display of prophetic power concerning the murder of the chief judge, some of the people acknowledged him as a prophet.[369] Others said, "Behold, he is a god, for except he was a god, he could not know all things."[370] Certainly there were others who were unmoved by the foregoing events, though for the moment they were silenced. "And it came to pass that there was a great division among the people." They all began to argue, and ostensibly, they completely forgot about Nephi, "insomuch that they divided hither and thither and went their ways, leaving Nephi alone, as he was standing in the midst of them."[371]

Nephi turned and made his way toward his home "pondering upon the things which the Lord had shown to him." He was filled with sorrow as he contemplated the wicked and rebellious state of the people. Then, the voice of the Lord came to him, saying,

> Blessed art thou Nephi, for those things which thou hast done; for I have beheld how thou hast with unwearyingness declared the word, which I have given thee, unto this people. And thou hast not feared them, and hast not sought thine own life, but hast sought my will, and to keep my commandments.
>
> And now, because thou hast done this with such unwearyingness, behold, I will bless thee forever; and I will make thee mighty in word and in deed, in faith and in works; yea, even that all things shall be done unto thee according to thy word, for thou shalt not ask that which is contrary to my will.
>
> Behold thou art Nephi, and I am God. Behold, I declare it unto thee in the presence of mine angels, that ye shall have power over this

> people, and shall smite the earth with famine, and with pestilence, and destruction, according to the wickedness of this people.
>
> Behold, I give unto you power, that whatsoever ye shall seal on earth shall be sealed in heaven; and whatsoever ye shall loose on earth shall be loosed in heaven; and thus shall ye have power among this people."[372]

Instead of going to his home, Nephi immediately turned about and went directly to the "multitudes who were scattered about upon the face of the land."[373] Again, he bore witness to them of their imminent destruction if they did not repent. Yet, notwithstanding the miraculous display of revelation, many of the same people who had witnessed his prophetic power were hostile to him. They sought to detain him and cast him into prison, but they could not, for he was conveyed by the Spirit out of their midst.

Over the following three years (23–21 BC), Nephi went forth in the Spirit across the land from multitude to multitude, and also sent others until all the people had been warned of the coming destruction.[374] The people refused to hearken to his warnings. His words merely provoked them to open rebellion against God. As 21 BC came to an end, the people "divided amongst themselves and began to slay one another with the sword."[375]

In 20 BC, the war escalated, "insomuch that there were wars throughout all the land among all the people of Nephi,"[376] all of which were caused by the Gadianton robbers.[377] The war continued throughout the year, and into 19 BC. When it seemed as though all of the people would be destroyed, Nephi prayed that the Lord[378] would send a famine to humble them that they might cease their fighting, and "repent and turn unto thee."[379]

## THE LORD'S JUDGMENT THROUGH NEPHI

In keeping with the Lord's covenant, "it was done, according to the words of Nephi. And there was a great famine in the land southward, among all the people of Nephi,"[380] among the Lamanites, as well as the Nephites.[381] Soon, they ceased their fighting and began to struggle just to survive. The famine continued throughout 18 and 17 BC, and the people "did perish by the thousands in the more wicked parts of the land."[382]

## THE NEPHITES ERADICATE THE ROBBERS TO END THE DROUGHT—THE SECRET PLANS ARE BURIED IN THE EARTH

Nephi had warned the people again and again of the great destruction that would come upon them. Now that it had arrived, they fully understood that Nephi held the key to their deliverance. In 17 BC, they "began to plead with their chief judges and their leaders, that they would say unto Nephi: Behold, we know that thou art a man of God, and therefore cry unto the Lord our God that he turn away from us this famine, lest all the words which thou hast spoken concerning our destruction be fulfilled."[383]

Only "when Nephi saw that the people had repented and did humble themselves in sackcloth,"[384] did he call upon the Lord. Only when he could say they have "swept away the band of Gadianton amongst them insomuch that they have become extinct, and they have concealed their secret plans in the earth,"[385] did he ask the Lord to end the famine, and he did so with great humility.[386]

## A FLEETING MOMENT OF REPENTANCE

Again as promised, the Lord responded according to Nephi's petition. In 16 BC, the drought came to an end. The rains returned, bringing fruit and grain in the time of their season.[387] All of the people rejoiced, and proclaimed Nephi to be a great prophet. "And the church did spread throughout the face of all the land; and the more part of the people, both the Nephites and the Lamanites, did belong to the church."[388]

For a short time (from 16 through 13 BC), there was peace throughout the land southward, among both the Nephites and the Lamanites. In 14 BC, some contention arose within the Church over points of doctrine, which escalated in 13 BC, but "Nephi, Lehi and many of their brethren" received many revelations daily, and therefore they "knew concerning the true points of doctrine."[389] They preached continually to the people throughout the same year and were able to put an end to the contention.

# PART 3

# THE SECOND PERIOD OF THE ROBBERS (12 BC–AD 25)

# CHAPTER 3.1

# THE REBIRTH OF THE ROBBERS—NEW LANDS OF HABITATION

## *12 BC*

ONLY FIVE YEARS AFTER the people "swept away" the Gadianton robbers and buried the secret plans in the earth,[390] and four years after the Lord had brought an end to the terrible drought,[391] there was a certain faction within the Lamanite land of Nephi, which once again rebelled against the principles of righteousness and "commenced a war with their brethren."[392] They were marauders who had moved into uninhabited mountain and wilderness areas. They would suddenly invade settlement areas to murder and plunder, and then, they would retreat back to their secret places.

They began recruiting among the Lamanites, and their numbers increased daily until they became a very large band of robbers. They searched out the secret plans of murder and re-established the Secret Society of Gadianton. Their identity comes as no surprise. As described in Helaman 11:24, they consisted of the following:

1. Dissenters "who had some years before gone over unto the Lamanites, and taken upon themselves the name of Lamanites." The specific identity of these dissenters is not revealed in Helaman 11, but is revealed later in the book of 3 Nephi.[393]
2. A "certain number who were real descendants of the Lamanites, being stirred up to anger by . . . those dissenters."

This scenario of dissenters stirring up the Lamanites to violence against the Nephites was a shot fired right out of the past. After taking place only once in Zarahemla during the reign of the kings,[394] it had occurred multiple times during the period of the judges leading to the

30 BC conversion of the Lamanite nation to Christ.[395] It was the first such occurrence, however, following the Lamanite conversion.

It was not the result of a great falling away of the converted Lamanites. Instead, it is the first indication, following the conversion of the Lamanite nation to Christ, that there remained a significant number of unconverted Lamanites, still under the influence of hardened dissenters living among them.

The re-establishment of the robbers by these Nephite dissenters confirms the fact that pagan dissenters and the Gadianton robbers were essentially one and the same. As such, they possessed the singular, unchanging goal of completely annihilating the Christian Nephites. This reorganized band of robbers grew rapidly as more and more Lamanites and Nephites joined them.[396]

Within less than a year, the number of robbers became so great that they threatened the security of Nephites and Lamanites throughout the entire land southward. The Nephites sent an army "into the wilderness and upon the mountains" during the same year, to seek out their hideouts and destroy them.[397] The robbers were so numerous, however, that the Nephite army was driven back to the land of Zarahemla.

In 11 BC, the army returned to the wilderness and engaged the robbers once more. There were many casualties on both sides. Again, the army was forced to retreat back into their own land. The robbers continued their attacks in many parts of the land. They would plunder and kill many, and carry away their women and children into the wilderness.[398]

## THE GROWTH OF THE ROBBERS THROUGH APOSTASY

The ranks of the robbers were continually bolstered by additional dissenters, which began to apostatize just as quickly as they had come into the Church.[399] It is thus apparent that they had joined the Church purely out of fear of being destroyed by the famine. As Nephi had said in his prayer, they had repented "because of the famine and the pestilence and destruction which [had] come upon them."[400] Therefore, only a short time after the famine ended, when they were no longer facing destruction, the lure of the sensual and devilish pagan religion captivated them once more.

At the same time, Nephites which did not apostatize from the Church quickly lost interest in the gospel and many fell back into transgression.[401] Their relationship with God was dictated entirely by the events of the day. In 11 BC, they had been stirred up to repentance because of their fear of the robbers.[402] In 10 BC, however, they began again to turn away from God,[403] and by 7 BC, "they were ripening again for destruction."[404]

Thus, only nine years after the drought ended, the people had returned to the same level of wickedness as before the drought. The Gadianton robbers had reorganized and regained all their power. Once again, they inflicted the entire land with a curse, while the people ceased to serve God and call upon Him for deliverance.

## THE WILDERNESS INHABITED BY THE REORGANIZED ROBBERS

After the re-establishment of the robbers, they occupied a wilderness region that at the time remained uninhabited, notwithstanding the expansion of both Nephite and Lamanite lands, which had taken place during the approximately 200 years following the initial settlement of Zarahemla. Following their expulsion from among the Lamanites and Nephites, the robbers began to inhabit this extensive region, consisting of both "wilderness" and "mountain" lands.[405] These lands were filled wild animals of every kind, which could provide food and sustenance,[406] when it was not available from plunder and looting.

Their habitation of the region, however, was not by choice. It had become a matter of necessity due to the situation which confronted them at that time. Indeed, it was the first time in which they had been expelled from both Nephite and Lamanite lands, as a result of the Lamanite conversion. Therefore, there was no other option, but to move into this uninhabited wilderness.

They began to attack and pillage small towns and villages across the lands of Zarahemla and Nephi. Then they would return to their hideaways in the wilderness and to their strongholds in the mountains. As their numbers increased through recruitment,[407] they attacked larger and larger cities—a factor not only of their increasing power and capability, but of their growing needs as well.

Gadianton had been the first robber to depart from Zarahemla into the wilderness,[408] which he had also done out of necessity. However, he did not launch attacks from the wilderness. Instead, it is apparent that he grew and developed his secret society within the land of Nephi among the Lamanites, which at that time were still twenty years away from their conversion to the gospel.

In Zarahemla during that first period, new recruits into the Gadianton Society did not always depart out of Zarahemla to join the robbers, but many worked in secret among the Nephites. Therefore, the survival of the robbers during the initial period was dependent neither upon pillaging, nor the acquisition of game within the wilderness.

## APPARENT INFERTILITY OF THE WILDERNESS

The reorganization of the robbers in 12 BC marked the first time in which the robbers began to inhabit wilderness regions within the land southward. From that time until AD 25, a period of thirty-seven years, their lands would be distinguished from both Nephite and Lamanite lands. Though they would grow by thousands and tens of thousands during that period, the lands of their habitation would still be denoted as wilderness.[409] This fact, coupled with the fact that the region remained wilderness approximately two hundred years after the settlement of the land of Zarahemla,[410] and seventy-five years after the expansion of the Lamanite lands of habitation all the way to the east sea, on the south of Jershon,[411] might very well indicate the region was infertile, with respect to the growing of crops.

The Nephites were unable to subdue the robbers at that time (12–11 BC).[412] It seems apparent that this was primarily an indication of the overwhelming denseness of the lowland forests, and the precipitous nature of the mountainous terrain, which enabled the robbers to remain shadowy and elusive. Alternatively, it may have been due to the great number of robbers, which had gathered there.

# CHAPTER 3.2

# THE PROPHECIES OF SAMUEL THE LAMANITE

### *6 BC*

IN THE EIGHTY-SIXTH YEAR of the judges, the Nephites remained in their wicked and rebellious state, while the Lamanites—twenty-four years after their miraculous conversion—still endeavored diligently to keep the commandments of God. Many of the Lamanite children had by this time been raised in the light of the gospel. In an unprecedented reversal of roles following almost 600 years of Lamanite darkness, a Lamanite prophet named Samuel traveled from the land of Nephi to the land of Zarahemla, to preach the gospel and to warn the Nephites of the Lord's coming judgment upon them because of their wickedness.

## SAMUEL IS REJECTED BY THE NEPHITES

"And it came to pass that [Samuel] did preach, many days, repentance unto the people, and they did cast him out."[413] As he turned in the direction of his homeland, "the voice of the Lord came unto him" and instructed him to return to the city of Zarahemla and "prophecy unto the people whatsoever things should come into his heart."[414]

When the guards at the entrance[415] would not allow him to re-enter the city, he climbed upon the wall and began to express his thoughts, which were given to him by the Spirit of the Lord. He told them that when he had come to the city the first time, he had been inspired to tell them of "glad tidings" of the coming of Christ into the world, but when they rejected his words and cast him out of the city, the Lord commanded him to return with warnings of destruction.

Samuel then began to prophesy concerning the Lord's judgments that would come upon the Nephites in AD 385.[416] Likely, this was not very frightening to the people. After all, everyone alive in 6 BC would long since be dead at the time of its fulfillment. His point, however, was that the same degree of sin and iniquity, which corrupted the Nephites at the present time, would result in their complete destruction and extinction 400 years later.[417]

Samuel then focused his prophecies on the present. He warned of the imminent destruction of the city of Zarahemla. He said that were it not for the righteous in the city, the Lord would send down fire from heaven to destroy it. "But behold," he said, "the time cometh, saith the Lord, that when ye shall cast out the righteous from among you, then shall ye be ripe for destruction."[418]

## A CURSE UPON THE LAND

Samuel spoke of a great curse that would soon come upon the land because of the "wickedness and abominations" of the people.[419] In fact, said he, "Behold, the anger of the Lord is already kindled against you; behold he has cursed the land because of your iniquity."[420] He described how the people had nothing but animosity for the "word of the Lord," and—referring to their response to his previous words of warning—would cast out the prophets of God for plainly telling them of their iniquity.[421]

At the same time, they welcomed false prophets who supported their wickedness. He said: "But behold, if a man shall come among you and shall say: Do this, and there is no iniquity; do that and ye shall not suffer; yea, he will say: Walk after the pride of your own hearts; yea, walk after the pride of your eyes, and do whatsoever your heart desireth—and if a man shall come among you and say this, ye will receive him, and say that he is a prophet."[422]

## THE LAW OF MOSES

In 6 BC, the Lamanites in the land of Nephi faithfully obeyed the commandments of God according to the law of Moses,[423] following their conversion through the teachings of Nephi and Lehi during their 30 BC mission.[424] The Nephites, on the other hand, had observed Mosaic Law from the beginning of Nephite history, which included animal sacrifice as a similitude of the sacrifice of Jesus Christ.

It was strictly observed by Lehi, while he and his family had lived in Jerusalem. This was demonstrated when Nephi and his brethren escaped from the murderous Laban and returned to their family in the wilderness. Lehi and Sariah rejoiced and "did offer sacrifice and burnt offerings unto the Lord."[425]

Furthermore, the law of Moses "was engraven upon the plates of brass," which Nephi obtained from Laban.[426] Its inclusion within the brass plates was important to the Nephites, for it would thereby be preserved for future generations following their departure from Jerusalem.

A few years after the people of Nephi separated from Laman and Lemuel, Nephi said, "We keep the law of Moses and look forward with steadfastness unto Christ, until the law shall be fulfilled. For, for this end was the law given; wherefore the law hath become dead unto us, and we are made alive in Christ because of our faith; yet we keep the law because of the commandments."[427]

Other scriptures in the Book of Mormon speak at great length about the law of Moses. The practice of animal sacrifice, as revealed in the Book of Mormon, stresses the great importance the Nephites placed upon looking forward to the coming of Christ. It was through the continual observance of the law of Moses that the idea of the coming of the Messiah remained firmly implanted in the minds of the Nephites.[428]

In 124 BC, when the Nephites gathered around the temple in Zarahemla to hear the words of King Benjamin, they offered "sacrifice and burnt offerings according to the law of Moses."[429] Later, the people of Anti-Nephi-Lehi, who were converted to the gospel through the teachings of King Mosiah's sons, observed the law of Moses:

> Yea, and they did keep the law of Moses; for it was expedient that they should keep the law of Moses as yet, for it was not all fulfilled. But notwithstanding the law of Moses, they did look forward to the coming of Christ, considering that the law of Moses was a type of his coming, and believing that they must keep those outward performances until the time that he should be revealed unto them.
>
> Now they did not suppose that salvation came by the law of Moses; but the law of Moses did serve to strengthen their faith in Christ; and thus they did retain a hope through faith, unto eternal salvation, relying upon the spirit of prophecy, which spake of those things to come.[430]

## THE LAW OF SACRIFICE

The law of sacrifice, which preceded the law of Moses, had been taught to the first parents, Adam and Eve:

> And Adam and Eve, his wife, called upon the name of the Lord, and they heard the voice of the Lord from the way toward the Garden of Eden, speaking unto them, and they saw him not; for they were shut out from his presence.
>
> And he gave unto them commandments, that they should worship the Lord their God, and should offer the firstlings of their flocks, for an offering unto the Lord. And Adam was obedient unto the commandments of the Lord.
>
> And after many days an angel of the Lord appeared unto Adam, saying: Why dost thou offer sacrifices unto the Lord? And Adam said unto him: I know not, save the Lord commanded me.
>
> And then the angel spake, saying: This thing is a similitude of the sacrifice of the Only Begotten of the Father, which is full of grace and truth. [431]

It was through Moses that "Israel received and practiced further ordinances to remind them daily of their duty toward God.[432] Types and symbols which were woven into the law of Moses taught God's people of the Savior's atoning sacrifice."[433]

## THE FULFILLMENT OF THE LAW OF MOSES

In 6 BC, Samuel prophesied to the Nephites concerning the coming of Jesus Christ into the world.[434] The law of sacrifice/law of Moses, which had been observed by mankind for approximately 4,000 years, would soon be replaced by a higher law. Fewer than forty years later, the sacrifice of the Savior, which had been symbolized countless times by men and women of faith since the days of Adam, would be freely offered for the salvation of all mankind.

This "great and last sacrifice" of the Son of God would be "infinite and eternal."[435] As Amulek had said in 74 BC to the Zoramites in Antionum, "then shall there be, or it is expedient that there should be, a stop to the shedding of blood," for "then shall the law of Moses be fulfilled."[436]

## THE SIGNS OF CHRIST'S BIRTH

One of the main purposes of Samuel's inspired discourse was that the people "might know of the signs of [Christ's] coming, to the intent that [they] might believe on his name."[437] Throughout the history of the Nephites, prophets of God had foretold of the coming of Christ into the world. It was one of the chief points of contention by which dissenters continually mocked the foolish traditions that had been handed down from the fathers.[438] Now, after centuries of prophecy (and ridicule), the prophet Samuel announced that the Savior's birth was imminent. He said:

> Behold, I give unto you a sign; for five years more cometh, and behold, then cometh the Son of God to redeem all those who shall believe on his name.
>
> And behold, this will I give unto you for a sign at the time of his coming; for behold, there shall be great lights in heaven, insomuch that in the night before he cometh there shall be no darkness, insomuch that it shall appear unto man as if it was day.
>
> Therefore, there shall be one day and a night and a day, as if it were one day and there were no night; and this shall be unto you for a sign; for ye shall know of the rising of the sun and also of its setting; therefore they shall know of a surety that there shall be two days and a night; nevertheless, the night shall not be darkened and it shall be the night before he is born.
>
> And behold, there shall a new star arise, such an one as ye never have beheld; and this also shall be a sign unto you.
>
> And behold this is not all, there shall be many signs and wonders in heaven.
>
> And it shall come to pass that ye shall all be amazed, and wonder, insomuch that ye shall fall to the earth. [439]

## THE SIGNS OF CHRIST'S DEATH

Next, Samuel prophesied concerning the signs that would accompany Christ's death. Whereas the signs of His birth would be visual signs only, the signs of His death would be an entirely different matter. Samuel plainly described the catastrophic phenomena,[440] which would accompany (and actually would cause) the darkness that would settle upon the land at that time. The phenomena are listed as follows:

1. There shall be thunder and lightning for the space of many hours.
2. The earth shall shake and tremble.
3. The rocks shall be broken up.

4. There shall be great tempests (windstorms).
5. There shall be many mountains laid low.
6. Many valleys shall become great mountains.
7. Many highways shall be broken up.
8. Many cities shall become desolate (without inhabitants).
9. "Many graves shall be opened . . . and many saints shall appear unto many."[441]
10. Darkness shall cover the face of the whole earth for the space of three days.

## THE SALIENT POINTS OF SAMUEL'S PROPHECY

Everything that Samuel prophesied in 6 BC from atop the wall of Zarahemla can be reduced to two key points, one related to His birth,and one related to His death:

1. On the night before the Savior's birth, there would be "great lights" in the heavens, and a new star would appear. As a result, there would follow a day and a night and a day, which would be as one day without darkness.[442]
2. On the day of His crucifixion, a great storm would destroy those who continued in their rebellious and wicked ways after seeing the signs of His birth,[443] and three days of darkness would follow.

If the people understood nothing else, it would serve them well to understand the two salient points. The great heavenly manifestation at the Lord's birth would serve as a wakeup call for the Nephites who had transgressed the commandments of God. It would be a sign of warning to those who continued to embrace the filthy pagan religion, which filled the land with violence. It would be a forewarning of destruction to those who continued to be antagonistic to the teachings of repentance and belief in Christ, and who actively sought to destroy the true Church of Christ.

The great storm would bring judgment and justice to those who ignored the wakeup call and continued in their evil ways.[444] It was a simple blueprint for deliverance. However, it would be extremely difficult to follow for the many who were so easily deceived and enticed by the evil one—who could not stay on the path of righteousness, and who refused to give heed to the prophets of the Lord.

## SAMUEL IS REJECTED ONCE AGAIN

At the time in which Samuel fearlessly declared the Lord's warning to the Nephites, Nephi, the son of Helaman, still resided in the city of Zarahemla. He was known by all, and everyone had acknowledged at one time or another that he was a great prophet of God.[445] By this time, however, though it had only been a few years since the devastating drought, Nephi was largely ignored by the majority of the people, notwithstanding the fact that he had not stopped "baptizing, and prophesying, and preaching, crying repentance unto the people, showing signs and wonders, [and] working miracles among the people, that they might know that the Christ must shortly come."[446] If they would not give heed to Nephi's warnings,[447] after all the miracles they had witnessed at his hand, then they certainly would not give heed to the words of a Lamanite.[448]

Nevertheless, there were many who did believe in the words of Samuel, especially when they saw that the power of God was upon him that he could not be hit by stones and arrows. These "went away unto Nephi to be baptized."[449] The majority, however, did not believe in his words, and when they could not kill him, they called on their "captains" to "take him and bind him, and away with him."[450] But as they attempted to capture him, he jumped down from the wall and fled out of the land of Zarahemla. He returned to his homeland "and began to preach and prophesy among his own people."[451]

## THE COUNTDOWN TO THE SAVIOR'S BIRTH

Following Samuel's prophecies in 6 BC, the majority of the people continued in their wicked ways, with hardly a pause for reflection. As the five years passed one by one, Christians of faith watched vigilantly for the heavenly signs. In 2 BC (the ninetieth year of the judges) there began to be "great signs given to the people, and wonders; and the words of the prophets began to be fulfilled,"[452] concerning the Savior's birth. "And angels did appear unto men, wise men, and did declare unto them glad tidings of great joy."[453]

After the first heavenly manifestations appeared, unbelievers began to speak out against Samuel's prophecies.[454] They said, "Why will he not show himself in this land as well as in the land of Jerusalem? But behold, we know that this is a wicked tradition, which has been handed down unto us by our fathers, to cause us that we should believe in some great and marvelous thing which should come to pass, but not among us, but in a land which is far distant, a land which we know not; therefore they can keep us in ignorance, for we cannot witness with our own eyes that they are true."[455]

The tone of this statement is considerably less arrogant than the former taunts of "silly or foolish Nephite traditions" encountered previously in the Book of Mormon. Likely it is indicative of the pagans' frustration and trepidation, as the prophecies began to be fulfilled.

However, in spite of the heavenly phenomena and miracles, which began to take place in abundance, "Satan did get great hold upon the hearts of the people upon all the face of the land."[456] Most of the people hardened their hearts to the teaching of the gospel. The year 2 BC came to an end, and then began the fifth year since Samuel's prophecy was given, which would soon be followed by the great sign of the Lord's birth.

## CHAPTER 3.3

# THE FIRST PROPHECY OF SAMUEL IS FULFILLED—THE GREAT SIGN OF THE SAVIOR'S BIRTH

### *1 BC*

At some point during the ninety-first year of the judges, the fifth anniversary of Samuel's prophecy arrived, for it was during the eighty-sixth year when he stood atop the wall of Zarahemla[457] and preached to the people of the city.[458] As referenced in the previous chapter, heavenly signs and wonders had begun to take place during the fourth year, the ninetieth year of the judges.[459]

Following the fifth anniversary, however, the followers of Christ surely began to watch the skies much more intently for the great sign of the Lord's birth. Shortly before the end of the fifth year, the prophet Nephi "departed out of the land of Zarahemla, giving charge unto his son Nephi, who was his eldest son, concerning the plates of brass, and all the records which had been kept, and all those things which had been kept sacred from the departure of Lehi out of Jerusalem."[460]

Then, like his great-grandfather Alma the Younger,[461] "he departed out of the land, and whither he went, no man knoweth; and his son Nephi did keep the records in his stead, yea, the record of this people."[462]

### PROPHETIC FULFULLMENT

As the ninety-second year of the judges (the sixth year) commenced, the heavenly signs began to increase, and "greater miracles" were "wrought among the people."[463] Still, the pagans began to celebrate, because the fifth year had passed and the great sign had not occurred. Given the frequent heavenly displays that had been taking place since the ninetieth year,[464] it was the only thing they could seize upon. In a bold display of the power they presumed to possess at that time, they publicly chose a date for the execution of all Christians, unless by that date, "the sign should come to pass, which had been prophesied by Samuel the prophet."[465]

When the pagans made their threats, "Lachoneus was the chief judge and the governor" of the Nephites.[466] Later, he would be identified as a Christian and a great spiritual leader. One might ask: Where was the rule of law in AD 1? As chief judge, was Lachoneus powerless to stop such actions? Where were military leaders like Moroni, who came to the aid of the Church in 73 BC, when Amalickiah rose up with other dissenters and attempted to murder Helaman and other church leaders?[467]

According to 3 Nephi 3:19, Lachoneus was chosen in a time of righteousness, principally because he was a great prophet. It is apparent that he had been elected shortly after the drought called down from heaven by the prophet Nephi. That was the only time, following Nephi's tenure as chief judge, when the Nephites were compelled briefly to repent and return to Christianity. His election to office likely occurred during the period from 16 to 14 BC. By AD 1, however, things had drastically changed.

As a Christian, Lachoneus would be killed as well. The pagans had gained a large following since his election, likely both religious and ethnic in nature. They had attained sufficient numbers to have the confidence to make such bold threats, whether or not they could be achieved.

Nephi, the son of Nephi, must surely have wished that his father had not departed out of the land, for now more than ever he needed the support of his father's faith and spiritual power. The pagans were threatening the lives of his entire family and his friends. His own life was of little consequence, compared with the people he loved. In despair, he "cried mightily to his God in behalf of his people, yea, those who were about to be destroyed because of their faith in the tradition of their fathers."[468] He prayed throughout the day. Finally, the voice of the Lord came to him, saying: "Lift up your head and be of good cheer; for behold, the time is at hand, and on this night shall the sign be given, and on the morrow come I into the world, to show unto the world that I will fulfill all that which I have caused to be spoken by the mouth of my holy prophets."[469]

What a marvelous and joyous announcement, and what a blessing it was for Nephi to receive it as a result of his great faith and obedience. The Lord's declaration heralded the fulfillment of a seemingly endless line of prophecies given by Nephite prophets for 600 years. Beginning with Lehi, Nephi, and Jacob, the prophets of every generation had tirelessly proclaimed the great prophecy of the coming of the Lord. It did not matter to the faithful that the prophecies were not fulfilled during their lifetime. They had lived and died in faith, believing that their descendants would one day see them come to pass.

Nephi's own father had wistfully spoken of prophets since the days of Melchizedek, more than 2,000 years earlier, who had prophesied concerning the Coming of Christ into the world.[470] He had desired that all might believe the prophecies of the coming of the Lord, and he looked forward with great anticipation to their fulfillment. Unlike the Second Coming of Christ, for which "no man knoweth the day or the hour,"[471] righteous Nephites knew at least the year of His coming, for it had been taught by the Nephi the son of Lehi that the Messiah would be "[raised] up among the Jews . . . 600 years from the time that [his] father Lehi left Jerusalem."[472] The moment at hand was truly a glorious moment, both on earth and in heaven. For the Nephites, it would be the most pivotal event in the history of mankind. Today, saints look forward to the Lord's Second Coming with the same longing, especially as the world plummets once again into sin and iniquity.

## EARTH'S LONGEST DAY—"ONE DAY AND A NIGHT AND A DAY AS ONE DAY"

The next day, as promised, the sign appeared. On the going down of the sun, it remained as bright outside as noon day. The new star shone brightly from the sky. The many pagans who had plotted the death of all Christians were astonished and overwhelmed by the marvelous event, for there was absolutely no way to explain it away. In a single moment, their taunts and jeers were transformed into trepidation and fear: "And there were many, who had not believed the words of the prophets, who fell to the earth and became as if they were dead, for they knew that the great plan of destruction which they had laid for those who believed in the words of the prophets had been frustrated; for the sign which had been given was already at hand."[473]

The significance of this great and marvelous sign and its implications with respect to their unbelief were understood throughout both the land southward and the land northward, for the prophecies of Samuel and other prophets before him had been published throughout the entire land: "And they began to know that the Son of God must shortly appear; yea, in fine, all the people upon the face of the whole earth from the west to the east, both in the land north, and the land south, were so exceedingly astonished that they fell to the earth. For they knew that the prophets had testified of these things for many years, and that the sign which had been given was already at hand; and they began to fear because of their iniquity and unbelief."[474]

## THE MAJORITY ARE ONCE AGAIN CONVERTED UNTO THE LORD

There was no more talk of violence at that time, though immediately after the sign was given, and "from [that] time forth, . . . there began to be lyings sent forth among the people by Satan, to harden their hearts, to the intent that they might not believe in those signs and wonders which they had seen."[475] In the aftermath of the great sign, however, the lies had little effect. The "more part of the people did believe, and were converted unto the Lord."[476] As a result of the sign, there was once more a great revival of Christian faith. Nephi the son of Nephi and many others went among the people "baptizing unto repentance in the which there was a great remission of sins."[477] But for a moment there was peace throughout the land.

## NEPHITE CALENDAR CHANGE

Throughout Nephite history to this point in time, the Nephites had maintained their calendar as the number of years since Lehi had departed from the land of Judah.[478] Though it was referred to as the year of the judges after 92 BC, the underlying count of years was still maintained, as referenced in 3 Nephi 1:1.[479] The sign of Christ's birth occurred shortly after the six hundredth year had come to an end. It marked the beginning of a new age—a new calendar period, for "the Nephites began to reckon their time from this period when the sign was given, or from the coming of Christ"[480] into the world. For the moment, the end of the former age was not yet punctuated by cataclysmic destruction, as prophesied by Samuel in Helaman 14.

## DISPUTATION CONCERNING THE LAW OF MOSES

After the sign was given, some members of the Church tried to "prove by the scriptures" that because Christ had been born, the law of Moses should no longer be observed. "Now in this thing they did err, having not understood the scriptures."[481] The law of Moses was the law of sacrifice. The sacrifice of a lamb without spot or blemish represented the sacrifice of the Holy One of Israel for the salvation of mankind. The Savior's great sacrifice would not take place until the end of His life. Only then should the law of Moses be fulfilled. Those who had misinterpreted the scriptures "were brought to a knowledge of their error and did confess their faults."[482]

# CHAPTER 3.4

# GADIANTON ROBBERS—UNDAUNTED BY THE HEAVENLY MANIFESTATIONS

Following the establishment of the secret society of Gadianton in 50 BC,[483] it immediately became the primary identity of pagan religion across the land southward. At that time, the robbers operated under the direction of their founder, Gadianton. Their close affiliation with idol worship during that first period is clearly shown in Helaman 6:21 and 31.

The two verses, considered in combination, identify this direct relationship through the common term "more part of the Nephites." Verse 21 reveals the sobering fact that by 25 BC, "the more part of the Nephites . . . did unite with those bands of robbers." Verse 31 then adds that "the more part of them . . . did build up unto themselves idols of their gold and their silver."

If the more part of the people could be identified as both robbers and idolators, then it can be directly concluded through a simple exercise of logic that the robbers practiced idolatry. It follows that the first period of the robbers from 52 BC to 17 BC was simply a late pre-Christ phase of the pagan conspiracy to destroy the Christian Nephite culture.

This close Gadianton relationship with pagan religion became much more obvious after the rebirth of the robbers, when a notorious pagan cult took control.[484] Still, even in the initial Gadianton period, the robbers became, in essence, the ruling power and the center of organization for the pagan conspiracy. They seized the responsibility of uniting the pagan factions, of multiplying their numbers through recruitment, and of focusing all of the pagan energy upon conquering the land southward.

## THE ROBBERS SEEK DOMINANCE OF THE ENTIRE LAND SOUTHWARD

Throughout the Gadianton period, the robbers worked feverishly to obtain the goal nearly attained by Amalickiah and Ammoron in 73 BC, which was to take control of the lands of Nephi and Zarahemla. Amalickiah had become the first Nephite dissenter to successfully overthrow a Lamanite king, rising to power in only a few months.[485] For a time, he and Ammoron had come dangerously close to defeating the Nephites and taking control of Zarahemla, but over the course of the thirteen-year military campaign, both men were slain, and the Lamanite armies under their command were soundly defeated and driven out of the land of Zarahemla. Nevertheless, though their bid for absolute power was unsuccessful, it raised dissenter expectations, and strengthened their belief that pagan dominance of the entire land southward was inevitable.

## EXTERNAL AND INTERNAL ATTACK

The tactics employed by Amalickiah and Ammoron were nothing new—to wit, they attacked the Nephites both externally and internally,[486] but the level of their success set a new standard. The external attack was conducted with a Lamanite army under their direction and control. The internal attack was conducted through the rebellion of the king-men. The two destructive forces—Lamanites and dissenters—were perennially aligned against the Christian Nephites throughout the pre-Christ Zarahemla period.

## EXTERNAL FORCES

The Lamanites had always acted as the opposing external force—even from the beginning when Nephi was forced to flee from Laman and Lemuel shortly after the death of their father Lehi. Approximately 400 years later, Mosiah's departure from the land of Nephi into the wilderness effectively eliminated the Lamanite threat throughout the period of the kings in Zarahemla—the singular exception being the attack that took place during the reign of King Benjamin. During the period of the judges, however, the external threat became greater and more frequent, as Lamanite support was repeatedly solicited by dissenters from within the land of Zarahemla.

## INTERNAL FORCES

The internal forces consisted of revolutionary pagan dissent groups, which it seems did not materialize among the Nephites until after the discovery of the Mulekites in Zarahemla and the merger of the two peoples into one. There is no indication in the Book of Mormon (as currently constituted)[487] of significant internal dissent during the first Nephite period while they lived in the land of Nephi. With the restoration of the 116 lost pages at some future time, this opinion might very well need revision, especially with respect to the dissolution of the Church of Christ, as alluded to in 3 Nephi 5:12.

Largely primitive and non-threatening during the first generation in Zarahemla, in the second generation, the Mulekites began to rise to intellectual equivalence. In time, pagan dissenters began to rise up against the Christian Nephites. Ultimately, they challenged the authority of King Benjamin. The account of their rebellion[488] is the first occurrence of "dissensions away unto the Lamanites"[489] to be recorded in the Book of Mormon.

## FORCES IN COMBINATION

The period of respite from Lamanite aggression, which was automatically created by the barrier of the wilderness, came to an end during the reign of King Benjamin with the first Lamanite attack. It was not the result of Lamanites spontaneously finding their way through the wilderness to Zarahemla. Rather, it resulted from the dissenters fleeing to the Lamanites and inciting them to go down against the Nephites. The external (Lamanite) attack during Benjamin's reign was thus solicited by the rebels. At that time, the dissenters did not pose a significant threat when acting alone.

That changed drastically in 87 BC, with Amlici's internal rebellion, four years after the commencement of the period of the judges.[490] Though they were defeated by "the voice of the people," they had sufficient numbers to pose a serious internal threat to the Christian Nephites.[491] When they were subsequently joined by a Lamanite army, they became an even more formidable force.[492] Only by the grace of God were they halted, as the Nephites, though greatly outnumbered, went forth in strength of the Lord to defeat the combined Amlicite and Lamanite forces and drive them out of the land of Zarahemla.

In the Amalickiah and Ammoron War (67–60 BC), an internal rebellion transformed the Lamanite offensive into a three-pronged attack, which posed a critical threat to the very existence of the Christian Nephite nation. Regardless of what brought the external and internal forces together during the conflict, the three-pronged attack was utilized to Amalickiah and Ammoron's advantage. Due to the near success of their offensive, it would continue to serve as a model for future generations of dissent, notwithstanding the fact that it ended with Nephite victory.[493]

## SECRECY COMPLICATES EVERYTHING

Multi-faceted attacks, similar to those described above, were conducted repeatedly during the first period of the robbers (50–17 BC). Through the weapon of calculated secrecy, the internal threat was greatly increased. Throughout that first period, whenever internal dissension surfaced within the land of Zarahemla, the precise source of the contention was frequently difficult to define, or even to identify.

During the second period of the robbers (12 BC–AD 25), they still operated in secrecy to recruit Nephites and Lamanites into their ranks. The secrecy was compromised to a certain extent, however, when new recruits would depart out of the land[494] to join the robbers in the wilderness. However, such vague knowledge of frequent departures merely indicated that trouble was brewing. It was insufficient to aid the Nephites in preparing for defense, because they did not know the precise nature of the forces being aligned against them, or the location of forthcoming attacks.

## THE TENACITY OF SECRET COMBINATIONS

The Gadianton robbers could quickly adapt to changing conditions. In 30 BC, following the Lamanite conversion, they immediately altered their mode of operation by focusing their efforts almost exclusively within the land of Zarahemla. They quickly rose to the pinnacle of Nephite political power without the people knowing they had returned to Zarahemla. They secretly maintained control of the government—until they were exposed by the Prophet Nephi in 23 BC.[495]

Between 22 and 20 BC, they became fully exposed to the Nephites, largely as a result of internal strife caused by their own greed. Subsequently, the drought of 18 and 17 BC,[496] humbled the people and in 16 BC, they "swept away the band of Gadianton from amongst them."[497] When the robbers reorganized,[498] again they adapted by departing from the inhabited regions of Zarahemla and Nephi, joining together within adjacent uninhabited wilderness regions.

One disturbing characteristic of secret combinations is that they will not dissolve on their own. They will not disband, and they will not lose interest in their works of darkness. They will not turn from their evil ways through spontaneous repentance.

The robbers were unaffected by the preaching of the gospel, the performance of miracles, or the occurrence of heavenly phenomena in fulfillment of prophecy. As recorded in the scriptural accounts of the two New World civilizations which preceded the Nephites, the termination of the secret combinations, which inflicted a terrible curse upon each culture, was achieved only by:

1. The total destruction of the Adamic culture in the waters of the Flood.
2. The complete extinction of the Jaredite culture through civil war.

In the Nephite culture, the Gadianton robbers exhibited a similar stubbornness and tenacity. The drought requested of God by Nephi forced the robbers to denounce their works of darkness and bury the secret oaths and covenants deep within the earth. Ostensibly, they became extinct.

Only five years passed away, however, before certain Nephite dissenters living in the land of Nephi overcame their fear and disavowed their repentance, which had come about only through duress from the drought. In 12 BC, "they did search out all the secret plans of Gadianton; and thus they became robbers of Gadianton."[499] Following the reestablishment of the robbers, they rose up with even greater power and influence than they had wielded before the drought.

## THE GADIANTON RESPONSE TO THE SIGN OF CHRIST'S BIRTH

The robbers' reaction to the great drought of 18 and 17 BC had resulted in their temporary extinction.[500] In contrast, it appears the reorganized robbers were largely unaffected by the great sign of the Lord's birth. There was, after all, no accompanying death or destruction to humble them and compel them to repent and return to Christ, as with the destructive drought.

Nevertheless, in AD 1 and 2, they made no detectable inroads into the Nephite or the Lamanite cultures, largely due to the people's response to the heavenly phenomena: "And thus the ninety and second year did pass away, bringing glad tidings unto the people because of the signs which did come to pass, according to the words of the prophecy of all the holy prophets."[501]

In their secret and formidable places of habitation, gospel principles and prophecies concerning the birth of Christ would have seldom, if ever, made their way into any conversation of the robbers, certainly not in any positive or meaningful way. Therefore, it is understandable that most of them reacted with little more than a momentary hesitation when faced with the prophesied celestial phenomenon that accompanied the Lord's birth, or the lesser signs which both preceded and followed it. Furthermore, the robbers were under the direct influence of evil. In the aftermath of the great sign, Gadianton agents almost immediately set out across the face of the land to publish the lyings of Satan, "to harden their hearts, to the intent that they might not believe in those signs and wonders which they had seen."[502]

As they went forth across the land, however, they quickly became aware of its dramatic impact upon the people. For two years, as the gospel was preached throughout the land and the people repented of their iniquities, the robbers had little success in their recruitment efforts. There is no doubt, however, that they countered every expression of belief and amazement with vitriolic denials of the Christian claims of miracles. They remained dedicated to their cause and waited for the moment when they could resume where they had left off, given the first indication of interest or support.

In AD 3, as the people recovered from their fear, the robbers suddenly enjoyed a great rebound, which immediately affected the mindset of many throughout the land southward. Not surprisingly, the stimulus for the change came from the robbers themselves. In that year, the "robbers, who dwelt upon the mountains" began "to commit many murders, and did do much slaughter among the people."[503]

While they committed these acts of violence across the face of the land, they continued to reach outward from their hideaways and strongholds to sound the waters of discontent. Notwithstanding all the signs which had occurred, once again, they began to have much success in their recruitment efforts. Within the land of Zarahemla, they successfully recruited many Nephites. These recruits, identified as "dissenters of the Nephites . . . did flee unto them, which did cause much sorrow unto those Nephites who did remain in the land."[504] The Nephite population thus contributed greatly to the rapid growth of the robbers.

Among the Lamanites, the robbers recruited primarily from among the "rising generation."[505] It was the first generation of Lamanites to be raised from their birth in the light of the gospel. It has been said that "familiarity breeds contempt."[506] Like previous generations of Nephites throughout Nephite history raised in the light of the gospel,[507] this latest generation of Lamanites considered the gospel as a thing of naught and rebelled against their parents when they reached adulthood.

## CHAPTER 3.5

# THE IDENTITY OF THE NEW ROBBER LEADERSHIP IS REVEALED

As first touched upon in Chapter 3.1, when the Gadianton robbers were reorganized, they operated under new leadership. Because of the scarcity and brevity of related references in the books of Helaman and 3 Nephi, the transformation is subtle indeed to the reader of the Book of Mormon, as to be almost imperceptible. In Helaman 11:24, the reorganizers are identified merely as "dissenters from the people of Nephi, who had some years before gone over unto the Lamanites and taken upon themselves the name of Lamanites." On the basis of that statement alone, any conclusion as to their precise identity is purely a matter of conjecture, for it could be any one of four known dissenter factions[508] and a couple of factions not identified by name.[509] Without specific information, one might reasonably conclude that it refers to a dissent faction never identified by name in the Book of Mormon.

In connection with the Gadianton upsurge of AD 3,[510] however, a clear, unambiguous identity is provided for this group of dissenters, which had unearthed the secret plans and resurrected the robbers. According to 3 Nephi 1, they were the Zoramites, who originally had lived at the southern boundary of Jershon in the city of Antionum.[511] In 75 BC, they reacted violently when Alma and his brethren preached the gospel in their city.

In 74 BC, they united with the Lamanites in a war against the Nephites.[512] At that time, they dissented over to the Lamanites, and moved to the land of Nephi. Now, in AD 3, they were directly involved in the recruitment of Lamanite youth to the robbers, as revealed in verse 29—the first and only verse to identify them by name in association with the reorganized robbers.

The land of Nephi became the official location of their residence after 74 BC. They remained in Nephi from that time until 24 BC when the newly converted Lamanites preached the gospel to the robbers, "utterly [destroying them] from among the Lamanites."[513] In 12 BC, they reestablished the robbers in the wilderness.[514] The Zoramites were not affiliated with the Order of Nehor and practiced a new form of pagan religion.

In 75 BC, Alma, Amulek, Zeezrom, and the sons of Mosiah were thoroughly familiar with the pagan cult of Nehor, having seen the edifices constructed by them, and having experienced much sorrow and tribulation at their hands during the period of Nehor aggression.[515] The Order of Nehor had spawned a series of wars between 91 and 77 BC.[516] The Zoramites, however, "did worship after a manner which Alma and his brethren had never beheld."[517] On the basis of their reaction, it can be concluded that it was a newly established pagan cult.

Amalekites and Amulonites belonged to the Order of Nehor, which took its name from a man in Zarahemla named Nehor,[518] though the original pagan religion actually preceded Nehor—in the land of Nephi, as well as in the land of Zarahemla.[519] The Zoramites practiced a religion that is described at length in Alma 31. Therefore, the term "Zoramite" represented not only the faction emanating from Zoram of Antionum,[520] but also, and perhaps more precisely, the pagan religion he established around 75 BC.[521] See Chapter 2.7 above.

The Zoramites were opportunists. When they departed from Zarahemla in 74 BC to join with the Lamanites in the land of Nephi, they stepped into the pagan void that had resulted from the virtual destruction of the Order of Nehor. It is possible that the Zoramites may have completed the demise of the weakened cult of Nehor. Given the hatred and obsession for power that characterized the two pagan religions, there was no room for both of them within the land of Nephi.

During the Zoramite War, which immediately followed their departure from Zarahemla, Zerahemnah, the Lamanite leader, utilized both Amalekites (who were of the Order of Nehor) and Zoramites as "chief captains over the Lamanites" because of their intense hatred for the Nephites.[522] After fighting side by side with the Zoramites and perhaps competing with them for positions of power, the Amalekites disappeared completely from the Book of Mormon. Thereafter, the Zoramite religion was the dominant religion in the land of Nephi, and no reference is ever again made to the Order of

Nehor, or to any other non-Zoramite pagan religion during the pre-Christ period. In contrast, there are a number of references to the Zoramites and their influences within the land of Nephi throughout the period from 74 BC to AD 25.[523]

It is thus concluded that shortly after 74 BC, the Zoramites replaced the Amalekites as the principle antagonists in the land of Nephi. Thereafter, they were the ones who stirred the pot of Lamanite hostility against the Christian Nephites. It is likely that pagan dissenters arriving in the land of Nephi from Zarahemla received support from the Order of Nehor during the Period of the Nehors, and from the Zoramites during the Period of the Zoramites.

Five years after the robbers were swept away by the people, the Zoramites "did search out the secret plans of Gadianton" and reestablished the Gadianton murder cult.[524] As they had previously moved in opportunistically to replace the weakened cult of Nehor, in like manner, they rushed in to fill the Gadianton power vacuum, establishing themselves at the top of the second generation of robbers. There are other indications that they had also played a role in the first generation of robbers.

CHAPTER 3.6

# PRE-CHRIST GADIANTON ROBBERS—TWO DISTINCT PERIODS

KNOWING THE PAGAN IDENTITY of the new robber leadership enables one to fully understand the underlying motivational purposes that stimulated the robbers throughout their entire history. It also enables the division of the pre-Christ era of the Gadianton robbers (52 BC–AD 25)[525] into two distinct, well-defined periods:

## PERIOD ONE

For thirty-six years (52–17 BC), the robbers were the organization initially established in the land of Zarahemla by Kishkumen and Gadianton. After Kishkumen was slain and the robbers were exposed to the Nephite government, Gadianton led them in their flight from the land of Zarahemla.[526] The land of Nephi then remained their base of operation until shortly after the 30 BC conversion of the Lamanites to the gospel. In 24 BC, the Lamanites preached the gospel to them, by which they were "utterly destroyed from among the Lamanites."

Still, they continued to operate secretly in both Nephi and Zarahemla until the drought of 17 BC. The drought extended across the entire land southward, "among the Lamanites as well as among the Nephites."[527] As a result, the robbers were completely eliminated, due to the lethal effects of the drought.

### *PRINCIPLES OF SECRECY*

During the first twenty-nine years of their existence (52–23 BC), the robbers were ghostlike in their secret operations. Other than the one recorded blunder in 50 BC at the time Gadianton took the reins—which saved Helaman's life and necessitated Gadianton's flight from the land of Zarahemla,[528]—the robbers were generally invisible to anyone outside of the Gadianton organization. In 43 BC, only seven years after their departure, Nephite officials "at the head of the government" were unaware that the robbers had secretly returned to Zarahemla.[529] In 23 BC, the prophet Nephi appears to have been the first to identify—by revelation—the full extent of their takeover of the Nephite government by that time.[530]

*EXPOSURE TO THE PEOPLE*

Shortly after Nephi exposed them in the streets of Zarahemla, the robbers initiated a war among themselves, which might be classified as "a gang war" in present day vernacular.[531] The war spread across the land of Zarahemla and became the means by which all of the people were finally brought into a full awareness of the robbers.[532]

The war was fundamentally similar to the previous genocidal war in the land northward, which had completely destroyed the Jaredite culture.[533] The robbers had already taken control of the Nephite government. Therefore, the conflict was apparently between various factions within the robbers, which began seeking supremacy over one another following the assassination of Seezoram and the conviction of Seantum. Ultimately, the war was interrupted by the drought, which brought a temporary end to the robbers, for it caused the people to repent and sweep them away.[534] In 17 BC, the secret plans of destruction were buried in the earth.

## PERIOD TWO

Five years passed, and then the Zoramites stepped forward. In 12 BC, they sought out the secret plans of murder and made them their own, taking control of the power structure previously engineered by Gadianton.[535] This time, however, the robbers operated in a completely different manner. The war had fully exposed them throughout the land southward, and in such a negative and destructive way that the people were much more wary the second time around.

With no place to operate among either the Nephites or the Lamanites, they found it necessary to separate from the people. They began to inhabit wilderness lands, which were isolated from both Nephite and Lamanite lands of habitation. The wilderness location was thus chosen out of necessity—not by preference. (For more on the wilderness location, see Part 5, Chapter 5.5.)

Throughout the following thirty-seven years (12 BC—AD 25),[536] the works of evil continued under the direction of the Zoramites. The revitalized organization became an appendage of the Zoramite religion, which supplied the intense religious hatred that characterized every activity. The existence of a pagan religious cause and purpose provides a viable explanation for the rapid growth of the robbers in spite of miraculous heavenly manifestations, such as the great sign of the Savior's birth, and the many signs and wonders that both preceded and followed it.

In that perspective, the robbers during the second period did not recruit new members; they proselyted them to their religion. Likely, most incoming members did not understand that to join the Zoramite religion was to join the Gadianton robbers. Once inside the secret society of Gadianton, however, it was very difficult to escape, if a person was so inclined.

Twelve years after the reorganization, the robbers were seemingly unaffected by the great sign of the Lord's birth. After only a momentary pause, they began once again to work tirelessly to ensure that their vehicle of destruction was finely tuned, which they hoped would carry them to absolute power in the land southward. It is apparent that the Zoramites were the very agents by which Satan sent forth his lies among the people in AD 1 "to harden their hearts, to the intent that they might not believe" that the Savior of mankind had been born.[537]

A small number of Zoramites had been instrumental in the wholesale conversion of the Lamanite culture in 30 BC.[538] However, the vast majority of them were not converted to Christianity at that time, and in fact were never converted. They remained enemies to the Nephites and to the cause of Christ. Regardless of the Lord's interventions, they were never diverted from their goal of planting the seeds of rebellion and enticing the youth across the entire face of the land southward to dissent away to the robbers.

### *THE UPSURGE OF AD 3*

The Gadianton tentacles reached out from their wilderness hideaways into the land of Zarahemla in AD 3. In that year, "there were many dissenters of the Nephites who did flee unto [the robbers], which did cause much sorrow unto those Nephites who did remain in the land [of Zarahemla]."[539] No one was exempt from the influence of the robbers, and they began making alarming advances throughout the land southward.

In the same year, the robbers for the first time began to entice many of the youth of the Lamanites, who had little or no direct knowledge of their horrendous record of murder and mayhem. For almost thirty-five years following their conversion, the Lamanites had remained true to the gospel. However, the "wickedness of the rising generation of Lamanites,"[540] suddenly caused a sharp decline in Lamanite righteousness.

Throughout the lands of Nephi and Zarahemla, "Satan . . . did blind their eyes and lead them away to believe that the doctrine of Christ was a foolish and vain thing."[541] As a result, in both lands, there was a great falling away[542] from the Church of Christ to the Zoramite religion. By AD 13, the gross wickedness of the rising generation would be reflected in the great number of robbers, who wreaked havoc across the face of the land: "And it came to pass in the thirteenth year there began to be wars and contentions throughout all the land; for the Gadianton robbers had become so numerous, and did slay so many of the people, and did lay waste so many cities, and did spread so much death and carnage throughout the land, that it became expedient that all the people, both the Nephites and the Lamanites, should take up arms against them."[543]

## LOOKING BACK TO PERIOD ONE

Within seventeen years of their initial establishment, the robbers had already made alarming advances in both the land of Zarahemla and the land of Nephi. In 35 BC, they were at the heart of the Lamanite invasion, which drove the Christian Nephites completely out of the land southward. An atmosphere of evil had settled over the Nephites, which intensified even as Moronihah led them over the next five years to retake half of their lands. As Nephi resigned from office in 30 BC, "they who chose evil were more numerous than they who chose good."[544] Things did not bode well for the future of the Christian Nephite nation. Indeed, the robbers were at that time only four years away from their rise to the seat of power in Zarahemla, which took place in 26 BC when Seezoram was elected as chief judge, following the assassination of Cezoram and his son.[545]

## THE LAMANITE CONVERSION—A SETBACK FOR THE ROBBERS

The sudden conversion of the Lamanites in 30 BC, however, injected new life into the Christian cause of freedom. Between 30 BC and AD 3, it infused a certain degree of stability into the land southward. In a substantial way it provided a counterbalance to the continually growing pagan movement within the land of Zarahemla. The combined effect of the Lamanite conversion, the drought of 18 and 17 BC, and the great sign of the Lord's birth kept the Gadianton robbers in check throughout that twenty-seven-year period.

Following the Lamanite conversion, there was no animosity between the Nephite and Lamanite nations. The borders became open, and both Nephites and Lamanites moved freely between the two lands.[546] They became united in purpose because of their newly-shared Christian beliefs and values.

## THE SETBACK IS ONLY TEMPORARY

In 12 BC, upon the reorganization of the Gadianton secret society, the robbers became, in effect, a third nation occupying previously uninhabited wilderness areas.[547] Though the second generation of robbers had much success proselyting among both the Nephites and the Lamanites, their numbers were not large enough (due to the Lamanite conversion) to pose a serious threat to the continued existence of the two nations—that is, until AD 3. The robbers' sudden growth spurt in that year[548] for the first time began to disturb the fragile balance of Nephite and Lamanite power, as the youth in both Zarahemla and Nephi began flocking to their ranks.

In AD 3, the primary purpose of the robbers was to destroy the Christian governments currently in power in Zarahemla and Nephi, which stood between them and political control of the entire land southward. Working secretly within both nations, they robbed them of the strength of their youth. The new recruits would apparently slip quietly out of the land of Nephi and the land of Zarahemla to join the ranks of the robbers in the wilderness. Their numbers increased rapidly until by AD 13 they threatened the two nations with complete destruction.[549]

## THE LAMANITES UNITE WITH THE NEPHITES

In AD 13, the Nephites and the Lamanites found it necessary to join together as one people to thereby combine their resources and manpower under one government for defense against the robbers. The Lamanites gave up their identity and became Nephites,[550] which was symbolic of their conversion to Christianity. It is yet another indication of the synonymous relationship between the terms "Nephite" and "Christian."[551] It is for this reason that the term "Christian Nephites" is used frequently in this book to describe the Nephites, though in essence, the term is redundant. The Nephites were never considered a pagan nation.

Prior to 30 BC, whenever Nephites dissented away to the Lamanites, they became Lamanites.[552] After the 30 BC conversion, dissenters fell away to the robbers, taking the name, Secret Society of Gadianton. Afterward, they no longer considered themselves to be Nephites. They became bitter enemies of the Nephites. Without exception, they denounced and ridiculed the Nephite belief in Jesus Christ.

## THE LAMANITE CURSE IS REMOVED

Following their merger with the Nephites, the curse was taken from the Lamanites, "and their skin became white like unto the Nephites . . . their young men and their daughters became exceedingly fair, and they were numbered among the Nephites, and were called Nephites."[553] Together, they fought against the Gadianton robbers for "the privileges of their church and of their worship, and their freedom and their liberty."[554]

## THE ROBBERS—A PRODUCT OF THE PAGAN CONSPIRACY

The Gadianton robbers operated under the influence of the Zoramite pagan religion—not just in the second period when the Zoramites stood at the head but in the first period as well. This is concluded from the fact that the robbers were idolators during the first period, as revealed in Helaman 6:21 and 31.[555] The Zoramites were the only identified pagan religion throughout the entire period of the robbers.

A small number of scriptures reveal the Zoramite presence and influence within the land of Nephi throughout the entire period from 74 BC[556]–24 BC[557] and in Zarahemla from 43 BC[558] to the great drought in 17 BC.[559] Their position at the head of the Gadianton robbers after

12 BC provides a powerful confirmation that the robbers were simply an extension of the pagan dissenters and from the beginning had practiced the Zoramite religion. Once again, it should be emphasized that the Zoramites were a religion and not an ethnic group. They were composed of both Nephites and Lamanites.

Combining the above information with other elements of the pagan conspiracy, the following scenario can be identified, with respect to the Lamanite conversion:

1. The Lamanites were the resource of choice for pagan Nephite dissenters until the conversion of largely the entire Lamanite nation in 30 BC. Not only did the Lamanites become completely unreceptive of dissenter hostility against the Nephites following their conversion, but in 24 BC, when they became aware of the continued operation of the robbers within the land of Nephi, they would no longer allow them to operate in their midst: "And it came to pass that the Lamanites did hunt the band of robbers of Gadianton; and they did preach the word of God among the more wicked part of them, insomuch that this band of robbers was utterly destroyed from among the Lamanites."[560]

   The cure for a bad case of the robbers was thus rooted in the Christian religion. The Lamanite conversion to Christianity destroyed the robbers' influence and control among the Lamanites in two ways. First, their conversion removed them from the pagan religion upon which the robber organization rested. Second, the gospel message taught them the principles of faith in God and love for their fellow man.
2. For the most part, the Gadianton robbers were not converted to the gospel through the preaching of the Lamanites in 24 BC. Neither did they become extinct but simply feigned repentance so they could remain in Nephi. Likely, many of them moved at that time to the land of Zarahemla, where robbers had filled the judgment seat since 26 BC, following the assassination of Cezoram and his son.[561]

   Due to the Lamanite conversion (see Chapter 2.5) and the great drought called down by Nephi (see Chapter 2.8), there was no place after 17 BC for the robbers to operate, either within the land of Nephi or the land of Zarahemla. Therefore, when the Zoramites reestablished the robbers, they had no choice but to occupy a neighboring wilderness region. From their hiding places, they secretly recruited from among the rising generation of Nephites and Lamanites and from all enemies of Christianity.

Due to their foundation of pagan religion, they resisted the gospel, notwithstanding frequent miracles of healing, fulfillment of prophecy, heavenly manifestations, and calamity. They became more and more enraged with each obstacle that delayed their rise to absolute power, which would enable them to destroy all Christians.[562]

*TABLE 2.0*

**TWO PERIODS OF THE GADIANTON ROBBERS (52 BC–AD 25)**

| LEADER | PERIOD | DURATION | MODE OF OPERATION |
|---|---|---|---|
| Gadianton | 52 BC to 17 BC | 36 YEARS | **51–30 BC:** Operated openly among the Lamanites. In Zarahemla they operated secretly, successfully infiltrated Nephite government.<br>**30 BC:** Following the great Lamanite conversion, the robbers were expelled from the land of Nephi.<br>**30–17 BC:** In Zarahemla, many Nephites embraced the robbers.<br>**17 BC:** As a result of the drought, the robbers were swept from among them, and became "extinct"[531] |
| FIVE YEAR HIATUS BETWEEN THE TWO GADIANTON PERIODS (17–12 BC) | | | |
| Zoramites | 12 BC to AD 25 | 37 YEARS | Separate and distinct lands of habitation, recruitment of Nephites[532] and Lamanite youth,[533] frequent violent attacks against villages, towns, and cities, which were looted for sustenance. |

## CHAPTER 3.7

# LACHONEUS AND GIDGIDDONI

### *AD 16*

IN "THE SIXTEENTH YEAR from the coming of Christ,"[566] the Nephites were reeling from the Gadianton assault over the past three years:

- In the thirteenth year, the robbers had moved out of their secret places, initiating a general offensive against both Nephites and Lamanites. No longer did they make surprise attacks on individual cities as they had done for twenty-five years.[567] Instead, they openly attacked cities throughout Zarahemla and Nephi. Therefore, it became necessary for the Nephites and Lamanites to unite politically. Afterward, the Lamanites considered themselves Nephites.[568]
- In the fourteenth year, the Nephites gathered their forces (both Nephite and Lamanite) and began to defend their lands and cities. The war became intense as the armies of the robbers attacked the armies of the Nephites. By the end of the year, the Nephites had gained some advantage over them. The robbers were driven out of Nephite lands and back into their own lands in the mountains and dense forest regions.
- In the fifteenth year, the robbers attacked again, and because of "contention and dissensions" among the Nephites, the robbers "gained many advantages over them."[569]

Looking closely at the above chain of events leading up to AD 16, a familiar pattern comes into focus—simultaneous internal and external attack. Though Mormon did not include a great deal of detail at this point, enough is provided to determine this manner of attack was essentially the same as every dissenter attack throughout the history of

Zarahemla. At the very moment in which the robbers were mounting their attacks, dissenters within Nephite lands were causing great disturbances. Likely, the secret agents involved in Gadianton recruitment (Zoramite proselyting) were the ones who fanned the flames of internal dissent. The twofold attack became a major factor in the success of the Gadianton offensive. As the fifteenth year ended, the Nephites were in imminent danger of being destroyed.

## GIDDIANHI'S ULTIMATUM TO LACHONEUS

Following the robbers' military success in AD 15, their leader Giddianhi sent an epistle to Lachoneus, the Nephite chief governor, threatening the Nephites with extinction if they did not surrender to the robbers and submit to their rule.[570] Giddianhi's correspondence reveals much about the nature of the robbers:

### *ENEMIES OF CHRISTIANITY*

He mocked the foolishness of the Nephites in claiming to have God-given rights and liberty, including the right to ownership of the lands currently within their possession. The import of the statement "ye do stand well, as if ye were supported by the hand of a god" is clear. As with all pagan dissenters, the robbers were enemies of the Christian faith and refused to acknowledge the existence of the Christian God. Instead, they attributed the Christian belief in God to the imagination of the Nephites.[571]

### *IDOLATRY AND SECRET COMBINATIONS—PASSED DOWN FROM ANCIENT TIMES*

He referenced the secret society and secret works as being of ancient date, having "been handed down unto us."[572] His claim seems ridiculous on the surface because the Gadianton organization was only fifty-six years old at that time.[573] Moreover, there had been no previous secret combinations among the Nephites.

Mormon had previously laid the groundwork for understanding Giddianhi's statement, when he traced the path of secret combinations from Cain to Gadianton. It was a path that passed across the three major cultures of the Western Hemisphere—pre-Flood, Jaredite, and Nephite. He said:

> Now behold, those secret oaths and covenants did not come forth unto Gadianton from the records which were delivered unto Helaman; but behold, they were put into the heart of Gadianton by that same being who did entice our first parents to partake of the forbidden fruit—
>
> Yea, that same being who did plot with Cain, that if he would murder his brother Abel it should not be known unto the world. And he did plot with Cain and his followers from that time forth.
>
> And also it is that same being who put it into the hearts of the people to build a tower sufficiently high that they might get to heaven. And it was that same being who led on the people who came from that tower into this land; who spread the works of darkness and abominations over all the face of the land , until he dragged the people down to an entire destruction, and to an everlasting hell.
>
> Yea, it is that same being who put it into the heart of Gadianton to still carry on the work of darkness, and of secret murder; and he has brought it forth from the beginning of man even down to this time.
>
> And behold, it is he who is the author of all sin. And behold, he doth carry on his works of darkness and secret murder, and doth hand down their plots, and their oaths, and their covenants, and their plans of awful wickedness, from generation to generation according as he can get hold upon the hearts of the children of men.[574]

Thus, the transfer did not depend upon direct contact between the various cultures but upon the devil. Though Giddianhi did not refer to direct discourse with the devil, it is certainly not outside the range of possibility. In 75 BC, Korihor had admitted to Alma that "the devil hath deceived me; for he appeared unto me in the form of an angel, and said unto me: Go and reclaim this people, for they have all gone astray after an unknown God."[575] In about 52 BC, shortly before Gadianton first introduced the secret oaths and covenants of evil to Kishkumen's gang,[576] "they were put into [his heart] by that same being who did entice our first parents to partake of the forbidden fruit."[577]

Still, Giddianhi referred to the secret plans as having been "handed down to us" from "ancient" times.[578] This seems to imply that in his view, they were passed directly from culture to culture. Interestingly enough, in each cultural transition—from pre-Flood to Jaredite, and from Jaredite to Nephite—there was a physical connection between the former and the latter culture.

## THE CONNECTION BETWEEN THE PRE-FLOOD AND JAREDITE CULTURES

The physical connection between these two cultures can be clearly observed by following the meandering pathway of sparse information found in the book of Genesis and the book of Ether. Noah and his family were the only survivors of the pre-Flood culture and the first parents of the post-Flood culture.[579] To Noah's great-grandson Nimrod[580] is attributed the re-establishment of idolatry in the post-Flood era.

Nimrod established an empire in the plain of Shinar, which included the cities of Babel, Erech, Accad, and Calneh.[581] In Babel, Nimrod's people built a tower under his direction "whose top," according to his purpose, would "reach unto heaven."[582] The tower exemplified his defiance of the power and supremacy of God through his own deification, and in the worship of idols.

Following its reestablishment by Nimrod, idolatry then returned to the land of the pre-Flood culture. It came by way of the Jaredites, who migrated from the Tower of Babel to the Western Hemisphere as a result of the confusion of tongues.[583] Prior to their departure, they had been subjects of Nimrod.[584] Therefore, the idolatry of Nimrod provides a physical connection between pre-Flood and Jaredite idolatry.

However, the Jaredites were connected even more closely to pre-Flood idolatry by the ruins of the former culture. pre-Flood ruins likely spread across the face of the land northward, which the Jaredites would inhabit for the next 2,000 years. Furthermore, their language was not confounded at Babel,[585] and they could read and understand the pre-Flood language, as preserved in the ruins. They would be enabled thereby to restore a relatively precise imitation of pre-Flood idolatry, if they were so inclined.

## THE CONNECTION BETWEEN THE JAREDITE AND NEPHITE CULTURES

The Mulekite link between Jaredite and Nephite idolatry was previously addressed in *The War Against Christianity*, Chapter 2.3, "The Order of the Nehors." In review, a primitive form of Jaredite idolatry was likely practiced by the Mulekites when they were discovered by the people of Mosiah. In Alma 1–28, there are frequent references to the Order of the Nehors. In time, the torch of pagan hatred was passed from the Order of the Nehors to the Zoramites, when the Zoramites rose to dominance in the land of Nephi.[586] When the Zoramites assumed the leadership of the Gadianton robbers in 12 BC,[587] the secret combinations were in effect handed down to them as well.

### *THE RIGHT TO RULE THE NEPHITES*

Giddianhi spoke of the robbers' right of rule over the Nephites, alluding to ethnic considerations, or ethnic flattery.[588] Likely, he was not exclusively championing Lamanite claims to power but was referring to king-men claims as well, for the robbers were made up of Mulekites, as well as Lamanites.

### *THE ROBBERS DID NOT CONSIDER THEMSELVES TO BE NEPHITES*

Giddianhi said that his warriors awaited his command to "[go] down and destroy the Nephites." Thus, regardless of bloodlines, he did not consider the robbers to be Nephites.[589] It is possible that dwelling in their own lands in the wilderness in such large numbers, the robbers considered themselves to be a separate nation. However, it is also possible that Giddianhi was referring to the religious dichotomy that existed between Christians and pagans, given the synonymous relationship of the terms "Nephite" and "Christian." This point was poignantly emphasized when the Lamanites became Nephites after their conversion to the gospel.

The correct interpretation could be either of the two ideas. Therefore when Giddianhi said, "Go down and destroy the Nephites," he may have meant the Nephite nation. He may also have meant, "Go down and destroy the Christians." His statement could also represent a combination of the two ideas, for each was equally valid in the minds of the robbers.

## LACHONEUS' RESPONSE TO GIDDIANHI'S DEMANDS

Lachoneus was "astonished" that Giddianhi would presume that the Nephites would be overcome by fear and give up the lands of their possession without further resistance, and also at the robber's claim that his followers had been wronged by the Nephites by retaining from them their rights of government.[590] If he was referring to the rights of the Mulekites, Giddianhi worked from the contrived premise of divine right to political control. It was a long standing argument which was first raised by Amlici in 87 BC. It was again set forth by the king-men in 67 BC. Perhaps the most ridiculous aspect of such a notion was the fact that the foundation of any claim of nobility or divine predilection that Giddianhi, the king-men, or Amlici might set forth, came originally through Jacob's priesthood blessing to his son Judah.[591] The power and authority of Jacob's blessing, however, came from the Christian God, the very existence of whom Giddianhi refused to acknowledge. His twisted and tangled logic can be explained as nothing more than the ranting of a power-hungry lunatic—under the influence of Satan.

Lachoneus "was a just man, and could not be frightened by the demands and threatenings of a robber."[592] He saw the robbers simply for what they were—usurpers,[593] who sought to eliminate the free government and destroy Christianity. He ignored Giddianhi's demands and exhorted his people to cry to the Lord for strength to withstand the impending attack.

## AN INSPIRED DEFENSIVE STRATEGY

Despite the vulnerability of the Nephites and their losses throughout AD 15,[594] Lachoneus had faith that by gathering the Lamanites and Nephites together in a single location surrounded by fortifications, they could prevail against the robbers. He was a man of action, as well as faith. Through inspiration, he devised a comprehensive defensive plan and immediately went into action. He sent a proclamation throughout the land southward and the land northward, which directed the people to evacuate the land northward, the land of Nephi, and the land of Jershon. They were instructed to gather with their families and possessions into a relatively small region within the land of Zarahemla: "And the land which was appointed was the land of Zarahemla, and the land which was between the land Zarahemla and the land Bountiful, yea, to the line which was between the land Bountiful and the land Desolation."[595]

To this point in the Book of Mormon account, the war with the robbers had been fought exclusively within the land southward. While that did not change in Lachoneus' defense against the robbers, the geographical area affected by the war was expanded from that of former wars. The Gadianton robbers threatened all Nephite and Lamanite lands, both in the land southward and in the land northward. This was evident in Lachoneus' instructions to his people, which called for the gathering of the people from the land northward, as well as from the land southward. The only region not under his control was the wilderness region occupied by the robbers.

It is noted that the specific locations from which the Nephites gathered—Zarahemla, Nephi, and the land northward—are not specifically set forth at the time of gathering.[596] However, the participation of Lamanites from the land of Nephi during the war under the direction of Lachoneus is clearly indicated in 3 Nephi 3:14. Furthermore, an explicit reference to the involvement of Nephite citizens from the land northward is provided at the end of the war. At that time, the Nephites "did return to their own lands and their possessions, both on the north and on the south, both on the land northward and on the land southward."[597]

The gathering of Nephites from the land northward in response to the proclamation demonstrated the fact that Nephites in that distant land had not moved outside the region of his jurisdiction. They too were under the power and influence of the chief judge. For that reason, their safety, like that of the Nephites in Zarahemla and Nephi, was his responsibility. His proclamation was therefore published across the entire face of the land—including the land northward, as well as the land southward.

## A PRIMARY REASON FOR NOT GATHERING IN THE LAND NORTHWARD

Within thirty years of the first Nephite northward migrations in 55 BC, the land northward had already fallen largely under the control of pagan dissenters, which likely were allied with the Gadianton robbers in the land of Nephi. The book of Helaman gives only a glimpse of such conditions in the land northward. It is a solitary statement, which describes the circumstances surrounding Nephi's return in 23 BC from the six-year mission he had served in that region with his brother Lehi: "For he had been forth among the people who were in the land northward, and did preach the word of God unto them, and did prophesy many things unto them. And they did reject all his words, insomuch that he could not stay among them, but returned again unto the land of his nativity."[598]

Thus, at that time, there was no place of sanctuary within the entire land northward for the servants of the Lord.

By AD 16, almost forty years after Nephi's mission, the wickedness and depravity in the land northward had continued to grow without restraint, and a great curse engulfed the region. For that reason the land northward was excluded as a candidate for the place of gathering.[599] However, given the fact that there were Nephites within the land northward in AD 17, which followed the directive of Lachoneus to gather to the appointed land within the land southward, it is an indication that pagans/robbers did not have complete control of the land northward, notwithstanding the curse. However, the number of Christian Nephites living north of the narrow neck apparently represented a small minority of the population living there, and likely, they maintained a low profile.

## PREPARATIONS FOR THE WAR

Within the region to which the Nephites gathered, Lachoneus "caused that fortifications should be built round about them, and the strength thereof should be exceedingly great." He instructed the armies of the Nephites and Lamanites to station their forces in and around the fortified cities "to guard [the people] from the robbers day and night."[600]

Lachoneus was a devout Christian. Therefore, he knew the recipe for victory against the robbers must begin with a large measure of repentance. Without repentance, it would be fruitless to cry unto the Lord for strength. "Yea, he said unto them: As the Lord liveth, except ye repent of all your iniquities, and cry unto the Lord, ye will in nowise be delivered out of the hands of those Gadianton robbers. And so great and marvelous were the words and prophecies of Lachoneus that they did cause fear to come upon all the people; and they did exert themselves in their might to do according to the words of Lachoneus."[601]

## CHIEF CAPTAIN GIDGIDDONI

In AD 16, Lachoneus appointed chief captains over all the armies of the Nephites. He selected Gidgiddoni to be "the great commander of all the armies of the Nephites."[602] "Now, it was the custom of the Nephites to appoint for their chief captains (save it were in their times of wickedness) someone that had the spirit of revelation and also prophecy; therefore, this Gidgiddoni was a great prophet among them, as also was the chief judge."[603]

## THE PREVIOUS ELECTION OF CHIEF JUDGE LACHONEUS

It should be emphasized, however, that Lachoneus chose Gidgiddoni as the chief commander of the Nephite forces.[604] As for Lachoneus, however, he had been the chief judge for more than fifteen years. He was elected prior to AD 1, for he held the office when the great sign was given to announce the Lord's birth.[605] He would continue to rule until at least AD 26, before passing the judgment seat to his son, Lachoneus II.[606]

Considering his Christian beliefs, it is likely that he was not elected at any time during the five-year period following Samuel's prophecy (6–1 BC). Throughout that entire period, the majority of the people were wicked and arrogant.[607] With each passing year, they became more and more "hardened in iniquity."[608] Therefore, it would be reasonable to examine the period leading up to 6 BC to find a more plausible time for his election.

The robbers had begun to govern the land of Zarahemla in 25 BC, when they first obtained the judgment seat following their assassination of Cezoram and his son.[609] The period of their rule continued until 17 BC, when the drought pronounced by the prophet Nephi forced the people to abandon and eliminate "the band of Gadianton" and to bury "their secret plans in the earth."[610] The drought came to an end in 16 BC.[611] A short period of peace throughout the land then followed: "And it came to pass that the seventy and sixth year [16 BC] did end in peace. And the seventy and seventh year [15 BC] began in peace; and the church did spread throughout the face of all the land; and the more part of the people, both the Nephites and the Lamanites, did belong to the church; and they did have exceedingly great peace in the land; and thus ended the seventy and seventh year."[612]

The most probable time for Lachoneus to be elected was the year 15 BC, while the people remained temporarily humbled by the adversity of the drought. It was the only year of peace, however, for strife would return in 14 BC[613] and would then increase during 13 and 12 BC.[614]

## A SECOND POSSIBLE ELECTION YEAR

There was only one other occasion when the people all across the face of the land repented and joined the Church of Christ. It took place in 11 BC when (momentarily) the people were stirred up once again "to a remembrance of the Lord their God."[615] Their repentance resulted explicitly from their fear of the robbers, who had reorganized the year before[616] and once again were causing great destruction across the face of the land.[617] However, if an election had been held at any time during the years which followed, it is doubtful that Lachoneus would have been chosen as chief judge, for the people had already returned to their wickedness, as described in the following verse: "And in the eighty and second year [10 BC] they began again to forget the Lord their God. And in the eighty and third year [9 BC] they began to wax strong in iniquity. And in the eighty and fourth year [8 BC] they did not mend their ways."[618]

## THE SELECTION OF GIDGIDONNAH

Considering the mindset of the people in AD 15, the year before Lachoneus sent forth his proclamation across the land, it was also a time of "many contentions and dissensions.[619] It is unlikely that Lachoneus would have been chosen if an election had been held during that year. Therefore, in AD 16 when Gidgiddoni was chosen by Lachoneus as the chief Nephite military commander, it was hardly a reflection of Nephite righteousness at that precise moment in time. Instead, it was a reflection of righteousness by compulsion during one of the two fleeting moments in 15 and 11 BC, when Lachoneus was chosen as the Nephite leader. On those two occasions, the Lord, for the sake of the truly righteous, and by way of adversity, had compelled the Nephites to repent and turn from their wicked ways.

## NEPHITE SPIRITUAL VACILLATION

Between 30 BC and AD 16, the obsessive and unrelenting violence of the robbers was countered only by the repeated intervention of Deity. During that period of seemingly erratic Nephite behavior, an illusion is created, for the reader of the Book of Mormon, of wild spiritual vacillation. In reality during this particular interval of time, the Nephites were cursed by the enticements of pagan religion and the hostility of ethnic pride.[620] As a result, they were extremely weak spiritually and behaved like the nation of Judah during the period of the kings.[621] Just as the succession of righteous and wicked kings in Judah created the appearance of a much more pronounced cycle between righteousness and wickedness than was actually occurring among the people of Judah, the chastening hand of the Lord[622] created the appearance of extreme spiritual inconsistency among the Nephites.

The sad truth is that, like the Israelites during the reign of the kings, the people of Nephi at this time were constantly drawn away from righteousness by the enticements of pagan religion. The sensual and devilish pagan cults[623] provided the substrate of evil upon which the Gadianton virus grew. Like Judah, the Nephites were actually quite consistent in their rebellion against righteousness. With each calamity or sign from heaven, they would enter a period of quasi-repentance, which, unlike the Lamanite conversion, was never permanent.

The prophet Mormon, who witnessed the same intense battle between good and evil during his day, lamented "the unsteadiness of the hearts of the children of men,"[624] and the natural predisposition of mankind to move toward evil. He said:

> O how foolish, and how vain, and how evil, and devilish, and how quick to do iniquity, and how slow to do good, are the children of men; yea, how quick to hearken unto the words of the evil one, and to set their hearts upon the vain things of the world!
>
> Yea, how quick to be lifted up in pride; yea, how quick to boast, and do all manner of that which is iniquity; and how slow are they to remember the Lord their God, and to give ear unto his counsels, yea, how slow to walk in wisdom's paths![625]

Truly, this is the predisposition of mankind in every age of the earth. Mormon acknowledged the absolute necessity of the Lord's chastening hand when he said: "And thus we see that except the Lord doth chasten his people with many afflictions, yea, except he doth visit them with death and with terror, and with famine and with all manner of pestilence, they will not remember him."[626]

## THE INVISIBLE HAND OF THE LORD

For Lachoneus to have retained his office as chief judge throughout a period of approximately thirty years, leading up to AD 16, while the righteousness of the Nephites rose and fell like the ocean tides, the Lord's direct intervention was required on more than one occasion. Lachoneus' presence was crucial to the Nephites when he directed them to gather in AD 16. Without his and Gidgidonni's righteous and inspired leadership, the Nephites may very well have fallen to the robbers at that time. Therefore, standing before the people as instruments of God and in critical positions of leadership, their very presence testified of the Lord's protective hand.

## SHOULD WE ATTACK, OR SHOULD WE WAIT?

As Gidgiddoni began to implement Lachoneus' defensive plan, the Nephites under his command had their own ideas about how to secure victory against the robbers. Likely, they were encouraged by the tremendous number of soldiers who had congregated in the place of gathering. They were optimistic that by shear numbers alone they could prevail. At the same time, they understood the importance of Gidgiddoni's leadership role and the critical nature of his faith and righteousness, for Lachoneus by the voice of the Spirit had planted the fear of the Lord within them.[627] They said unto Gidgiddoni, "Pray unto the Lord, and let us go up upon the mountains and into the wilderness, that we may fall upon the robbers and destroy them in their own lands."[628] By structuring their request in this manner, they simultaneously made the following points:

1. They acknowledged Gidgiddoni as their leader.
2. They viewed him as their mediator with God.
3. They acknowledged the Lord as the source of their strength, without which they could not defeat the robbers.
4. They asked Gidgiddoni to pray unto the Lord and obtain His approval and support to destroy the robbers in their own lands.

There are many examples in the scriptures in which men of God have been raised up by the Lord to stand as an intermediary between the Lord and the people. To name a few, the brother of Jared,[629] Moses,[630] Nephi, the son of Lehi,[631] Mosiah I,[632] Benjamin,[633] Alma the Elder,[634] Alma the Younger,[635] the sons of Mosiah,[636] Nephi the son of Helaman,[637] and Mormon[638] became intermediaries between God and man during difficult times. Through revelation, Gidgiddoni gave the people an immediate answer from the Lord. There were five important points in his response: [639]

1. If we should go up against them the Lord would deliver us into their hands.
2. Therefore we will prepare ourselves in the center of our lands.
3. We will gather our armies together, but only for defensive purposes.

4. We will wait until they come against us.
5. If we do this, the Lord will deliver them into our hands.

Gidgiddoni's army accepted his counsel and followed his orders explicitly.

In AD 363, Mormon responded in the same way at the city of Desolation, refusing to lead the Nephites against the Lamanites and Gadianton robbers in their own lands.[640] However, at that time the Nephite armies were not dissuaded. They proceeded without Mormon—with disastrous results.[641]

# CHAPTER 3.8

# THE GADIANTON ROBBER WAR

THE FOLLOWING IS A summary of the recorded events of the Nephite war with the robbers:

## *AD 13–15*

In AD 13, the robbers began to attack cities throughout the land southward.[642] As a result, all Lamanites who had accepted the gospel in 30 BC "did unite with their brethren, the Nephites."[643] Afterward, "they were numbered among the Nephites, and were called Nephites."[644] The merger of the Nephites and Lamanites was completely necessary, due to the massive numbers within the growing body of robbers.

At that time it became necessary, "for the safety of their lives and their women and their children, to take up arms against those Gadianton robbers."[645] They had some success against the robbers in AD 14, but due to a continuous flow of dissenters to the robbers, by the end of AD 15, the robbers had gained "many advantages over them."[646]

## *AD 16*

Giddianhi, the leader of the robbers then sent his communique to Chief Judge Lachoneus, demanding that to avoid extermination, the Nephites must surrender their cities and their lands—all of their possessions to them.[647]

## *AD 17–18*

The Nephites prepared continuously throughout the two years following Giddianhi's warning. They gathered from all across the land southward into the heartland of Zarahemla, bringing with them all of their possessions and enough food to last for a period of seven years.

Due to the alliance between the Nephite and Lamanite nations, all of the people were under the rule of Lachoneus. Therefore, the people in both lands willingly obeyed his directive to gather within the land of Zarahemla.[648] They came to the region of gathering from the land of Nephi, as well as from outlying lands in Zarahemla. Others journeyed there from the land northward.

### AD 18

The robbers had no idea that, under the direction of their righteous and God-fearing leaders, the Nephites were fully prepared to defend against their great offensive. They believed that no amount of preparation would enable the Nephites to withstand the attack. Victory was a certainty, due to their vast numbers, and the prowess of their many great warriors.[649] "And it came to pass that in the latter end of the eighteenth year those armies of robbers had prepared for battle, and began to come down and to sally forth from the hills, and out of the mountains, and the wilderness, and their strongholds and their secret places, and began to take possession of all the lands which had been deserted by the Nephites, and the cities which had been left desolate."[650]

## THE DESERTED NEPHITE LANDS ARE LEFT DESOLATE

Over the previous two years, as the Nephites had gathered within the heartland region, all of their abandoned lands were purposefully left barren.[651] And "behold, there were no wild beasts nor game in those lands which had been deserted by the Nephites."[652] No food of any kind had been left behind, neither crops, nor animals—wild or domestic.

For that reason, the robbers' initial jubilation surrounding this seeming victory quickly transformed into desperation. At that time, there were no wilderness regions within any of the deserted Nephite lands where the robbers might go to get game.[653] Furthermore, they could not spread out within the deserted lands to plant crops and "raise grain, lest the Nephites should come upon them and slay them."[654]

### AD 19

## THE ROBBERS ATTACK THE NEPHITES

In the sixth month of the nineteenth year—six months after taking possession of the deserted Nephite lands—Giddianhi commanded the robbers to "go up to battle against the Nephites."[655] Third Nephi 4:7–14 records the account of the following intense battle, which the Nephites won because of their great faith in God. By "supplicating" the Lord, they received the necessary strength to achieve victory.

The robbers were thoroughly defeated and driven back to their wilderness lands. The Nephites continued to "pursue" and "slay" them only until they reached the wilderness.[656] Giddianhi was one of the casualties, being "overtaken and slain" before he could reach the borders of the wilderness.[657] The robbers would remain in the wilderness for about a year and a half, during which time Zemnarihah would be chosen to replace Giddianhi.[658]

The following question might be asked: Upon their return to their wilderness lands, why did they not immediately begin to produce food through farming? Their lands were not far away and were off limits to Nephite attack.[659] The Nephites had never attacked their enemies within their own lands. It was the traditional Nephite standard of defense.

In the wilderness, the robbers could therefore have spread out and raised crops, without fear of Nephite attack. Raising grain was apparently not beneath them, since spreading out in Nephite lands for that purpose was a definite consideration.[660] In their starved condition, it certainly was not beneath them. Is it possible that the wilderness regions inhabited by the robbers were unsuitable for farming, due to steep, rocky terrain, swampy lowland, and/or nutrient-poor soils?

The idea that this wilderness region may have been unfit for farming was addressed in Chapter 3.1.[661] It was considered simply from the fact that it remained wilderness many years after other neighboring regions had been settled. Furthermore, it was still referred to as wilderness, even after tens of thousands of robbers began to occupy the region. The failure of the robbers to spread out and farm these wilderness lands, even when threatened with starvation, lends further credence to this possibility.

### *AD 21*

In "the twenty and first year," Zemnarihah ordered the robbers to lay siege against the Nephites on every side.[662] It was a move based on the premise that sooner or later they would run out of food. "But behold, this was an advantage to the Nephites; for it was impossible to lay siege sufficiently long to have any effect upon the Nephites, because of their much provision which they had laid up in store."[663]

The robbers had no idea the people of Lachoneus had reserved enough provisions to last seven years. It was a period that could be further lengthened by growing additional crops and breeding the "cattle, and flocks of every kind," which they had brought with them.[664]

This final stage of the Gadianton Robber War, in which the robbers encircled and laid siege against the Nephites, is described in 3 Nephi 4:16–28. The siege lasted five years (AD 21–25), though that detail is not divulged until 3 Nephi 5:7. Therefore, defeating the robbers was no easy task.

The entire five-year period is contained within thirteen verses of 3 Nephi 4.[665] In contrast, the last seven years of the Amalickiah and Ammoron War comprise 394 verses in twelve chapters of the book of Alma.[666] That is less than one page, compared with twenty-nine pages. Needless to say, the Gadianton Robber War is briefly summarized.

## THE ROBBERS ATTEMPT TO FLEE NORTHWARD

Near the end of AD 25, Zemnarihah ordered the robbers to "withdraw themselves from the siege, and march into the furthermost parts of the land northward."[667] However, Chief Captain Gidgiddoni was aware of their intentions and "of their weakness from the want of food."[668] He ordered the Nephite armies to move out in front of the fleeing robbers. In their weakened state, the robbers were easily defeated. Other robbers attempted to return to the wilderness located southward of the place of gathering.[669] These in turn were cut off before they could reach the borders of the wilderness and were captured by the Nephite armies.

Zemnarihah was hanged from a tree. The tree was cut down as a symbol of their desire that they must never again allow a secret combination to get above them.[670] As the tree toppled to the ground, they cried: "May the Lord preserve his people in righteousness and in holiness of heart, that they may cause to be felled to the earth all who shall seek to slay them because of power and secret combinations, even as this man has been felled to the earth." [671]

## THE END OF THE ROBBERS

The defeat and dissolution of the robbers was thorough and complete. No robbers escaped either on the north or on the south. All were taken as prisoners,

> Insomuch that none did escape who were not slain, they did cast their prisoners into prison, and did cause the word of God to be preached unto them; and as many as would repent of their sins and enter into a covenant that they would murder no more were set at liberty.
>
> But as many as there were who would not enter into a covenant, and who did still continue to have those secret murders in their hearts, yea, as many as were found breathing out threatenings against their brethren were condemned and punished according to the law.[672]

Robbers which "entered into a covenant to keep the peace of the land," and which "were desirous to remain Lamanites," were given lands, "that they might have, with their labors, wherewith to subsist upon."[673] This is the third indication of the unproductive nature of the wilderness regions previously inhabited by the robbers. They did not return to their lands in the wilderness. Instead, these repentant robbers were given lands within the land of Nephi, specifically so they could subsist by tilling the land.

Through these actions, the Gadianton robbers were defeated and thoroughly dissolved by AD 25. They are never again identified by name in the pre-Christ period. Once again, the Nephites, by laboring with all the might of both body and soul, reestablished peace across the entire land.

## *AD 26*

### THE NEPHITES RETURN TO THEIR HOMES

When the war came to an end, the Nephites returned to their lands of habitation. Each man took his "family, his flock and his herds, his horses and his cattle, and all things whatsoever did belong unto them." They also carried with them all provisions that had not been consumed during the course of the war.

Some returned to the land northward.[674] If they had known that great destruction would be coming to that region on the fourth day of AD 34, however, they would surely have remained in the land southward. Only there would they survive the Great Storm.[675] Only there would they experience the joy of the Savior's visitation.

### INDICATIONS OF AN INFERTILE WILDERNESS—A REVIEW

As noted in this chapter, three conditions can be observed in the account of the second period of the robbers, which seem to indicate the wilderness occupied by the robbers between 12 BC and AD 25 was unfit for farming. They are listed as follows.

### INDICATION 1

As first considered in Chapter 3.1, the robber lands remained wilderness though they bordered upon the heartland regions of both Nephi and Zarahemla. The heartland region of highland Nephi had been inhabited by either Nephites or Lamanites for more than 550 years. Zarahemla's heartland along the Sidon had been inhabited by the Nephites for approximately 200 years.

Long after other nearby regions had been settled, it remained wilderness. Furthermore, after tens of thousands of robbers moved into the region,[676] it was still referred to as wilderness. Thus, the robbers did not settle the region, but apparently "infested the mountains and the wilderness"[677] only out of necessity.

### INDICATION 2

The failure of the robbers to spread out during the course of the war and farm their own lands even when threatened with starvation lends further credence to the idea of the unproductive nature of this wilderness region. The Nephites would not,[678] and during the course of the war did not,[679] attack them in their own lands.

### INDICATION 3

At the conclusion of the war, those robbers which "entered into a covenant to keep the peace of the land," and which "were desirous to remain Lamanites," were given lands, "that they might have, with their labors, wherewith to subsist upon."[680] This is the third indication of the unproductive character of the wilderness regions previously inhabited by the robbers. Rather than return to the wilderness, repentant robbers chose to remain in the land of Nephi, specifically so they could subsist by tilling the land.

## REFLECTIONS ON THE OUTCOME OF THE WAR

In his "epistle" to Lachoneus, Giddianhi had threatened the Nephites with extinction.[681] Based on similar threats by secret combinations against the Nephites and the Jaredites, when each of their civilizations came to an end, and against various pre-Flood cultures, it was not an idle threat. If the Nephites had lost the war, the robbers would have been intent on their complete annihilation at that time, prior to the appearance of the Savior.

That has always been the mindset of secret combinations throughout the history of mankind. The book of Moses records such diabolical actions at the hands of the Canaanites, who were guilty of the sins of Cain. They completely destroyed the people of Shum and seized their lands.[682] When the Jaredites came under the power of secret combinations, they were completely destroyed down to a single man.[683] During the final phase of the Nephite pre-Christ period, the Gadianton robbers had gained a tremendous following. They had the power—and under the influence of the devil, they had the predisposition—to completely destroy the Nephites. However, the Lord shaped the outcome of those events through intervention, though based fully upon the repentance of His people.

The Nephite victory resulted in the complete elimination of the Gadianton secret combination.[684] As will be considered throughout Part 4, however, other dissenters would rise up almost immediately. Though they would not assume the Gadianton name, they would resume the war against Christianity.

## MORMON'S PERSONAL PERSPECTIVE

Ironically for Mormon, as he inscribed the story of the Gadianton robbers on the plates of Mormon, the Nephites were embroiled in the terminal Nephite wars, which also involved the Gadianton robbers.[685] The conclusion of the Gadianton Robber War in AD 25 would not be reflective of the outcome in his day. As he led the Nephites during the final series of wars—which began in AD 322 when he was eleven and would continue until AD 385—Mormon was fully aware of the prophecies of Alma the Younger[686] and Samuel the Lamanite,[687] which foretold the complete extinction of the Nephites. According to the prophecies, it would occur 400 years after the sign was given of Christ's birth—the very time during which Mormon lived.

Furthermore, through the whisperings of the Spirit, as well as revelations he received during his own life, he knew without doubt that the prophesied time was at hand. Though he prayed continually for his people and desired that they would repent and be saved from destruction,[688] he had little hope that they would do so, for their wicked and unrepentant state was in perfect alignment with the prophecies.

# CHAPTER 3.9

# THE CURSE OF CAIN

Much has been said concerning the curse of Cain.[689] It is not the purpose of this book to expound on the subject, except as it relates to secret combinations. As it pertains to the Gadianton robbers, the curse of Cain has nothing to do with genealogy or lineage. It is the curse that accompanies idolatry and its close associate, secret combinations—both of which originated with Cain. The curse of Cain was a curse upon the robbers themselves.

However, in a completely different sense, the robbers are the greatest curse to be associated with Cain. It was not a curse upon them but upon the victims of their violence, for they have destroyed entire nations, to include the Jaredites and the Christian Nephites. The waters of the Flood covered the earth because of violence—likely at the hands of secret combinations.[690]

The curse of idolatry and secret combinations thus afflicted all three of the scriptural cultures that inhabited the Western Hemisphere. It is only through modern revelation that we know all three of these cultures inhabited the "New World," including the pre-Flood culture. The Western Hemispheric setting was not revealed to mankind until it was revealed to the Prophet Joseph Smith, and other prophets who followed him. We are greatly blessed that such revelations have been given to the inhabitants of the earth during this last dispensation—the dispensation of the fulness of times.

Genesis 4 refers to the curse of Cain, a curse that was placed upon him individually. Cain was a "tiller of the ground." His younger brother Abel "was a keeper of sheep."[691] The two brothers presented offerings to the Lord. Cain offered up the best of his vegetable crops to God, while Abel sacrificed "of the firstlings of his flock and of the fat thereof."[692] Cain's "countenance fell"[693] when God accepted Abel's offering, but rejected his offering.[694] It should be emphasized that Abel's offering was a similitude of the sacrifice of Jesus Christ, which was the only acceptable offering to God. Diced carrots or sliced peaches has little if any significance as a meaningful representation of the Lord's sacrifice.

After complaining to Satan, who had purposely instructed him to present a meaningless offering to the Lord, Cain fell into the trap that was carefully prepared for him. The first secret combination was a murder pact between Cain and Satan to murder his brother Abel, and thereby take possession of all his property and possessions.[695]

After Cain had committed the evil deed,[696] the Lord God confronted him about Abel's death. Cain actually tried to hide his sin—from the Lord, no less—who responded, by saying:

> What hast thou done? The voice of thy brother's blood crieth unto me from the ground.
>
> And now art thou cursed from the earth, which hath opened her mouth to receive thy brother's blood from thy hand;
>
> When thou tillest the ground, it shall not henceforth yield unto thee her strength; a fugitive and a vagabond shalt thou be in the earth."[697, 698]

According to the Genesis and the book of Moses accounts, Cain's curse was not the blackness that was placed upon him by the Lord. Rather, he was cursed that the earth would no longer produce crops for him, for his pride and disobedience were directly related to his skill in agriculture. The blackness was actually a softening of the curse.[699]

With respect to the earth's resistance to Cain's partaking of its bounty, a curse had already been placed upon mankind because of Adam's transgression. It resulted from Adam's eating of the fruit of the tree of knowledge of good and evil, when he had been commanded of God to never partake of it. Though the fall of man was necessary, and salvation could only come through the fall, still, for every transgression, there is a punishment affixed,[700] "for behold, justice exerciseth all his demands."[701]

Adam's transgression pertained to the partaking of a fruit of the earth, though he was specifically forbidden of God to do so. His punishment was that he could partake of the earth's bounty only through great effort (sweat), both on his part and on the part of his descendants. It would not be easy, for "thorns . . . and thistles" would spring forth spontaneously, which would strangle and out-compete the food-producing plants unless they were repeatedly and persistently weeded out. What gardener has not experienced the curse of Adam's transgression?

Cain's curse, however, was much more destructive, because it did not matter how hard he worked. His perspiration would always turn to exasperation, for the earth would not produce anything, regardless of how much effort he expended. The curse of Cain was a curse of drought and famine, which was superimposed upon the curse of thorns and thistles.

The curse of Cain was upon the Gadianton robbers, not because they were descendants of Cain, but because they restored the oaths and covenants originally embraced by Cain. The robbers were a secret combination, patterned after Cain's, which, like Cain, received their oaths directly from Satan.[702] As a result, the ground would not yield up its strength to them. It had occurred between 19 and 16 BC, when Nephi, in following the direction of the Spirit of God, pronounced a drought upon the land southward to compel the Gadianton robbers to cease their destructive war.

In the present war, a related phenomenon took place, in which once again they could not obtain of the earth's bounty. This time, however, the curse was upon the robbers, but not upon their victims. This can be seen in the fact that they suffered greatly from a lack of food, though there was not a famine in the land.

The Nephites did not suffer likewise because of the seven-year supply of food they had accumulated.[703] The scarcity of food was experienced only by the robbers, who were smitten with the curse of Cain because of the abominable secret combinations. However, when a culture allows the secret combinations to overcome them, the curse extends to the people as well.[704] This can be seen in the previous drought pronounced by Nephi upon the Nephites. Thousands of people died in the more wicked parts of the land. Only when the people repented and forcibly extracted the robbers from their midst did the drought end.

## CHAPTER 3.10

# PRE-CHRIST ZARAHEMLA—DIVIDED INTO TWO PAGAN PERIODS

DURING THE PRE-CHRIST ERA in the land of Zarahemla, the Christian Nephites were constantly tormented by pagan dissenters. The persecution came at the hands of two religious cults, which were first considered in *The War Against Christianity*.[705] There was a slight overlap between the periods of the two cults. Having reached the end of the Zoramite period with the extinction of the robbers, the two pagan periods can now be reviewed in their entirety.

## THE ORDER OF THE NEHORS

The Order of Nehor was introduced into the Nephite culture by the people of Zarahemla (Mulekites), albeit in a primitive form, considering their illiteracy. At the time of their discovery by the Nephites, the history of the people of Zarahemla, as well as their religion, was maintained exclusively in the memory of the people, rather than in writing. However, as they ascended in knowledge and learning through the Nephite influence, the pagan religion took on greater complexity and sophistication. At some point, many Nephites were enticed to join the religion because of its sensual appeal and carnal freedom.

The eventual name by which it was identified, as well as other telltale signs, reveal its Jaredite roots. Therefore, it can only have come from the Mulekites, who had lived in the land northward next to the Jaredites throughout the first 400–year period following their arrival from Jerusalem.[706] The Nephites had lived exclusively within the land southward from 589 BC until they discovered the people of Zarahemla on the banks of the Sidon River in *ca.* 200 BC.[707] They were completely unaware of the Jaredites until they learned of them from the people of Zarahemla.[708]

Many of the people of Zarahemla had Jaredite names. Nephites, such as Alma the Younger, who for a time became involved in this Mulekite idolatry,[709] gave their children Jaredite names—another indication of the Jaredite influence. Indeed, the naming of children might very well provide one of the most lucid windows into the lives of the rising generation of Nephites near the end of Mosiah's reign, when the Order of Nehor began to entice many to denounce Christianity.

## WHAT'S IN A NAME?

The names given to Alma the Younger's children might be used to reconstruct the pathway of his life, which led to his "road to Damascus" experience.[710] Based upon the name of his firstborn son, it is determined that Alma the Younger grew up in the Church, apparently in the land of Helam.[711] Helaman's name might well mean that Alma had not left the Church at the time of his birth and still had a fondness for the place of his youth.

Alma was then drawn to the Jaredite pagan religion and named his next two sons Shiblon and Corianton—the names of Jaredite kings.[712] He returned to the Church shortly before 92 BC. Chief Captain Zoram may very well have had the same life experience, for he named his first son Lehi but gave his second son the name Aha, a Jaredite name from the list of kings. Thus, like Alma the Younger, Zoram may have briefly become involved in the Jaredite pagan religion for a time, and the two may have been friends throughout that period of time. Hence, Zoram returned to the Church and was made chief captain by Alma. It is noted that the above scenario is only speculation, which springs simply from the names given to Alma's and Zoram's offspring. However, the foundation for such reasoning rests upon the fact that for an unknown period of time, Alma did indeed join with the idolators[713] and did seek to destroy the Church of God.[714]

## THE PERIOD OF THE NEHORS

As pertaining to Nephite history, the period of the Nehors began simultaneously with the arrival of the people of Mosiah in the land of Zarahemla. The Nehor period is projected to have lasted from approximately 200 BC to 77 BC, or about 123 years. See Table 3.0.

*TABLE 3.0*

## THE ORDER OF NEHOR—ZARAHEMLA'S FIRST PAGAN RELIGION

| Year BC | Events |
|---|---|
| *Ca.* 200 | The Nephites arrive in the land of Zarahemla and discover the people of Zarahemla (Omni 1:13–14). |
| 200–91 | Many of the people of Zarahemla deny the being of their Creator and practice a primitive form of religion (Omni 1:17). Through time, the pagan religion takes on a more complex and erudite form, as the Mulekites become literate under the influence of the Nephites. |
| Sometime Before 124 | Amalekites establish the Mulekite pagan religion in the land of Nephi, which they had practiced in the land of Zarahemla before dissenting away to the Lamanites. The manner of construction of the edifices of the religion is similar to those constructed by the Order of Nehor in the land of Zarahemla, as inferred in Alma 21:4. |
| 91 | The Lamanite cities of Jerusalem, Middoni, and the village of Ani Anti are controlled by the Amalekites and Amulonites, which practice the Mulekite pagan religion. A synagogue previously constructed in the city of Jerusalem is constructed after the same manner as the Order of Nehor would be constructed in the land of Zarahemla. |
| 91 | Nehor establishes a church in the land of Zarahemla. |
| 87 | The Amlicites practice the Order of Nehor, declare war on the Nephites, and enlist the support of Lamanites from the land of Nephi. |
| 82 | The Nephite city of Ammonihah is governed by the Order of Nehor. |
| 81 | Desolation of Nehors—The city of Ammonihah is destroyed by a Lamanite/Amalekite/Amulonite army from the land of Nephi. Unbeknownst to one another, the city of Ammonihah and the army from Nephi both practiced the religion of Nehor. |
| 81 | The Lamanite/Amalekite/Amulonite army flees into the East Wilderness. The Amulonites anger the Lamanites and are virtually destroyed (Alma 25:7–9). |

| | |
|---|---|
| 78 | The Lamanite/Amalekite army (minus the Amulonites) returns to the land of Nephi. They begin to attack the people of Anti-Nephi-Lehi. |
| 77 | The people of Anti-Nephi-Lehi flee from the land of Nephi with the sons of Mosiah to the land of Zarahemla, and the Nephites allow them to settle in the land of Jershon. |
| 77 | The Lamanite/Amalekite army pursues the people of Anti-Nephi-Lehi to the Nephite land of Jershon. They meet the Nephite armies in battle and are smitten and driven into the east wilderness. A death blow is thus inflicted upon the Order of Nehors, which is never again referenced in the Book of Mormon. |
| 74 | Zerahemnah, the Lamanite leader in the Zoramite War utilizes Amalekites and Zoramites as his captains. There is no further reference to Amalekites following the Zoramite War. This may be a result of Zoramite hostility, though they may have simply united with the Zoramites at that time, abandoning their separate identity. |

Amalekites and Amulonites embraced the order of Nehor.[715] After the Nephites thoroughly defeated the Amalekites and Lamanites in 77 BC in the borders of Jershon,[716] the order of Nehor disappears from the Book of Mormon, and afterward exerted no visible influence among either Nephites or Lamanites. Following the Zoramite War in 74 BC, there is no further mention of the Amalekites. Though it could be maintained that the Nehor and Zoramite periods had a three-year overlap, the Nehor era is considered to have ended at basically the same time the Zoramites established the city of Antionum, having been dealt a death blow in the battle of 77 BC.

## THE ZORAMITES

Not long after 77 BC, Zoram established a new pagan religion in Antionum.[717] Throughout the following 102 years, his followers inflicted great trauma upon the Christian Nephites. The Lamanites also became victims of the murderous cult after they were converted to the gospel in 30 BC.

Chapter 2.4 in *The War Against Christianity* describes the rise of the Zoramites in the land of Antionum. The Zoramite War of 74 BC was the immediate result of their dissent over to the Lamanites. Following their defeat in the land of Manti,[718] they fled to the land of Nephi. It is likely that they became members of Gadianton's band in 50 BC, after he fled from Zarahemla and began to recruit many Lamanites.[719]

They remained in Nephi until 12 BC, at which time they reestablished the Gadianton robbers and moved into an uninhabited mountain and wilderness region, from which they could launch attacks against the Nephites and the Lamanites.[720] The defeat of the robbers in AD 25 brought the Zoramite era to an end. The final thirty-seven–year period can therefore be described as both the last period of the robbers, and the last period of the Zoramites.

Throughout their history, the Zoramites were continuously obsessed with the overthrow of the Nephite government. The Book of Mormon makes a number of direct references to them during the sixty-two years they remained in the land of Nephi. Two additional references are given while they directed the robbers from the wilderness, during the last period. The references are summarized as follows:

1. In 73 BC, Amalickiah utilized Zoramites as chief captains. They were chosen for two reasons—first, because of their extreme hatred for the Nephites, and second, because of their knowledge of Nephite military strengths and weaknesses.[721] This was little more than a year after the Zoramite War, and much of their knowledge was based on information obtained during the war. Furthermore, like Amalickiah, they were recent citizens of Zarahemla and had firsthand knowledge of Nephite lands from an internal perspective. Amalickiah also had a kinship with the Zoramites, both having descended from Zoram.[722]

   Unbeknownst to Amalickiah and the Zoramites, Moroni had implemented his defensive fortifications in cities along the western perimeter of Nephite lands following the Zoramite war. This included Ammonihah and Noah,[723] both of which lay at the western border of Nephite lands, as settled in 72 BC.[724] Their immediate designs were frustrated when they found the weakest cities had been strengthened, making them the strongest points of defense.[725]

   The period of Zoramites lasted from *ca.* 77 BC until AD 25. As noted in Table 4.0 (see page 168), Amalekite leaders (the Order of Nehor) who had participated in the Zoramite

War[726] are curiously absent from the ranks of Amalickiah's army. They are never again mentioned in the Book of Mormon, possibly a result of either Zoramite hostility or Amalekite acquiescence to Zoramite dominance.

2. The next reference to the Zoramites concerns an event that took place in 30 BC. It is found in Helaman 5:41, in connection with the miraculous conversion of the Lamanites, approximately forty-five years after the Zoramite War.[727] Great and marvelous heavenly manifestations filled the Lamanites with fear. Aminadab, a dissenter from the Nephites, exhorted the other Lamanites to have faith in Christ, "who was taught unto you by Alma, and Amulek, and Zeezrom."

   The only reference in the Book of Mormon to all three men of God preaching the gospel together occurred during their mission to the Zoramites.[728] Immediately afterward, the Zoramites dissented away to the Lamanites. In 73 BC (one year after their defection), Alma disappeared from the land of Zarahemla,[729] so any other reference to the teaching of Alma, Amulek, and Zeezrom would have occurred at an even earlier time.

   It is concluded that Aminadab was a Zoramite and was speaking to other Zoramites previously from Antionum living among the Lamanites in 30 BC. Over the previous forty-four years, they had shaped and influenced, even dominated the Lamanite culture. Due to their pagan religion and their hatred of Christianity, they continuously sought to destroy the Nephites.

3. Another reference is made to the Zoramites as the faction responsible for the 12 BC reestablishment of the Gadianton robbers in the wilderness and mountain regions of the land southward. It should be noted that the Zoramites are not identified by name in this passage:

   > And it came to pass that in the eightieth year of the reign of the judges over the people of Nephi, there were a certain number of the dissenters from the people of Nephi, who had some years before gone over unto the Lamanites, and taken upon themselves the name of Lamanites, and also a certain number who were real descendants of the

> Lamanites, being stirred up to anger by them, or by those dissenters, therefore they commenced a war with their brethren.
>
> And they did commit murder and plunder; and then they would retreat back into the mountains, and into the wilderness and secret places, hiding themselves that they could not be discovered, receiving daily an addition to their numbers, inasmuch as there were dissenters that went forth unto them.
>
> And thus in time, yea, even the space of not many years, they became an exceedingly great band of robbers; and they did search out all the secret plans of Gadianton; and thus they became robbers of Gadianton. [730]

It is only in the light of the final reference (Item 4 below) that the Zoramite identity can be clearly seen in the above verse.

4. In AD 3, only two years after the sign was given of the birth of Christ, the robbers began to grow in number, as more and more Nephites dissented over to them.[731] They also began to actively recruit the rising generation of Lamanites in the land of Nephi: "And there was also a cause of much sorrow among the Lamanites; for behold, they had many children who did grow up and began to wax strong in years, that they became for themselves, and were led away by some who were Zoramites, by their lyings and their flattering words, to join those Gadianton robbers."[732]

## THE END OF THE ZORAMITES

Notwithstanding the destruction of the Gadianton robbers in AD 25, the Zoramite identity may have persisted among both Lamanites and Nephites until they were finally destroyed in the Great Storm of AD 34, though there is no record of any further activity. The events of the Zoramite era are summarized in Table 4.0:

### *TABLE 4.0*
### THE ZORAMITES—ZARAHEMLA'S SECOND PAGAN RELIGION

| Year | Events | Base of Operations |
|---|---|---|
| *CA.* 77 BC | The Zoramites establish the city of Antionum and practice a new religion. | Zarahemla |
| 75 BC | Korihor, an anti-Christ, begins to preach among the Nephites. After being stricken dumb, he returns to Antionum and is slain by the Zoramites.(Alma 30:59) | Zarahemla |
| 75 BC | Alma, Ammon, Aaron, Omner, Amulek, Zeezrom, Shiblon, and Corianton go on a mission to the Zoramites (Alma 31–35; 35:12). | Zarahemla |
| 74 BC | The Zoramites dissent over to the Lamanites and join forces with Lamanites in the east wilderness. The only battle of the Zoramite War is fought in the land of Manti. The Nephites are led by Chief Captain Moroni. Following their defeat, they depart into the land of Nephi (Alma 35:10–13; Alma 43–44). | Zarahemla |
| 74–12 BC | For sixty-two years, the Zoramites live among the Lamanites and are likely involved in every Lamanite attack throughout the period. | Nephi |
| 30 BC | The conversion of the Lamanites is aided by a Zoramite in the land of Nephi. Notwithstanding the beneficial nature of his involvement, which is completely out of character, it serves as an indicator that the Zoramites are still active and very influential as leaders in the land of Nephi (Helaman 5:35–52). | Nephi |
| 12 BC | The Zoramites reestablish the Gadianton robbers in mountain and wilderness regions of the land southward (Helaman 11:24–27). | Wilderness |

| | | |
|---|---|---|
| AD 3 | The Zoramites entice many of the Nephite and Lamanite youth to join the Gadianton robbers (3 Nephi 1:29–30). | Wilderness |
| AD 16–25 | The Gadianton Robber War (3 Nephi 3–5). | Wilderness |
| AD 25 | The Zoramite era ends with the defeat of the Gadianton robbers. | Disbanded |

## ONE PAGAN CONTINUUM IN THE LAND OF ZARAHEMLA

The conclusion of the Zoramite era enables a complete view of both pagan periods. Together, the two cults (the Order of Nehor and the Zoramites) caused continual contention within the land of Zarahemla from the time of the *ca.* 200 BC Nephite arrival in the land of Zarahemla until the defeat of the robbers at the end of AD 25,[733] a period of approximately 225 years. The two periods literally constituted one continuous pagan era, due to the fact that the Zoramite era began even as the era of the Nehors was coming to an end. Actually, there was a slight overlap, for both pagan religions were represented in the Zoramite War.[734] See Table 5.0 on the following page.

Though the two pagan cults were markedly distinct from one another, the two periods were similar in a number of ways. Each cult in turn became more and more violent with the acquisition of power until each was destroyed by the violence, which is attributed in the Book of Mormon to the judgment of God, upon reaching the fulness of their iniquity. Both cults openly expressed intense hatred for Christianity, which without exception led to violence and bloodshed.

Proponents of both pagan cults continually ridiculed the "traditions of their fathers,"[735] which they had rejected, referring to them as "silly," or "foolish." The term "foolish traditions" became a worn out cliché that was employed with derision by the Order of Nehor—first in 91 BC against Aaron in the land of Nephi,[736] and in 82 BC when they maligned Alma and Amulek in the city of Ammonihah.[737] It was used repeatedly by Korihor in his rantings as he traveled throughout the land of Zarahemla in 75 BC.[738] In the land of Antionum during the same year (75 BC), the Zoramites were observed by Alma and his missionary companions utilizing the same term in a disparaging way as part of their repetitive babblings.[739]

### *TABLE 5.0*

### PRE-CHRIST ZARAHEMLA: TWO PAGAN PERIODS

| RELIGION | PERIOD | DURATION | LAND OF OPERATION |
|---|---|---|---|
| Nehor | *ca.* 200 BC<br>to<br>77 BC | 123 years | **ZARAHEMLA** (*ca.* 200–77 BC)—Began with the arrival of the Nephites and merger with Mulekites. Ended with the 77 BC defeat of the Lamanites and Amalekites in the borders of Jershon.<br>**NEPHI** (*ca.* 150–74 BC)—Began with the arrival of the Amalekites, ended with the arrival of the Zoramites. |
| Zoramite | 77 BC<br>to<br>AD 25 | 102 years | **ZARAHEMLA** (77–74 BC)—Established city of Antionum, joined with Lamanites in Nephi, whom they incited to wage the Zoramite War.<br>**NEPHI** (74–12 BC)—From Zoramite War to rebirth of the robbers.<br>**WILDERNESS** (12 BC–AD 25)—Zoramites headed the Gadianton robbers. |

# PART 4

# THE PEOPLE OF THE LORD—A NEW PERIOD OF PERSECUTION (AD 25–AD 34)

# CHAPTER 4.1

# DISSOLUTION OF THE CHURCH OF CHRIST

### *AD 25*

THE THREAT OF ABSOLUTE destruction, which had hovered over the Nephites for thirteen long years,[740] was finally removed. The robbers had launched their first attacks at the beginning of AD 13[741] and were not defeated until the end of AD 25.[742] The war was therefore similar in length to Amalickiah and Ammoron's thirteen-year war, which had taken place from the beginning of 73 BC[743] to the end of 61 BC.[744]

When the robbers were finally defeated, the Nephites were filled with glorious relief and indescribable joy. In that moment of joy and humility before God, they acknowledged His hand in the great victory: "And their hearts were swollen with joy, unto the gushing out of many tears, because of the great goodness of God in delivering them out of the hands of their enemies; and they knew it was because of their repentance and their humility that they had been delivered from an everlasting destruction."[745]

### *AD 26*

### AN ILLUSION OF PEACE AND PROSPERITY

The people "returned to their own lands, and their possessions, both on the north and on the south, both on the land northward and on the land southward."[746] The seeming redundancy in the use of the words north/south and northward/southward is likely due to the Lamanite involvement in the gathering. Had it been only Nephites that gathered, a sole reference to the lands northward and southward would have sufficed. The reference to the people returning to their lands "both on the north and south" seems to relate to the Nephites returning to their homes across the land of Zarahemla, while the Lamanites returned to the land of Nephi. Zarahemla was on the north, and Nephi was on the south.

As peace settled upon the land, the people began to be prosperous once more. Many cities were repaired and new cities were established. Highways and roads were constructed throughout the land southward, which connected "land to land," "city to city," and "place to place."[747] The robbers had been completely eliminated, and there was no one to threaten the harmony and good will that settled in the hearts and the minds of all the people.[748] With such sincere humility, genuine repentance, rededication of their lives to God, and commitment to serve the Lord diligently both "day and night," surely the Nephites could enjoy a lasting period of peace and prosperity. However, it was not to be.

## *AD 29*

## PRIDE GOETH BEFORE DESTRUCTION[749]

Only three years after the end of the war, the Nephites plummeted once again into transgression. According to 3 Nephi 6:6–14, the return of peaceful conditions resulted in unfettered commerce throughout all regions of the land, both in the land of Zarahemla and in the land of Nephi—in the land northward as well as the land southward. Some of the people profited greatly and the distinctions between the rich and the poor suddenly became more pronounced. The riches of many "merchants," "lawyers," and "officers"[750] caused them to become lifted up in pride and to create class divisions, for they considered themselves to be elite and of greater importance than the lower classes.

Thus, the pride of the elite appears to have been the basic reason for the contention. It might well be projected, however, that for the most part, the wealth, which divided the people into classes at that time, was not a recent development. This was made evident as the people returned to their homes in AD 26, immediately following the defeat of the robbers: "And it came to pass that they had not eaten up all their provisions; therefore they did take with them all that they had not devoured, of all their grain of every kind, and their gold, and their silver, and all their precious things, and they did return to their own lands and their possession."[751]

They had taken with them all of their earthly possessions when they traveled to the place of gathering, "save it were their land,"[752] to which they returned at the conclusion of the war. Everything they owned was preserved during the conflict, for the robbers never penetrated the outer perimeter of the land of gathering. Therefore, the class distinctions, as they related to material wealth, were likely established long before the war. It follows that the elite were the greatest benefactors of the subsequent flurry of activity.

Therefore, the division of the people into ranks of rich versus poor likely reflected a spiritual decline, rather than a newly developed division of wealth. There was a great inequality, as the rich had many advantages over the poor. Many were ignorant and uneducated because of their poverty, while the rich were lifted up with "great learning."[753] Again, this was most likely not a new class distinction, but an indication of pride and condescension to a degree seldom displayed by the Nephite aristocracy.

It was the arrogance of the affluent, which became the primary driving force behind the "disputings" and "great persecutions" that first surfaced in AD 29.[754] In their growing decadence and pride, they ridiculed and viciously maligned the poor. In so doing, they rejected one of the most basic requirements of the gospel, and in fact its very essence.[755] Some of the poor retaliated against such attacks and "did return railing for railing, while others would receive railing and persecution and all manner of afflictions, and would not turn and revile again, but were humble and penitent before God."[756] "Now the cause of this iniquity of the people was this—Satan had great power, unto the stirring up of the people to do all manner of iniquity, and to the puffing them up with pride, tempting them to seek for power, and authority, and riches, and the vain things of the world."[757]

## *AD 30*

## THE BREAKUP OF THE CHURCH

The following happened as a result of this "great inequality" that had developed in AD 29: "In the thirtieth year, the church was broken up in all the land save it were among a few of the Lamanites who were converted to the true faith; and they would not depart from it, for they were firm and steadfast, and immovable, willing with all diligence to keep the commandments of the Lord."[758]

It had now been sixty years since the conversion of the Lamanites, and it is likely that it was the second and third generation that clung firmly and resolutely to the gospel of Jesus Christ.

The scope and degree of this cultural strife and spiritual decline was profound, as it spread across the entire face of the land. To members of the Church today, it may seem unnatural and unreasonable, because the Church was strong coming out of the war with the robbers, and the people were serving God both "day and night."[759] Yet within a single year following the first contentions, the Church was completely dissolved in the land of Zarahemla, and severely weakened within the land of Nephi.

Such a sudden and widespread development is best explained in the context of a destructive ethnic and pagan religious movement, which would be halted from time to time by the adversity of drought or warfare. Afterward, however, it would quickly regain a new following and once again advance from region to region across the land southward. Considering the outcome, it is all too apparent that the Church was the focal point of the contentions. Intense persecution and even violence may have permeated the halls of various church bodies across the land. The reference to "railing and persecution" in 3 Nephi 6:13 may have concerned attacks specifically within and against the Church.

## REVIEWING THE FIRST INSTANCE OF HOSTILITY AGAINST THE CHURCH

The Church in Zarahemla was first established by Alma the Elder in about 120 BC.[760] Approximately twenty years later in *ca.* 100 BC, the first attack against the Church took place.[761] At that time, the seeds of contention were planted by unbelievers, which through "flattering words," enticed church members to commit grievous sins.[762] Following the excommunication of members who transgressed the commandments of God, persecution against the Church grew. A rapidly growing body of apostates and unbelievers subjected the Church to a continually escalating level of persecution until King Mosiah issued a proclamation forbidding persecution shortly before 92 BC.[763]

The contention in AD 29 may have followed a similar pattern to that of Mosiah's time. However, there is no record of a proclamation similar to Mosiah's being issued against the persecution, which continued unchecked until it culminated with the breakup of the Church. More will be said concerning this phenomenon of unresponsive government in the following chapter.

The Nephite repentance during the war with the robbers was likely heartfelt in the distress of the moment. However, the dissolution of the

Church in such a short period of time exposes the sad reality that their repentance had resulted exclusively from the grave physical threat to life and limb presented by the robbers. When the threat was removed, the people once again became weak as to things of the flesh.[764] As with the signs accompanying the Lord's birth, they found a way to rationalize and justify their immediate departure from the faith. They returned to their sins and to their pagan religion like a freshly washed pig returns to wallow in the mire.[765]

CHAPTER 4.2

# A HISTORY OF PERSECUTION AGAINST THE CHURCH

## AD 30

THE CONTENTIONS OF AD 29 resulted in the collapse of the Church in only one year. The abruptness of the collapse served as a harbinger of an impending calamity of epic proportions—the disintegration of the Christian government—which was soon to follow. Such a collapse had occurred once before, during the first Nephite period in the land of Nephi. Ultimately, it was followed by the loss of their beloved homeland of almost 400 years, when it became necessary for King Mosiah to flee with his people into the wilderness.[766]

The account of the first dissolution of the Church while the Nephites inhabited the land of Nephi is not recorded in the Book of Mormon, as comprised today. It would not be surprising to one day find that it is included in the 116 lost pages of Mormon's abridgement. Without Mormon's brief statement in 3 Nephi 5:12, the previous existence of a church in the land of Nephi and its ultimate breakup—identified simply as "the transgression"—would be completely hidden from us today.

### THE RESTORATION OF THE CHURCH OF CHRIST IN ZARAHEMLA

Following the breakup of the Church in Nephi, an unknown number of years passed before the Church was re-established through Alma the Elder in the borders of Nephi in about 147 BC.[767] Upon the 120 BC arrival of the people of Alma in Zarahemla, King Mosiah II authorized Alma to establish the Church throughout the land.[768] Seven churches were established in Zarahemla, and in each church body, the priests taught the word of God "according as it was delivered to [them] by the mouth of Alma."[769]

It is therefore apparent that the Church organization had been lost in the land of Nephi before Mosiah I led his people into the wilderness, for there is no prior mention of a church, or of baptism in Zarahemla, even when Benjamin gave his people a new name—the "children of Christ."[770] Under Benjamin's direction, they took upon themselves the name of Christ, but were not baptized to become members of a church organization.

It is also apparent, however, that the authority of the priesthood was never lost, for it seems to have been passed down from generation to generation, with no lapse even during the absence of an organized church structure. The Nephites still performed the ordinances pertaining to the law of sacrifice first given to Adam,[771] which they referred to as the law of Moses.[772] The three kings of Zarahemla apparently possessed the keys of the Melchizedek Priesthood and thus had the authority to perform all the ordinances thereof.

Furthermore, they possessed the Urim and Thummim and held the greatest gift of priesthood power that can be given by God to man.[773] By that power, Mosiah I translated the words inscribed on the large stone that was brought to him,[774] which gave a brief account of the Jaredite destruction.[775] His grandson Mosiah II translated the twenty-four gold plates of Ether by the same power. As Ammon[776] told King Limhi, it was well known among the Nephites that King Mosiah II was a prophet, seer, and revelator with great power and authority given to him by God.[777] There is no difference between the tenor of Ammon's declaration concerning the prophet Mosiah and our testimony of the prophets in the Church today.

In the days of King Benjamin, they had built a temple, yet there was no church organization surrounding it. As implied in 3 Nephi 5:12, there had been such an organization prior to "their transgression." In 124 BC, Benjamin had called his people together:

1. To announce the ascension of his son Mosiah to the throne.
2. To preach the Word of God to them.
3. To give them a name by which they should be known from that time forth.

He did not call them the people of Nephi, the people of Benjamin, or the people of Mosiah. Instead, he called them the "children of

Christ."[778] During his sermon, he referred repeatedly to the Nephites receiving "a remission of their sins."[779] He never mentioned baptism or the idea of entering into the Church of God. In the Church today, and as frequently set forth in the New Testament, the terms "remission of sin" and "baptism" are inseparable. There can be no remission of sin without baptism.[780]

Unbeknownst to King Benjamin and his people, his words were preparing them to receive the Church of Christ. At that very moment in the land of Helam, the Lord had already established His church through the prophet Alma. In his sermon, King Benjamin laid the foundation for their acceptance of the Church of Christ, but he was not ordained of God to establish the Church. It was not his calling, though he was worthy in every way and held the priesthood of God.

Only three years later, King Mosiah II sent sixteen strong men, led by Ammon, into the wilderness in search of the people of Zeniff. This he did because his people "wearied him with their teasings."[781] The question might be posed: Was the intensity of their curiosity due purely to a desire to know the state of the people of Zeniff who had departed Zarahemla almost 100 years previously, or were they moved upon by the Holy Ghost according to the purposes of God? Their pleadings to Mosiah set in motion a series of events, which delivered the people of Limhi from Lamanite bondage in Nephi and granted them peace and refuge in the land of Zarahemla.

At almost the same time in which the people of Limhi were being led by Ammon to the land of Zarahemla, the voice of the Lord came to Alma in Helam, "saying: Be of good comfort, for on the morrow I will deliver you out of bondage."[782] The Lord then miraculously delivered the people of Alma from Lamanite bondage, and through revelations given to Alma, He led them to the land of Zarahemla. Through such intricate workings, the Lord simultaneously brought blessed relief to the people of Limhi and the people of Alma. He also brought to pass the restoration of the Church of Christ to the Nephites in Zarahemla, and to the people of Limhi as well.

The designs of God are far beyond our ability to comprehend, and they are intended for the benefit of his righteous peoples, who have been distributed through time and space throughout man's tenure on earth. Today, the Lord unfailingly watches over His people in the same way He watched over the "children of Christ,"[783] as the Nephites were called from the day King Benjamin gave them a new name.[784] Members of the Church of Christ were called "Christians" by unbelievers in 73 BC. They wore this name gladly.[785] Many times the children of Christ must walk by faith like the people of Nephi, and the Lord in His infinite wisdom will at the proper time reward our faith and obedience with great and marvelous blessings.

## THE PAGAN OFFENSIVE AGAINST THE CHURCH OF CHRIST

Following the establishment of the Church in Zarahemla, it was only a few years before the "unbelievers" initiated their first offensive.[786] From that time forth, they were unrelenting in their war against the Church of Christ. They continued their campaign for 150 years before finally achieving success when the Church collapsed in AD 30.

The "unbelievers," as identified in Mosiah 26 and 27, can be more appropriately identified as pagan worshippers, according to the following verse: "And they would not be baptized; neither would they join the church. And they became a separate people as to their faith, and remained so ever after."[787]

From this verse, it is apparent that the "unbelievers" were of a different faith, which is in agreement with their practice of sorcery and idolatry.[788] They were not simply unbelievers from the standpoint of not believing in Jesus Christ. Indeed, their idols were graven images of pagan gods.

To a great degree, the survival of the Church until AD 30 can be attributed to the protection afforded by King Mosiah II, Alma the Younger, Nephihah, Chief Captain Moroni, and many others—righteous Nephite political and military leaders which stood guard over the Lord's Church. Sometime between 100 and 92 BC, Mosiah had required that the government of the Church must remain separate from Nephite government,[789] which prevented the Church from coming under direct governmental control. This may have been a critical factor in the very survival of the Church after 30 BC, when unbelievers first took control of the government.[790]

At Mosiah's insistence,[791] Alma the Elder had established regulations for acceptable Christian conduct. The standard of Christian conduct was given to Alma by direct revelation from the Lord.[792] It was sanctioned and upheld by the Church "from [that] time forward," according to the Lord's accompanying commandment.[793]

There were two basic rules in the new regulations given to Alma with respect to those who transgressed against the commandments of God:

1. If they would confess their sins and repent, Alma was commanded to forgive them, regardless of how often they transgressed.[794]
2. If they refused to repent of their sins, they would no longer be numbered among the believers.[795]

When Alma began to administer the new regulations, it became necessary to withdraw from those who grievously disobeyed the commandments of God and refused to repent. Many church members were excommunicated at that time. Following these actions, persecution against the Church quickly escalated:

> The church began to murmur, and complain to their leaders concerning the matter; and they did complain to Alma. And Alma laid the case before their king, Mosiah. And Mosiah consulted with his priests.
>
> And it came to pass that king Mosiah sent a proclamation throughout the land round about that there should not any unbeliever persecute any of those who belonged to the church of God.
>
> And there was a strict command throughout all the churches that there should be no persecutions among them, that there should be an equality[796] among all men.[797]

Only through the support of King Mosiah was the Church able to survive those initial contentions.

The same was true when Alma the Younger became the first Nephite chief judge in 91 BC. As chief judge, he enforced the laws that had been given by King Mosiah.[798] After he resigned from office in 83 BC to devote all his time to re-establishing the regulations of the Church, as set forth by his father,[799] were it not for the political support of Nephihah (Alma's appointed replacement as chief judge),[800] it is likely the Church would have been subjected to a barrage of attacks from unbelievers and dissenters.

Following Alma's departure from the land of Zarahemla in 74 BC, Helaman went forth among the people to re-establish church regulations.[801] Again, there were many which refused to abide by the rules of the Church.[802] Contention quickly escalated, and apostates, led by

Amalickiah, rose up with the intention of destroying Helaman and other church leaders.[803] Without the military support of Chief Captain Moroni, it is likely the Church would have been destroyed at that time.[804]

In 35 BC, when dissenters rose up at the beginning of Nephi's reign,[805] the contention was directed against the Church.[806] The government protected the Church, and "there was much bloodshed. And the rebellious part were slain and driven out of the land."[807]

The Gadianton robbers gained control of Nephite government in 26 BC.[808] It is probable that without the drought called down from heaven by the prophet Nephi, which humbled the people and brought about the temporary extinction of the robbers, the Church would soon have been destroyed.[809] Thus, where the righteous could not protect themselves through the power of the government, the Lord intervened through the priesthood power given to the prophet Nephi.

In AD 29, it is likely that Lachoneus II had already taken office.[810] It is quite apparent, however, that he was unable to provide the kind of support necessary to protect the Church from such an attack. The attack was too widespread, and the forces of evil were too great to overcome. Without doubt, the apostasy of the majority of the people was the primary underlying factor. As a result of such wickedness, many local government leaders elected at that time were personally involved in the movement to destroy the Church. This will be further considered in the following chapter. As the pagan attack against the Church continued throughout that year, heavenly intervention was not immediately forthcoming, though in time it would come (see Chapter 4.5).

## RECURRING PAGAN CORRUPTION WITHIN THE CHURCH

There are multiple instances in the Book of Mormon in which converts flocked to the Church of Christ as a result of trauma from war and drought. Many entered the Church without true repentance and without an actual conversion to the gospel.[811] In each case, they brought with them their wickedness and their pride, and frequently a pagan mindset, which inevitably brought the doctrines of the Church into question. As a result, contention quickly developed. Four instances of this phenomenon are considered below:

1. In 87 BC, following the Amlicite War, the first recorded sequence of such events took place. In the aftermath of the

war, there was a great influx of converts into the Church,[812] many of which may have joined as a reaction to, or perhaps even as a kind of retaliation against the Order of Nehor for the suffering they had caused.[813] Almost immediately, pride became a serious problem and a source of contention, not only between church members and unbelievers, but also between members of the Church.[814] The apparent source of both aspects of contention was the new members, who only shortly before had fallen into "wickedness and . . . abominations." Many had joined the Church[815] because they believed that the "afflictions" of the Amlicite War were just punishments according to "the judgments of God."[816]

The contention continued over the following four years. By 83 BC, Alma found it necessary to resign from his office as chief judge so that he could "go forth" among the people of the Church "that he might preach the word of God unto them, to stir them up in remembrance of their duty, and that he might pull down, by the word of God, all the pride and craftiness and all the contentions which were among his people, seeing no way that he might reclaim them save it were in bearing down in pure testimony against them."[817]

During the course of his ministry, as he preached in the city of Gideon, Alma spoke of pride and the worship of idols, which he had observed within the Church in the city of Zarahemla.[818] Thus, many of the new members had not relinquished their pagan gods when they joined the Church.

2. In 43 BC, during the latter part of Helaman II's reign as chief judge, and only a few years after the establishment of the Gadianton robbers,[819] a similar development took place in which "tens of thousands" were baptized into the Church, to the complete amazement of church leaders.[820] Only two years later (41 BC), pride had become a serious problem among the new members.[821] By 38 BC, the pride led to apostasy, which resulted in contention and "much bloodshed in the land of Zarahemla."[822]

   The violence did not stop there. The apostates (dissenters) were driven out of the land and went to the Lamanites to stir them up to war against the Nephites.[823] Two years later, they were followed by other apostates, who joined with them, and together they succeeded in stirring up the Lamanites to go to battle against the Nephites.[824] The ensuing Lamanite invasion marked the first time the Nephites were driven out of the land southward.[825]

3. Between 16 and 13 BC,[826] a third such sequence of events occurred when the drought, which came by the commandment of Nephi, humbled the people and brought them to repentance.[827] As a result of the drought, many thousands were "converted" to the Church of Christ in both the land of Nephi and the land of Zarahemla.[828] Strife began almost immediately, which not surprisingly, concerned "points of doctrine."[829] Though Nephi, Lehi, and the elders of the Church were able to restore order for a time through continual daily revelation,[830] it was demonstrated that despite the appearance of peace and prosperity throughout the land southward at that moment in time, all was not well within the Church. Thus, repentance under stress from the drought did not bring about a true or complete conversion, but stimulated wolves to enter the flock during a brief moment of humility.
4. Between AD 15 and 30, the fourth such sequence of events took place. The fear, which was generated by the threat of the robbers served well to turn the people's hearts to repentance. As long as the threat of destruction remained, they continued to call upon the name of the Lord.

    Following the war, "there was not a living soul among all the people of the Nephites who did doubt in the least the words of all the holy prophets who had spoken."[831] "Therefore, they did forsake all their sins, and their abominations, and their whoredoms, and did serve God with all diligence day and night."[832] Though it is not recorded in the account of the war, it is likely that most of the people, which repented in response to the "words and prophecies" of Lachoneus[833] and which attributed the victory over the robbers to the mercy of God,[834] joined the Church of Christ.

However, many of those, which entered the Church during that traumatic period, were never truly converted to the gospel of Jesus Christ. They never overcame the allure of the pagan religion, which had a magnetic appeal to their carnal appetites. Once again, when peace returned to the land, and their lives

> were no longer in peril, they were quickly enticed to return to their former pagan world.[835] Once the movement of apostasy began, the Church was completely "broken up" within a single year.[836]

Thus, the negative effect of large influxes of new members into the Church, purely as a result of political distress, warfare, or drought, was a frequent source of contention within the Church. Generally, it would lead to contention within the Church, and many dissensions would follow. Ultimately, it caused the dissolution of the Church in most parts of the land.

## CHAPTER 4.3

# THE ASSASSINATION OF LACHONEUS II—A LAND DIVIDED

AT AN UNDISCLOSED TIME between AD 26 and AD 30, Lachoneus II ascended to the judgment seat. Concerning the year AD 30, Mormon said the following: "And now it was in the days of Lachoneus, the son of Lachoneus, for Lachoneus did fill the seat of his father and did govern the people that year."[837] It is not stated that he ascended to the judgment seat that year, but rather that he "did govern the people that year."

His father, Lachoneus I, was one of the more successful judges of the Nephites, especially since he was able to endure the spiritual and political roller coaster ride surrounding the birth of Christ. It seems likely that either he died or retired from office, and the judgment seat passed to his son by rights of lineage, as ratified by the voice of the people.[838]

Due to the intensity of the previous war, and the length of his tenure in office, it is likely that Lachoneus stepped down shortly after the war ended, possibly as early as AD 26.[839] Almost certainly, he stepped down within the first three years,[840] given the "disputings" and the "pride" that surfaced in the fourth year (AD 29),[841] which was so intense that it brought about the dissolution of the Church in only one year.[842] Based on the above reasoning, as well as other factors related to the beginning of his reign, Lachoneus I had been the chief judge for a period of around forty years. Still, the details of his son's appointment to the judgment seat are not provided in the Book of Mormon.

## LACHONEUS I—THE PERIOD OF HIS REIGN

As previously considered in Chapter 3.7,[843] there were only two plausible times for the election of Lachoneus I as chief judge—15 and 11 BC. Only in those two years did the people momentarily flock to the Church as a result of drought or fear of the robbers. They appear to be the only times during that period when the people would elect a Christian to the highest office in the land.

As outlined above in this chapter, the only logical time for the end of his reign was during the three-year period of peace immediately following the Gadianton Robber War. At that time, the people had great respect for Lachoneus, due to the great victory he had delivered, and the peace which filled the land. Only in a time of peace and harmony could Lachoneus pass the judgment seat to his son without insurmountable opposition from the pagan dissenters, who as in previous times would surely have called for a vote of the people.[844] This was especially true in this time of extreme instability.

### *TABLE 6.0*

### POTENTIAL LENGTHS OF THE REIGN OF LACHONEUS I

| Beginning—Reason | End—Reason | Length |
|---|---|---|
| 15 BC—The People Humbled by Drought | AD 28—Peace Throughout the Land | 43 Years |
| 15 BC—The People Humbled by Drought | AD 27—Peace Throughout the Land | 42 Years |
| 15 BC—The People Humbled by Drought | AD 26— Peace Throughout the Land | 41 Years |
| 11 BC—The People's Fear of Robbers | AD 28—Peace Throughout the Land | 39 Years |
| 11 BC—The People's Fear of Robbers | AD 27—Peace Throughout the Land | 38 Years |
| 11 BC—The People's Fear of Robbers | AD 26— Peace Throughout the Land | 37 Years |

Table 6.0 denotes the only plausible times for the beginning and the end of the reign of Lachoneus I. Admittedly, the reasoning rests exclusively upon Mormon's assessment of the precise conditions of the people from year to year throughout that volatile period. They are included primarily to further emphasize the sharpness of Nephite spiritual fluctuations throughout that final period leading to the Great Storm, and the miraculous preservation of the Lord's true followers—those who did not waver—in the face of pure evil.

## THE WANING POWER OF THE CHIEF JUDGE

Almost immediately after the Gadianton Robber War ended, the wonderful peace that had come through the inspired leadership of Lachoneus I began to erode. Shortly after Lachoneus II ascended to the judgment seat, the power and authority of the central government was compromised. Lower judges, emboldened as a new rebellion commenced, began to exceed the authority granted to them.

As the Church came under attack in AD 29, Lachoneus was therefore unable to use the power of his office to protect it from persecution. Without doubt, he became frustrated when the attacks against the Church became widespread, and the local judges would not enforce his directives. Thus, there was no way to enforce the laws against persecution, which had been decreed by Mosiah many years before,[845] which were likely still in force. In AD 30, as the Church was broken up across the face of the land, Lachoneus was powerless to stop it.

## PROPHETS OF GOD ARE PUT TO DEATH

During that same year, following the breakup of the Church, the wickedness of the Nephites continued to escalate. As in Lehi's day in the city of Jerusalem,[846] many prophets of God went forth among the people all across the face of the land to condemn them for their iniquity and to warn them of the coming judgment of God if they did not repent. Their warnings had no positive effect on the people to motivate them to repent. Instead, these messengers from God[847] were apprehended and taken before the local chief judges to be judged for alleged crimes. Many were tried secretly and put to death, which was forbidden without authorization "from the governor of the land."[848]

## LACHONEUS II ATTEMPTS TO ADMINISTER JUSTICE

When he received word in the city of Zarahemla concerning the execution of the prophets, Lachoneus had the responsible judges brought before him to be judged for their crimes. If possible, he would restore order in the land and reclaim the power that was vested in him as chief judge. However, if he had understood the murderous intent and the full extent of the movement to overthrow the free government, he would surely have called in the army to counter the force that was soon aligned against him.

## THE ASSASSINATION OF LACHONEUS II—THE COLLAPSE OF THE GOVERNMENT

"Now it came to pass that those judges had many friends and kindreds; and the remainder, yea, even almost all the lawyers and high priests, did gather themselves together, and unite with the kindreds of those judges who were to be tried according to the law."[849]

Their purpose in gathering was to deliver their friends from the judgment of Lachoneus. It was imperative that they move with secrecy. Their plans were not only criminal, but were treasonable as well.

The first order of business was to organize a secret combination,[850] which would irreversibly require the unwavering commitment of everyone involved, with the penalty of death attached, should anyone try to withdraw, or divulge their intentions to anyone outside the organization.[851] A plan was then devised to assassinate Lachoneus, and assassins were chosen to carry out the plan. Soon, Lachoneus was murdered as he sat upon the judgment seat.[852]

His assassination was not designed merely to "deliver those who were guilty of murder from the grasp of justice . . . according to the law,"[853] but to overthrow the government and "to establish a king over the land."[854] Their ultimate goal, however, was "to destroy" "the people of the Lord."[855] In this vein, the establishment of the secret combination was simply a further development of the conspiracy that had already achieved the breakup of the Church,[856] and the murder of the prophets.[857]

Compared to the initial rise of the Gadianton robbers in 52 BC,[858] the forces which gathered to destroy the government in 30 BC were much greater in number. Whereas the Nephite government was left intact following the assassination of Pahoran and Pacumeni,[859] and Gadianton had found it necessary to flee from the land of Zarahemla following the attempted murder of Helaman,[860] the only secrecy required in AD 30 may have been related to the element of surprise in the assassination of Lachoneus. Upon his death, the government immediately disintegrated, and the forces of the insurrection overwhelmed the powers of government in the city of Zarahemla. The series of events, which led to the overthrow of the government, are summarized in Table 7.0 below on the following page.

As mentioned previously, two basic elements of dissent are woven into the fabric of this series of events:

1. The most basic and fundamental element was pagan hatred for Christianity, which underlay and set the tone for the entire sequence of events which led to the collapse of the government. A natural consequence of pagan hatred is the pagan conspiracy, which plagued the Nephites throughout their history, and which from 52 BC to AD 30 was generally present in its most evil and destructive form.[861]
2. Ethnicity, a major element in Book of Mormon conflict, is clearly identified in events 6 and 11. Only when the people were separated through civil strife and violence into discrete factions or alliances, is the tribal nature of the divisions clearly identified.

### *TABLE 7.0*

### EVENTS LEADING TO THE OVERTHROW OF THE NEPHITE GOVERNMENT

| SEQUENCE | ALL EVENTS OCCURRED DURING THE YEAR 30 BC |
|---|---|
| 1 | The Church of Christ "was broken up" across the entire land, except "among a few of the Lamanites" (3 Nephi 6:14). |
| 2 | The sins and depravity of the people had spawned the contention that destroyed the Church of Christ. As a result, inspired men of God went forth among the people, boldly condemning them for their wickedness, and testifying of the redemption of Christ through His suffering, death, and resurrection (3 Nephi 6:20). |
| 3 | There were "many of the people . . . chiefly the chief judges, and they who had been high priests and lawyers," which "were angry with those who testified of these things" (3 Nephi 6:21). |
| 4 | The men of God, who had testified of Christ, were condemned by the judges and put to death secretly, without the required authority from the chief judge over all the land (3 Nephi 6:23). |
| 5 | "Therefore, a complaint came up unto the land of Zarahemla, to the governor of the land against these judges who had condemned the prophets of the Lord unto death, not according to the law," (3 Nephi 6:25), and "they were taken and brought up before the [chief] judge to be judged of the crime which they had done" (3 Nephi 6:26). |

| | |
|---|---|
| 6 | The accused "judges had many friends and kindreds; and the remainder, yea, even almost all the lawyers and the high priests, did gather themselves together, and unite with the kindred of those judges who were to be tried according to the law" (3 Nephi 6:27). |
| 7 | "And they did enter into a covenant one with another, yea, even into that covenant which was given to them of old, which covenant was given and administered by the devil, to combine against all righteousness" (3 Nephi 6:28). |
| 8 | "Therefore, they did combine against the people of the Lord, and enter into a covenant to destroy them, and to deliver those who were guilty of murder from the grasp of justice, which was about to be administered according to the law" (3 Nephi 6:29). |
| 9 | They "did covenant one with another to destroy the governor, and to establish a king over the land" (3 Nephi 6:30). |
| 10 | Lachoneus was assassinated "upon the judgment seat," and the government immediately collapsed. |
| 11 | The people divided into tribes, which were made up of family, kindred, and friends (3 Nephi 7:2). |

## FINAL THOUGHTS CONCERNING THE ASSASSINATION OF LACHONEUS II

The AD 30 assassination of Chief Judge Lachoneus II within the city of Zarahemla was arranged by a tribe of unidentified lineage.[862] In preparation for the revolutionary act, they entered into a pact of secret murder, according to the pattern first established by Gadianton eighty years earlier.[863] In effect, their murder of the prophets, which had led to the confrontation with Lachoneus, had also been committed secretly. Though it may have been performed openly within their own community, it was done without the knowledge of the chief judge.[864]

Of necessity, the assassination of the chief judge required a higher level of secrecy than the murders committed at the local level where the perpetrators were in power. Once the assassination was carried out, however, and the government collapsed, the rebels discarded their cover of secrecy. They immediately made known to all their objective of taking control of the Nephite nation, which at that time included both Zarahemla and Nephi.

In AD 30, the land of Nephi had been part of the Nephite nation since the Lamanite union with the Nephites in AD 13 to defend against the robbers.[865] Throughout that seventeen–year period, they remained subject to the Nephites. For that reason, the order of Lachoneus I to gather in the center of the land of Zarahemla was obeyed by Lamanites, as well as Nephites, obeyed, and the land of Nephi was evacuated at that time. Being numbered with the Nephites, the Lamanites participated in the defensive effort against the robbers.[866] Their alliance with the Nephites was a direct result of their belief in Christ. The fact that they began in AD 13 to refer to themselves as Nephites[867] further signifies the synonymous relationship of the terms "Christian" and "Nephite."

The conversion of the Lamanites and their alliance with the Nephites comprise the last major events of Lamanite history during the pre-Christ Era leading to the Great Storm, which boldly announced the Lord's appearance to the Nephites in the land of Bountiful.[868] Table 8.0 provides a summary of Lamanite history from 589 BC to AD 34.

### *TABLE 8.0*

### LAMANITE HISTORY FROM 589 BC TO AD 34

| Year BC | Event |
|---|---|
| ~589 BC | Laman and Lemuel plan the murder of Nephi, who escapes with his followers into the wilderness. |
| ~589 to ~200 BC | Lamanites make war with the Nephites again and again throughout the period until the departure of the people of Mosiah from the land of Nephi. |
| ~200 BC | The Lamanite king Laman allows the people of Zeniff to occupy the cities of Nephi and Shilom. |
| ~190 BC | Lamanites attack the people of Zeniff and are defeated. |
| ~155 BC | Amalekites dissent away to the Lamanites from King Benjamn. They incite the Lamanites to anger; Lamanites return with Amalekites and attack the Nephites. Are defeated by an army led by King Benjamin. |
| ~150 BC | Lamanites make war with the people of King Noah and are defeated. |
| ~145 BC | Lamanites attack the people of Noah and defeat them. Noah dies at the hands of his own people. See Chapter 2.5. |

| | |
|---|---|
| ~143 to ~121 BC | In retaliation for the Amulonite abduction of the Lamanite maidens, the Lamanites subject the people of Limhi to bondage for approximately twenty-two years. Thrice during that period, they put down revolts of the people of Limhi. |
| 121 BC | Ammon arrives from Zarahemla with the party of sixteen. The people of Limhi depart with Ammon for Zarahemla. The Lamanites pursue them, become lost and unexpectedly discover the land of Amulon. |
| 121 BC | The Lamanites take the priests of Amulon with them and discover the people of Alma in the land of Helam. They take control of Helam and set Amulon over them. Alma teaches geography to the Lamanites. |
| 121–91 BC | Lamanites expand their understanding of the wilderness from the knowledge base taught by Alma. |
| 91 BC | Lamanites (people of Anti-Nephi-Lehi) are converted to Christianity through the ministry of the sons of Mosiah. |
| 87 BC | Lamanites join with the Amlicites to attack the Nephites in Zarahemla. |
| 83 BC | Lamanites retaliate for the conversion of Anti-Nephi-Lehites, join with Amalekites and Amulonites. They destroy Ammonihah and are driven into the east wilderness. Remain in east wilderness for three years before returning to Nephi. |
| 77 BC | Lamanites follow the people of Anti-Nephi-Lehi to Zarahemla. They are smitten and driven into the east wilderness. |
| 74 BC | Lamanites are incited by the Zoramites and attack the land of Zarahemla. |
| 73 BC | Amalickiah sends a Lamanite army to attack the city of Ammonihah. They are intimidated by the fortifications at Ammonihah. They attack Noah and are defeated. |
| 67–61 BC | Amalickiah and Ammoron lead the Lamanites in a war against the land of Zarahemla. They are defeated after seven years of warfare. |
| 51 BC | During the reign of the Lamanite king Tubaloth, Coriantumr leads a Lamanite army to attack the land of Zarahemla. |
| 35 BC | Lamanites are incited by dissenters to attack the land of Zarahemla. Drive the Nephites into the borders of the land Desolation. |

| | |
|---|---|
| 30 BC | The Lamanite nation is converted to Christianity through the ministry of Nephi and Lehi. From that time forth, many Lamanites support the cause of Christ throughout the remainder of the pre-Christ period—a period of 64 years, which would end at the Savior's appearance in Bountiful in AD 34. |
| AD 13 | The Lamanites unite with the Nephites and are numbered among the Nephites. |
| AD 18–25 | The Lamanites gather with Nephites in the center of the land to defend against the Gadianton robbers. |
| AD 25–34 | Many Lamanites remain steadfast in the gospel and are righteous for a total period of sixty-four years, including the period of escalating wickedness and turmoil across the land southward, leading to the Great Storm of 34 AD. They are spared from destruction. |

## GRAND EXPECTATIONS

In AD 30, when Lachoneus II was assassinated, the insurgent tribe apparently expected to immediately assume full control of the entire land southward—both Zarahemla and Nephi—just by assassinating him.[869] From the beginning of the movement, this had been their plan—to "destroy the governor, and to establish a king over the land."[870] They selected a man by the name of Jacob to be their king.

This is the first mention of kings since the Amalickiah and Ammoron War.[871] It was previously observed in Chapter 3.1 that with the rise of the robbers, dissenters began to seek power within the system of judges. This mode of operation continued until the chief judge was assassinated, and the free government was destroyed. The revolutionaries immediately returned to their preferred goal of monarchy, which would give them total power over the people. Because of their tunnel vision and overconfidence, they did not expect the chain of events that immediately followed the assassination.

When the government fell, all of the people divided into tribes. The insurgent tribe immediately found themselves outnumbered by the other tribes, who "were united in the hatred of those who had entered into a covenant to destroy the government."[872] Therefore, King Jacob ordered them to "take their flight into the northernmost part of the land. . . . And so speedy was their march that it could not be impeded until they had gone forth out of the reach of the people."[873] In the land northward, they would wait for others to join them, at which time Jacob believed they would be able to achieve their ultimate goal. Their plans never came to fruition. Four years later, they were completely destroyed in the catastrophic storm.[874]

## RELIGIOUS HATRED AND ETHNIC PRIDE

Considering the entire scenario that began with the contentions of AD 29[875] and culminated during the following year with the breakup of the Church,[876] the murder of the prophets,[877] the assassination of Lachoneus II,[878] and anarchy,[879] the initial controversy seems (on the surface) to have revolved almost exclusively around issues of wealth versus poverty,[880] as described in Chapter 4.1 above. However, while the initial turmoil did result from animosity leveled by the rich against the poor, the most basic underlying factors, which constituted the deepest roots of the contention, revolved around religious hatred and ethnic pride. This conclusion is not drawn from the disputings in AD 29 (as described in 3 Nephi 6:10–13), but from the following:

1. The resulting developments of AD 30—the dissolution of the Church[881] and the murder of the prophets.[882]
2. The ethnic nature of the cultural divisions that formed after the government was overthrown.[883]

Through the developments of AD 30 the true nature of the problem rose to the surface and became fully exposed. The pride of the rich and their contempt for the poor did not lead to class warfare, that is, to war between the rich and the poor, as one might expect if that was indeed the actual root of the discord. Rather, it led to the breakup of the Church. Furthermore, the fact that the dissolution of the Church was caused by religious hatred can be seen in the murder of the Christian prophets, which quickly followed, and through which the contention quickly mushroomed into anarchy.

## ANARCHY REIGNS—TRIBAL DIVISIONS

As considered above, the dissenters believed that once the chief judge Lachoneus was eliminated, the people would accept a new king and acquiesce to his commands.[884] However, in this they were mistaken, for though the people had accepted the breakup of the Church and the murder of the prophets with little reaction, they had no desire to be ruled over by the secret combination, which was tribal in nature. Its ethnic character is not clearly communicated in the Book of Mormon until 3 Nephi 7:2–4, but there is no doubt that the people themselves were fully aware of the ethnic nature of the conflict long before they separated into tribes.

In their immoral and depraved state, the conflict no longer revolved around good versus evil. As their faith had weakened and their righteousness had declined, their sense of ethnicity had become stronger than any allegiance to religious beliefs. Therefore, kinship and lineage had become the primary determining factors as to religious affiliation. In other words, religion was no longer a focal point or bastion of belief, but of tradition. The same conditions would also develop near the end of Nephite civilization.

Even before the Church of Christ was broken up, it had lost its magnetic appeal to transcend ethnic barriers and draw the people together. Whenever the Church was strong and the members were righteous, converts to the gospel were drawn from every ethnic group within the Nephite nation. When the Church weakened through transgression and the members ceased walking in righteousness and obedience, every tribe returned to the traditions of their fathers.

In connection with the continuously declining standards of righteousness, tribal relationships had thus become the principle element of division. The other tribes or leagues of tribes did not wish to be subjugated by a king from a different lineage, especially a lineage which considered them to be inferior[885] and sought dominion over them.

When Lachoneus was assassinated, it is apparent that the people were already segregated along tribal lines, for as the government collapsed, they immediately divided into tribes, each of which was very substantial in size, comprising many thousands of people. It is also apparent that much earlier in the Book of Mormon and long before the contentions of AD 29, the people were already segregated into ethnic and religious cities,[886] and into ethnic barrios or districts within large cities, such as the city of Zarahemla. In fact, they had been divided in that manner since the Nephite arrival in the land of Zarahemla.[887] Therefore, for the most part, it was not necessary to separate—they were already separated.

In spite of a number of previous indicators in the Book of Mormon that divisions and contentions among the people were frequently ethnic in character,[888] the tribal nature of the final divisions of the people at this time is unexpected, based upon the text of 3 Nephi. It is especially surprising, if one takes note of the initial description of the contentions (rich versus poor) in Chapter 6:10–12 and contrasts them with the ethnic character of the divisions that appeared suddenly at the beginning of the following chapter.

## A ROBBER BY ANY OTHER NAME IS STILL A ROBBER

The Nephite war effort, which had been masterfully engineered by Chief Judge Lachoneus I and flawlessly executed by Chief Captain Gidgiddoni, ended with the second extinction of the Gadianton robbers by the end of AD 25.[889] At first inspection, it appears to be the last of the robbers during the pre-Christ era. According to the Book of Mormon, the robbers would not rise up again until approximately 234 years later (AD 260),[890] following the Nephite golden age of love and peace.[891]

However, though the new secret combination that rose up in AD 30 was not identified as Gadianton robbers, in actuality, it was nothing more or less than a second rebirth of the same organization, similar to the rebirth of 12 BC. In each case, the time-frame from the destruction to the rebirth was five years:

1. The robbers were first destroyed in 17 BC. The rebirth took place in 12 BC.[892]
2. The robbers were then destroyed in AD 25. The rebirth occurred in AD 30.[893]

Every action taken by the people of Jacob was characteristic of the Gadianton robbers. Like the robbers, they formed a secret combination, and in all probability used the same oaths and covenants previously searched out by the Zoramites.[894] They committed murder like the Gadianton robbers. They sought to take control of the government like the robbers. For all intents and purposes, they were Gadianton robbers, but after they destroyed the democratic government, and openly sought to establish a king, only then is it discovered that they were an ethnic group, for they gathered together as a tribe of kindred and friends.[895]

## ETHNIC UNDERTONES—A PERENNIAL SOURCE OF DISSENT?

The question then follows: How long had the contentions among the Nephites been structured along tribal lines? In some cases, it is impossible to tell if dissent emanated from ethnic differences. However, in a number of cases, the connection is clear and undeniable. A case in point is the king-men rebellion of 67 BC, which took place during the Amalickiah and Ammoron War.[896] The king-men were men of nobility or high birth, which contended for power in Zarahemla according to their inherent rights, or birthright. Upon close inspection, it becomes apparent that ethnic differences provided a primary basis for dissent at that time and perhaps even earlier in 87 BC, when a large contingent of the people sought to overturn the system of judges and raise up Amlici as king.

Re-examining the epistle of the Gadianton robber Giddiani to Lachoneus in AD 16, ethnic undertones of the same nature as those used to describe the king-men are observed, to wit, "And I write this epistle unto you, Lachoneus, and I hope that ye will deliver up your lands and your possessions, without the shedding of blood, that this my people may recover their rights and government, who have dissented away from you because of your wickedness in retaining from them their rights of government."[897] Returning to the events of AD 30, when Jacob's tribe sought to raise him up as king of the Nephites, it was merely the continuation of the long-standing dispute against the Nephites, which was centered on claims of nobility. Thus, whether it was the king-men, the Gadianton robbers, or the tribe of Jacob, it is apparent that ethnic pride[898] defined their cause, and ethnic flattery[899] provided the magnet by which new recruits were drawn to them. On the basis of these similarities, it might well be concluded that many dissenters throughout the pre-Christ period in Zarahemla shared the same ethnic background—having descended from Judah, the kingly tribe of Israel, through Mulek, the son of King Zedekiah.[900]

## ZORAM'S LINEAGE

Zoram is not generally considered to be a descendant of Judah. Some have concluded that he may have descended from Manasseh. However, nothing concrete is found within the Book of Mormon text that would point undeniably to a specific lineage. Therefore, any conclusion with respect to his lineage is nothing more than speculation.

The Zoramites were followers of a man named Zoram of Antionum.[901] It is likely that some of his followers were related to him, and others were friends. It is assumed purely on the basis of Zoram's name that he, like Ammoron,[902] was a descendant of the original Zoram, who came with the people of Lehi from Jerusalem.[903]

Ammoron, like his brother Amalickiah,[904] sought to defeat the Nephites in war, and to rule over them as king. However, his justification for his quest was not founded upon the nobility of the original Zoram as a descendant of Judah. Instead it rested upon Lamanite claims against the Nephites, for as he said to Chief Captain Moroni: "I am Ammoron, and a descendant of Zoram, whom your fathers pressed and brought out of Jerusalem. And behold now, I am a bold Lamanite; behold, this war hath been waged to avenge their wrongs, and to maintain and to obtain their rights of government; and I close my epistle to Moroni."[905]

On the basis of this scripture, it is concluded that Zoram, who came with Lehi, was not a descendant of the kingly tribe of Judah, for that would surely have eclipsed Lamanite claims.

## THE REMAINING TRIBES MAINTAIN A TENTATIVE AND UNSETTLED PEACE

Following Jacob's departure into the land northward, the tribes remaining in the land southward were not righteous, and their actions revealed a newfound hatred for Christianity. Furthermore, they were enemies, and the only thing which had united them following the collapse of the Nephite government was their shared hatred for the band of Jacob. Following his departure, they established a rigid separation and somehow maintained a tentative peace, as described in the following verse: "Nevertheless, they had come to an agreement that they would not go to war one with another; but they were not united as to their laws, and their manner of government, for they were established according to the minds of those who were their chiefs and their leaders. But they did establish very strict laws that one tribe should not trespass against another, insomuch that in some degree they had peace in the land; nevertheless, their hearts were turned from the Lord their God, and they did stone the prophets and did cast them out from among them."[906]

## CHAPTER 4.4

# THE END OF THE PERIOD OF THE JUDGES

Following the assassination of Lachoneus II in AD 30 and the resulting destruction of the Nephite government, there were no additional chief judges in the pre-Christ era. The following table thus provides a quick-reference guide to all chief judges that governed Zarahemla from 91 BC to AD 30:

### *TABLE 9.0*

### NEPHITE CHIEF JUDGES DURING THE PRE-CHRIST ERA

| Year of Judges | Time Interval | Years of Reign | Name | Scripture |
|---|---|---|---|---|
| 1–8 | 91–83 BC | 8 | Alma the Younger | Mosiah 29:42–47; Alma 4:20 |
| 8–23 | 83–68 BC | 15 | Nephihah | Alma 4:16–20; 50:37–38 |
| 23–39 | 68–53 BC | 16 | Pahoran I | Alma 50:39–40; Helaman 1:2 |
| 40 | 52 BC | <1 | Pahoran II | Helaman 1:5–9 |
| 40–41 | 52–51 BC | 1 | Pacumeni | Helaman 1:13–21 |
| 42–53 | 50–39 BC | 11 | Helaman II | Helaman 2:1–2; 3:37 |
| 53–62 | 39–30 BC | 9 | Nephi | Helaman 3:37; 4:18; 5:1–4 |
| 62–66 | 30–26 BC | 4 | Cezoram | Helaman 5:1; 6:15–19 |

| 66 | 26 BC | <1 | Son of Cezoram | Helaman 6:15–19 |
|---|---|---|---|---|
| 66–69 | 26–23 BC | 3 | Seezoram | Helaman 6:15; 8:27–28; 9:26–37[907] |
| 69–92 | 23 BC-AD1 | 23 | Unknown | Helaman 9:26–37; 10:19; 11:8–9, 35–38; 13:1; 16:8–13, 24; 3 Nephi 1:1 |
| 92–121 | AD 1–30 | 29 | Lachoneus I | 3 Nephi 1:1; 6:1, 6, 19[908] |
| 121 | AD 30 | 1 | Lachoneus II | 3 Nephi 6:19; 7:1 |

## NEPHITE RECORDS: TRANSFERRED TO ALMA THE YOUNGER

Throughout the entire period of the kings, the Nephite records were always kept by the kings, who stood at the head of government. It did not change when Mosiah II changed the form of government from kings to judges. He transferred the records to Alma the Younger, the first chief judge.

When Alma left office eight years later, he appointed Nephihah to be his successor. At that time, he attempted to follow the same tradition by transferring the records to Nephihah, but the new chief judge refused to take them. The Nephite record thus remained in Alma's family throughout the remainder of Nephite civilization, or at least through Ammaron. Without doubt, this fulfilled the purposes of God, considering their righteousness through generation after generation.

## MORMON AND MORONI: DIRECT DESCENDANTS OF ALMA THE ELDER?

The precise lineage of the prophets Mormon and Moroni is not provided in the Book of Mormon, but consider the following: Mormon was a "pure descendant of Lehi,"[909] who descended from Joseph, the son of Jacob.[910] Mormon 1:5 states that Mormon was a "descendant of Nephi," though his kindred relationship to Ammoron—who transferred the plates to him[911]—is not revealed.

However, it is concluded that he was a descendant of Alma the Elder. This assumption comes from the information that both Mormon and his father were named after the Waters of Mormon, where Alma the Elder, "having authority from God,"[912] reestablished the Church of Christ among the Nephites.[913] Every point of evidence seems to imply that he was a descendant of Alma the Elder, including the simple fact that Ammaron, a direct descendant of Alma passed the record to Mormon. It is likely that Ammaron followed the established tradition of passing the records to someone within the family—someone he knew quite well and could therefore judge his character.

## THE END OF THE PRE-CHRIST ERA

When the period of the judges came to an end, the Crucifixion and Resurrection of Jesus Christ was only four years away. The Savior's appearance to the Nephites would take place immediately thereafter and would mark the end of the pre-Christ era. For comparison with Table 9.0, Table 10.0 provides a list of all record keepers during the Zarahemla pre-Christ period.

### *TABLE 10.0*

### KEEPERS OF THE NEPHITE RECORD IN PRE-CHRIST ZARAHEMLA

| Interval | Years | Name | Scripture | Comments |
|---|---|---|---|---|
| Ca. 200– ? | ? | King Mosiah I | Omni 1:11, 12–23; Mos. 2:32 | Mosiah's death not included in the account—It may have been recorded in the 116 lost pages. |
| ?–124 BC | ? | King Benjamin | W. of Mor. 1:12–18; Om. 1:23–25; Mos. 1:1–3, 6; 6:5; Chap. 1–6 | The total length of the reigns of Mosiah I and Benjamin was *Ca.* 76 yrs. |
| 124–92 BC | 32 | King Mosiah II | Mos. 1:15–16; 6:4; 29:41–47 | Mosiah changed the government from kings to judges. |

| 91–74 BC | 17 | Alma, Younger | Mosiah 28:20; 29:44; Alma 1:1–2; 44:24 | First chief judge, son of Alma the Elder. No record of death. |
|---|---|---|---|---|
| 73–57 BC | 16 | Helaman I | Alma 37:1–12, 45, 62:52 | Son of Alma the Younger. Led the 2,000 stripling warriors. |
| 56–53 BC | 3 | Shiblon | Alma 63:1–10 | Brother of Helaman I. |
| 53–39 BC | 14 | Helaman II | Al. 63:11–13; Helaman 3:37 | Sixth chief judge, son of Helaman I. |
| 39 BC-AD 1 | 39 | Nephi | Helaman 3:37; 3 Nephi 1:2, 3 | Seventh chief judge, son of Helaman II. No record of death. |
| AD 1–34 | 33 | Nephi, Disciple | 3 Nephi 1:2–3, 23:7–13 | Son of Nephi. No record of death. |

CHAPTER 4.5

# THE STAGE IS SET FOR THE COMING OF THE LORD

By AD 33, ALL of Samuel the Lamanite's prophecies concerning the signs of Christ's birth had long since been fulfilled. Some of the signs of the Lord's death had also come to pass. These signs did not include celestial signs, such as those which had heralded the Lord's birth. As pertaining to the Lord's death, Samuel did not forecast any advance signs from the heavens for the period leading up to the great sign of His death.[914] Neither are any precursory astronomical events or signs recorded in 3 Nephi. It is therefore concluded that there were no periodic heavenly signs to warn of the approaching Great Storm.

The signs that preceded the Crucifixion of Christ could be observed only in the depravity of the people, which had continually increased in scope and degree. First, they had participated (in many cases through apathy) in the AD 30 dissolution of the Church.[915] Subsequently, they had willingly descended into the depths of wickedness, with many turning their heads when the prophets of God were slain by the local judges.[916] Following the departure of Jacob and his followers into the land northward, the wickedness of the people remaining in the land southward continued to grow.

In AD 31, they began to openly stone the prophets,[917] as the people of Jacob had done in AD 30. Notwithstanding the great miracles performed by Nephi "in the sight of the people, in the name of Jesus,"[918] "there were but few who were converted unto the Lord."[919] The majority only became more infuriated with each miracle.

## THE RIGHTEOUS ARE CAST OUT FROM THE WICKED

At that time, they began to cast the righteous "out from among them,"[920] which was the last and perhaps the most crucial of all the signs that were prophesied to precede the Great Storm. In review of that particular prophecy, the prophet Samuel had said:

> Yea, wo unto this great city of Zarahemla; for behold, it is because of those who are righteous that it is saved; yea, wo unto this great city, for I perceive, saith the Lord, that there are many, yea, even the more part of this great city, that will harden their hearts against me, saith the Lord.
>
> But blessed are they who will repent, for them will I spare. But behold, if it were not for the righteous who are in this great city, behold, I would cause that fire should come down out of heaven and destroy it.
>
> But behold, it is for the righteous' sake that it is spared. But behold, the time cometh, saith the Lord, that when ye shall cast out the righteous from among you, then shall ye be ripe for destruction.[921]

Beginning in AD 31, the wickedness of the people had become so advanced that they did indeed begin to openly murder the prophets and to expel the righteous from among them.[922] It was the essence of the Lord's final condition. After the righteous were ejected from the cities of the wicked, the table was fully set for the Lord's judgment, and they were then "ripe for destruction."

## THE WORK OF THE LORD GOES FORWARD

Expelled from the cities of the wicked, the people of the Lord gathered together in the land of Bountiful, which may have been the very land abandoned by the people of Jacob when they departed into the land northward. The reasoning for placing Jacob's tribe in Bountiful near the narrow neck of land is thus:

If inhabited by the people of Jacob, then no other tribe would have been in position to cut them off when they fled into the land northward. Unimpeded, they would simply have moved northward along the narrow neck of land into the land northward. However, if any other tribe had inhabited that region, the scenario described in 3 Nephi 7:12–13 could not have occurred, for Jacob would have likewise been cut off purely as a result of positioning and would have found it necessary to contend with them to obtain passage.

If this scenario did in fact take place, Jacob departed the very land which would be spared in the coming destruction, migrating to the region where the greatest destruction would occur.[923] The righteous were then cast out from among the wicked.[924] Ultimately, they moved into the lands vacated by the people of Jacob, where they would be blessed to endure the Great Storm.

The Church of Christ had been broken up across the face of the land,[925] but it had not been destroyed. The prophet Nephi still stood at its head. At his direction, the Lord's work continued:

> And it came to pass that Nephi—having been visited by angels and also the voice of the Lord, therefore having seen angels, and being eye-witness, and having had power given unto him that he might know concerning the ministry of Christ, and also being eye-witness to their quick return from righteousness unto their wickedness and abominations;
>
> Therefore, being grieved for the hardness of their hearts and the blindness of their minds—went forth among them in that same year, and began to testify, boldly, repentance and remission of sins through faith on the Lord Jesus Christ.
>
> And he did minister many things unto them; and all of them cannot be written, and a part of them would not suffice, therefore they are not written in this book. And Nephi did minister with power and with great authority.
>
> And it came to pass that they were angry with him, even because he had greater power than they, for it were not possible that they could disbelieve his words, for so great was his faith on the Lord Jesus Christ that angels did minister unto him daily.
>
> And in the name of Jesus did he cast out devils and unclean spirits; and even his brother did he raise from the dead, after he had been stoned and suffered death by the people.
>
> And the people saw it, and did witness of it, and were angry with him because of his power; and he did also do many more miracles, in the sight of the people, in the name of Jesus.
>
> And it came to pass that the thirty and first year did pass away, and there were but few who were converted unto the Lord; but as many as were converted did truly signify unto the people that they had been visited by the power and Spirit of God, which was in Jesus Christ, in whom they believed.
>
> And as many as had devils cast out from them, and were healed of their sicknesses and their infirmities, did truly manifest unto the people that they had been wrought upon by the Spirit of God, and had been healed; and they did show forth signs also and did do some miracles among the people.

> Thus passed away the thirty and second year also. And Nephi did cry unto the people in the commencement of the thirty and third year; and he did preach unto them repentance and remission of sins.
>
> Now I would have you to remember also, that there were none who were brought unto repentance who were not baptized with water.
>
> Therefore, there were ordained of Nephi, men unto this ministry, that all such as should come unto them should be baptized with water, and this as a witness and a testimony before God, and unto the people, that they had repented and received a remission of their sins.
>
> And there were many in the commencement of this year that were baptized unto repentance; and thus the more part of the year did pass away.[926]

## THE FINAL DAYS OF THE PRE-CHRIST PERIOD

The above verses reveal that in the final period leading to the Great Storm, the followers of Christ were still preaching the gospel. They ventured among the wicked in the hope that they might reach some.[927] In AD 31, they went forth through inspiration from God at the risk of their own lives. It was during that time that Nephi raised his brother from the dead "after he had been stoned and suffered death by the people."[928]

The Lord continued to work through His people throughout the thirty-second and thirty-third years,[929] though the land was cursed with iniquity. His miraculous power was continually manifested among them, as they went forth preaching the gospel across the face of the land. As the thirty-third year proceeded, the people of the Lord knew the time was drawing near for the fulfillment of Samuel's second prophecy: "And the people began to look with great earnestness for the sign which had been given by the prophet, Samuel, the Lamanite, yea, for the time that there should be darkness for the space of three days over the face of the land."[930]

CHAPTER 4.6

# THE SECOND PROPHECY OF SAMUEL IS FULFILLED—THE GREAT SIGN OF THE SAVIOR'S DEATH

## *AD 34, DAY FOUR*

THE THIRTY-THIRD YEAR FOLLOWING the sign of Christ's birth came to an end, and the thirty-fourth year commenced without incident. No one was prepared, however, for what was about to happen, certainly not the wicked, which in their rebellious state refused to lend any credence to Samuel's prophecies, and not even the righteous, though they were looking for the sign of Christ's death with yearning and great anticipation. Suddenly, on the fourth day of the thirty-fourth year, a great storm arose, the likes of which had never been seen before, with fierce winds, sharp lightning, terrible thunder, and earthquakes that violently shook the earth.

## THE FURY OF THE STORM: 3 NEPHI 8

The Book of Mormon provides no direct statement as to the specific physical elements, which joined together at the beginning of AD 34 to create the perfect storm. Neither does it provide any indication that there were any visible precursors to the storm in the days preceding it. When the storm struck with overwhelming intensity, it is doubtful that anyone was aware of its full magnitude and scope. There were no satellite images to monitor its initial development.

The only information available to the people was that which had been described in Samuel's prophecy (which only the righteous believed), and that which each individual could see as they observed the approaching storm. Each person watched the local developments of the day without knowing what was happening in other parts of the land—having no understanding of the nature and immensity of the storm.

The atmosphere became completely unstable as the great storm advanced across the face of the land. There were tempests, which are defined today (as well as in the dictionary of Joseph Smith's day)[931] as violent wind storms, which may or may not be accompanied by rain, hail, or snow. As the powerful winds struck suddenly, though it is not mentioned, debris likely filled the air, including flying missiles of every kind.

The sky became treacherous, as sizzling bolts of lightning struck frequently, illuminating the landscape with an eerie strobe-like effect that filled the people's hearts with fear, especially when laced with the staccato-like sounds of booming thunder that rattled their heads and their houses, and shook the earth "as if it was about to divide asunder."[932] There were powerful whirlwinds, by which "some . . . were carried away"[933] never to be seen again.

It is difficult to visualize conditions that would generate earthquakes so powerful ("quaking of the whole earth") that they deformed the entire face of the land,[934] in company with hurricane-like winds ("tempests") with many entrained killer tornados ("whirlwinds"),[935] and violent thunder and lightning.[936] Unlike hurricanes, the winds did not dissipate at landfall, but continued unabated across the face of the land. In many places, fire fell from the skies destroying cities,[937] which seems to imply an extraterrestrial origin for the Great Storm. Astronomical causes would explain the immense scope and overwhelming intensity of the cataclysm and the simultaneous occurrence of so many violent phenomena.

The violence of the storm was so great that some cities were buried under water.[938] Others were buried deep within the earth.[939] Valleys became mountains, and mountains became valleys,[940] as the surface of the earth was warped and twisted by powerful forces that fractured the previously unfractured layers[941] of the earth's strata into fragments, fissures, and faults.[942] As a result, highways were broken up all across the face of the land, and cities were left desolate.[943] Everything took place exactly as prophesied by Samuel. According to Nephi, the storm lasted approximately three hours,[944] and then there was intense darkness across the face of the land.

## A GREATER DESTRUCTION WITHIN THE LAND NORTHWARD

The Great Storm inflicted much greater devastation in the land northward than in the land southward, "for behold, the whole face of the land was changed."[945] In that regard, wickedness is the precise reason given for the destruction of specific Nephite cities,[946] to include Jacob's city of Jacobugath.[947] It is thus concluded that the relatively intense and widespread devastation within the land northward[948] occurred specifically because of the wickedness there, which covered the entire face of the land.

The wickedness was not limited to the people of Jacob, but included many who had lived in the region since 55 BC. This idea is based on the fact that Nephi and Lehi had found extreme wickedness and the total rejection of Christianity during their mission to the land northward between 29 and 23 BC.[949] Ultimately, they "could not stay among them" and returned to the land of Zarahemla.[950] Their mission ended fifty-six years before the Great Storm.

The involuntary departure of the two missionaries from the land northward is a strong indication that few, if any, righteous Nephites resided there during their visit—no location where they could find refuge from the storm of evil. When the people of Jacob arrived in AD 30, through their influence, the wickedness could only increase. Accordingly, the wickedness in the city of Jacobugath is described as being "above all the wickedness of the whole earth, because of their secret murders and combinations,"[951] by which they had quickly brought the entire region under their influence and control.

## AFTERMATH

When the storm finally came to an end, the survivors lay transfixed in total and complete darkness, in which there was not so much as an impression of light: "And there was not any light seen, neither fire, nor glimmer, neither the sun, nor the moon, nor the stars, for so great were the mists of darkness which were upon the face of the land . . . neither candles, [nor] torches; neither could there be fire kindled with their fine and exceedingly dry wood, so that there could not be any light at all."[952]

As they endured the darkness, at times, any hope for survival weakened to the point of sheer hopelessness. Cries of anguish could be heard among all of the survivors:

> And it came to pass that it did last for the space of three days that there was no light seen; and there was great mourning and howling and weeping among all the people continually; yea, great were the groanings of the people, because of the darkness and the great destruction which had come upon them.
>
> And in one place they were heard to cry, saying: O that we had repented before this great and terrible day, and then would our brethren have been spared, and they would not have been burned in that great city Zarahemla.
>
> And in another place they were heard to cry and mourn, saying: O that we had repented before this great and terrible day, and had not killed and stoned the prophets, and cast them out; then would our mothers and our fair daughters, and our children have been spared, and not have been buried up in that great city Moronihah. And thus were the howlings of the people great and terrible.[953]

## THE VOICE OF THE LORD: 3 NEPHI 9

At length, as the people wept, groaned, and howled in the darkness with complete anguish of soul, a voice was heard by all the inhabitants throughout the land, crying:

> Wo, wo, wo unto this people; wo unto the inhabitants of the whole earth except they shall repent; for the devil laugheth, and his angels rejoice, because of the slain of the fair sons and daughters of my people; and it is because of their iniquity and abominations that they are fallen!
>
> Behold, that great city Zarahemla have I burned with fire, and the inhabitants thereof.
>
> And behold, that great city Moroni have I caused to be sunk in the depths of the sea, and the inhabitants thereof to be drowned.
>
> And behold, that great city Moronihah have I covered with earth, and the inhabitants thereof, to hide their iniquities and their abominations from before my face, that the blood of the prophets and the saints shall not come any more unto me against them.
>
> And behold, the city of Gilgal have I caused to be sunk, and the inhabitants thereof to be buried up in the depths of the earth;
>
> Yea, and the city of Onihah and the inhabitants thereof, and the city of Mocum and the inhabitants thereof, and the city of Jerusalem and the inhabitants thereof; and waters have I caused to come up in the stead thereof, to hide their wickedness and abominations from

before my face, that the blood of the prophets and the saints shall not come up any more unto me against them.

And behold, the city of Gadiandi, and the city of Gadiomnah, and the city of Jacob, and the city of Gimgimno, all these have I caused to be sunk, and made hills and valleys in the places thereof; and the inhabitants thereof have I buried up in the depths of the earth, to hide their wickedness and abominations from before my face, that the blood of the prophets and the saints should not come up any more unto me against them.

And behold, that great city Jacobugath, which was inhabited by the people of king Jacob, have I caused to be burned with fire because of their sins and their wickedness, which was above all the wickedness of the whole earth, because of their secret murders and combinations; for it was they that did destroy the peace of my people and the government of the land; therefore I did cause them to be burned, to destroy them from before my face, that the blood of the prophets and the saints should not come up unto me any more against them.

And behold, the city of Laman, and the city of Josh, and the city of Gad, and the city of Kishkumen, have I caused to be burned with fire, and the inhabitants thereof, because of their wickedness in casting out the prophets, and stoning those whom I did send to declare unto them concerning their wickedness and their abominations.

And because they did cast them all out, that there were none righteous among them, I did send down fire and destroy them, that their wickedness and abominations might be hid from before my face, that the blood of the prophets and the saints whom I sent among them might not cry unto me from the ground against them.

And many great destructions have I caused to come upon this land, and upon this people, because of their wickedness and their abominations.

O all ye that are spared because ye were more righteous than they.[954]

The words of the Lord struck the people with great force. Was it possible that there had been precision and purpose in the chaos, which had finally come to an end? It must be so, for the voice had declared that they were spared because they were more righteous than those who were destroyed. He then called them to repentance, saying,

Will ye not now return to me, and repent of your sins, and be converted, that I may heal you?

> Yea, verily I say unto you, if ye will come unto me ye shall have eternal life. Behold, mine arm of mercy is extended towards you, and whosoever will come, him will I receive; and blessed are those who come unto me.
>
> Behold, I am Jesus Christ the Son of God. I created the heavens and the earth, and all things that in them are. I was with the Father from the beginning. I am in the Father and the Father in me, and in me hath the Father glorified his name. [955]

Thus, compared with the wicked, which had been destroyed from before the Lord's face, the survivors were relatively righteous, though it was necessary for them to repent of their sins and come to Christ in faith that they might be healed. He then said, "I came unto my own, and my own received me not. And the scriptures concerning my coming are fulfilled."[956]

During the three-year period of the Lord's ministry on earth among the Jews, which had ended only three days earlier, He had made a similar statement in a temple in the city of Nazareth concerning the fact that His coming was the fulfillment of scripture.[957] His proclamation was not well received. At length, He was cast out of the city, and a futile attempt was made to cast Him off a cliff.[958] Now, however, He spoke with great power as the resurrected Savior of the world. No one doubted or dared to dispute the truthfulness of His words.

In the last days, the Saints of God face the same circumstances as those endured by the Savior during His earthly ministry, and by the righteous Nephites during the final years preceding His appearance to them. More and more, the wicked rise up and with swelling words denounce Christ, and persecute believers throughout the world.

According to scriptural prophecy, the animosity and hatred will continue to escalate as the day of the Lord approaches. As our Savior has decreed, however, the time will come that they too shall mourn, for He will not allow the wicked to continue in their wickedness. As in the Book of Mormon account of the Great Storm that preceded His appearance to the Nephites—which destroyed the wicked and ended their day of probation—the end of man's probation will come suddenly at the time of the Lord's Second Coming.

## THE FULFILLMENT OF THE LAW OF MOSES

Jesus then told the Nephites, "And as many as have received me, to them have I given to become the sons of God; and even so will I to as many as shall believe in my name, for behold, by me redemption cometh, and in me is the law of Moses fulfilled."[959]

He said, "And ye shall offer up unto me no more the shedding of blood; yea, your sacrifices and your burnt offerings shall be done away, for I will accept none of your sacrifices and your burnt offerings."[960]

From that time forth, sacrifice would consist of the following: "And ye shall offer for a sacrifice unto me a broken heart and a contrite spirit. And whoso cometh unto me with a broken heart and a contrite spirit, him will I baptize with fire and with the Holy Ghost, even as the Lamanites, because of their faith in me at the time of their conversion, were baptized with fire and with the Holy Ghost, and they knew it not. Behold, I have come unto the world to bring redemption unto the world, to save the world from sin."[961]

When He ceased speaking, the people in their astonishment lay motionless in the darkness. There was complete silence, as they pondered with awe the words they had just heard. The impossible had just been witnessed, and it was beyond their ability to grasp—an immortal God, the Savior of the world, had just spoken to them!

## THE DISCONTINUANCE OF "SACRIFICES" AND "BURNT OFFERINGS"

According to the above verses (3 Nephi 9:19–21), the law of Moses—the sacrifice of the firstlings of the flock to the Lord—was terminated following the Savior's death and resurrection. Thus, the shedding of blood as a gospel ordinance ended with His great sacrifice. Upon reflection, it is apparent that the sacrifices and burnt offerings required of God in the pre-Christ world had provided the only visual and graphic representation of the Lord's great sacrifice, and offering them was purely a matter of faith. Following the offering of His life for mankind, His sacrifice stands alone and requires only that we believe in Him with all our heart, mind, might, and soul. The law of sacrifice was therefore replaced by the sacrament of the bread and the water, in remembrance of the Lord's great sacrifice.[962]

## THE LORD SPEAKS THE SECOND TIME: 3 NEPHI 10

After many hours of silence throughout the land following the Lord's first communication,[963] His voice once again could be heard by all the people, saying:

> O ye people of these great cities which have fallen, who are descendants of Jacob, yea, who are of the house of Israel, how oft have I gathered you as a hen gathereth her chickens under her wings, and have nourished you.
>
> And again, how oft would I have gathered you as a hen gathereth her chickens under her wings, yea, O ye people of the house of Israel, who have fallen; yea, O ye people of the house of Israel, ye that dwell at Jerusalem, as ye that have fallen; yea, how oft would I have gathered you as a hen gathereth her chickens, and ye would not.
>
> O ye house of Israel whom I have spared, how oft will I gather you as a hen gathereth her chickens under her wings, if ye will repent and return unto me with full purpose of heart.
>
> But if not, O house of Israel, the places of your dwellings shall become desolate until the time of the fulfilling of the covenant to your fathers.[964]

After the Lord finished speaking, His words weighed deeply upon the people. All across the face of the land, they began to mourn and weep once more because of the loss of their loved ones, while the earth continued to tremble and settle with tumultuous noises: "And now it came to pass that after the people had heard these words, behold, they began to weep and howl again because of the loss of their kindred and friends. And it came to pass that thus did the three days pass away."[965]

## CHRONOLOGICAL VERACITY

Mormon presents two thoughts in 3 Nephi 8:1–2 concerning the accuracy of the calendar date, as recorded for the Great Storm. Verse 1 speaks of Nephi's integrity from the standpoint that he would not intentionally alter the record. The date that was recorded for the Great Storm (thirty-three years and four days after the sign of the Lord's birth) is correct, because Nephi was a just man, and he performed "many miracles in the name of Jesus." Then was added, "And there was not any man who could do a miracle in the name of Jesus save he were cleansed every whit from his iniquity."

Thus, it is implied that the highest moral fiber a man can possess is witnessed by the singular phrase, "He performed miracles in the name of Christ."[966] According to Mormon, it is the best evidence that he tells the truth. A man cannot be approved to receive the power and authority of the priesthood, unless he is filled with righteousness and integrity at all times and in all places.[967]

Verse 2 speaks of correctness. The calendar date is correct, if no mistake was made by Nephi. Standing spotless before God does not mean we will not make human errors or mistakes.[968] However, Nephi was not referring to an obscure date from a previous scriptural era, or a date from Nephite history that was relatively unimportant. It was a date that he personally experienced, and an event that abruptly and completely changed the Nephite culture.

Recording an incorrect date would imply that the entire culture was mistaken about the date on which their world turned upside down. It would be of much greater magnitude than if American history erroneously placed the signing of the Declaration of Independence on a date other than July 4, 1776, or more recently, if the date of the attack on the World Trade Center in New York City was somehow placed on a date other than September 11, 2001, for it personally affected each and every Nephite—physically, emotionally, and materially. Therefore, given Nephi's unquestioned integrity, in combination with the prominence of the Great Storm in Nephite history, there is no possibility that the recorded date is incorrect.

The prophet Mormon had absolutely no reason to doubt the correctness of the record. Thus, his comments in these verses may have been offered in reaction to false claims and contrived accusations put forward by unbelievers during his day—fables with no foundation other than a wicked imagination.

## THE LENGTH OF THE SAVIOR'S LIFE, AS REVEALED IN THE BIBLE

The Bible does not provide the Savior's precise age at the time of His Crucifixion. According to the Gospel of Luke, He was baptized by John the Baptist when He was "about thirty years of age."[969] Immediately thereafter, He was "tempted of the devil" for forty days.[970] Then, He began His ministry of two to three years, which length is indicated by the observance of at least three Passovers, as recorded in the gospel of John.[971] This series of events—the Savior's baptism, temptation, and ministry—is concisely set forth in Mark 1:9–14.

Notwithstanding the paucity of information concerning the length of the Savior's ministry, it is considered by many for various reasons to have lasted approximately three years. Furthermore, if His ministry did indeed last for three years, and ended precisely at the time of the Passover, as set forth in the book of John,[972] it can be concluded that there was a fourth Passover during that period of time. Two possible references to a fourth Passover feast are found in John 4:45 and 5:1. If four Passover events did in fact occur during the Savior's ministry, including one at the beginning and one at the end during His trial and crucifixion, it becomes poignantly symbolic, considering the purpose and meaning of the Passover.[973]

## THE PRECISE LENGTH OF THE SAVIOR'S LIFE

Thanks to the restoration of the gospel through the Prophet Joseph Smith and the coming forth of the Book of Mormon, Latter-day Saints are privileged to know the length of the Lord's life on earth to the very day. As prophesied in 6 BC by Samuel the Lamanite,[974] the day of His birth was announced to the Nephites by a night without darkness. At that time, the Nephite calendar was reset to begin on the day He was born.

On the fourth day of the thirty-fourth year of the new calendar, the great storm struck, destroying the wicked, while proclaiming the crucifixion of the Savior of mankind. As a result, we know that Jesus lived upon the earth for precisely thirty-three years and four days. No math was required to calculate the time since the great sign of His birth had occurred—just a glance at the calendar. It could not have been any simpler, or more easily retained in their collective memory.

The length of the Savior's life, at thirty-three years and four days, in combination with the biblical indication that His ministry lasted for three years, takes the symbolism set forth throughout His life to a new level. Indeed, we learn that the Passover was woven into the very fabric of His entire life—He was born during the Passover. He began His ministry at the time of the Passover, and He was crucified during the Passover.

The Book of Mormon thus corroborates the length of the Savior's life, as indicated in the Bible, yet provides precise calendrical data, which is not provided in the four New Testament accounts. For the Nephites, the symbolism of the two days was graphically portrayed as only God, our Father could do—light on the day of the Savior's birth, and darkness on the day of His death.

## THE DATE OF THE SAVIOR'S BIRTH

It was revealed to the Prophet Joseph Smith that the Savior was born on April 6. This date was corroborated by later prophets of the Church, as stated in the *Encyclopedia of Mormonism*: "Presidents of the

Church, including Harold B. Lee and Spencer W. Kimball, have reaffirmed that April 6 is the true anniversary of Christ's birth." However, they "have encouraged Church members to join with other Christians in observing Christmas as a special day for remembering Jesus' birth and teachings."[975]

The April 6 date correlates very well with the Passover, as observed in Israel today. The Passover is a spring festival, which begins on the fifteenth of Nissan—the day in the Jewish calendar when Moses led the children of Israel out of Egypt. Similar to the Christian holiday Easter,[976] Passover typically begins on the night of a full moon following the northern vernal equinox. As a result, it occasionally begins in late March, but generally occurs during the month of April. See the following table:

*TABLE 11.0*

THE TIME OF PASSOVER IN ISRAEL TODAY

| YEAR | BEGINS | ENDS |
|---|---|---|
| 2000 | April 19 | April 27 |
| 2001 | April 7 | April 15 |
| 2002 | March 27 | April 4 |
| 2003 | April 16 | April 24 |
| 2004 | April 5 | April 13 |
| 2005 | April 23 | May 1 |
| 2006 | April 12 | April 20 |
| 2007 | April 2 | April 10 |
| 2008 | April 19 | April 27 |
| 2009 | April 8 | April 16 |
| 2010 | March 29 | April 6 |
| 2011 | April | April 26 |
| 2012 | April 6 | April 14 |
| 2013 | March 25 | April 2 |
| 2014 | April 14 | April 22 |
| 2015 | April 3 | April 10 |

| 2016 | April 22 | April 30 |
|---|---|---|
| 2017 | April 10 | April 18 |
| 2018 | March 30 | April 7 |
| 2019 | April 19 | April 27 |
| 2020 | April 8 | April 16 |

The first Passover took place while Israel was in bondage in the land of Egypt.[977] To compel the Pharaoh to let His people go, the Lord sent His destroying angel to slay the firstborn of every Egyptian family. Moses prophesied to his people that they must sacrifice a first-born lamb without spot or blemish and apply its blood to the doorposts of their homes, or they would suffer the same fate. The scriptures teach that as the children of Israel were shielded from God's judgment in Egypt by the blood of the innocent Passover lamb, we are forgiven and protected through the blood of Jesus Christ, the Lamb of God.

## THE REST OF THE STORY

The pre-Christ Nephite era came to an end on the fourth day of the thirty-fourth year following the Savior's birth. The catastrophe, which accompanied the crucifixion of Jesus Christ, brought a violent end to the period. At face value, the impression is given that it was not a happy ending, though it was indeed. The Great Storm brought rest to a land suffering in torment from the forces of evil. In the intense darkness and quietude that followed the turmoil of the storm, the people, even as they suffered in their miserable and forlorn condition, were poised on the brink of joy.

The account of the post-Christ Nephite era will be presented in a subsequent publication. Whereas the pre-Christ period ended with judgment and death, and all of the pain and sorrow associated with it, the post-Christ period would begin with the Lord's love and approbation, and all of the well-being and happiness associated with it. It would begin with a great healing, as the Lord healed the Nephites of all their infirmities, including those suffered in the Great Storm.

The setting of this book has been the land southward. An upcoming book by this author will begin in the land southward as well, with the account of Christ's visitation to the Nephites. The prophet Nephi's account of the Great Storm and all that immediately preceded and followed it was written from the city of Bountiful. It was the land where Nephi and the righteous lived after being cast out of the cities of the wicked.[978] It was the location where the Savior first appeared.[979]

However, in Mormon's personal account of events that took place during his lifetime, and which brought to pass the extinction of the Christian Nephite culture, the geographical perspective of the Book of Mormon moves permanently into the land northward, where he was born. As will be presented in the upcoming publication, Mormon lived in the former land of the Jaredites and traveled into the land southward only once during his childhood and once during his early years as chief commander of the Nephite armies.

Mormon's personal account of those things which occurred immediately before and during his lifetime, was written for the most part in the land northward—the last being written from the Hill Cumorah in present-day upstate New York. That, however, is a story for another day. For the moment, let us bask in the joy of the Lord's peace, when the wickedness and violence of the pre-Christ period were brought to a sudden and dramatic end, and the stage was set for the Nephite golden age of love, peace, and prosperity.

# CHAPTER 4.7

# THE BOOK OF MORMON— ANOTHER TESTAMENT OF JESUS CHRIST

No one should doubt that the history of the Christian Nephite nation is a principle theme of the Book of Mormon. Many other subordinate themes are provided only as they affected Nephite history. However, while Nephite history is the core subject matter and the setting for the entire work, the primary theme that completely supersedes and overshadows it is the theme of its role as another testament of Jesus Christ.

Without the primary theme, the gold plates of the Book of Mormon would remain where they were buried by the prophet Moroni. We could even go a few steps further. Metal plates would not have been prepared by Nephi. The history of the Nephites would not have been tediously and meticulously placed upon those plates through generation after generation. The prophet Mormon would not have abridged those records and created the text of the Book of Mormon. He would not have been inspired to insert the small plates of Nephi.

The prophet Moroni would not have made his essential final remarks and sealed up the record in the earth. He would not have directed Joseph Smith to the Hill Cumorah to bring forth the record to the Latter-day inhabitants of the earth. The power of God would not have rested upon the Prophet of the Restoration, as he prepared that 'most correct' of all records for publication.

In 1830, the Book of Mormon united with the Holy Bible as a second witness to the divinity of the Savior of the world, and to the covenants the Lord has made with mankind.[980] As the scriptures declare, "In the mouth of two or three witnesses shall every word be established."[981] "And this gospel of the kingdom shall be preached in all the world for a witness unto all nations; and then shall the end come."[982]

The primary purpose of the Book of Mormon and the reason it graces our lives today is to provide another testament of Jesus Christ. Notwithstanding the fact that it is a history of the Nephites, written by Nephite prophets from the beginning to the end of their civilization, the theme that dominates its pages is the good news of the gospel of Jesus Christ. Thus are laid out with painstaking care many of the prophecies given by Nephite prophets of the coming of Christ at the meridian of time.

The first Nephite prophecies of Christ were given to Lehi,[983] followed immediately by revelations given to his fourth son, Nephi.[984] Only a few years later, while Lehi was still alive, Nephi's brother Jacob, the fifth son of Lehi, became a third witness of Jesus Christ.[985] Thus, the Nephite traditions of the Savior, already founded in the prophecies of the brass plates, were confirmed and given new legitimacy within the Nephite culture through the instrumentality of the first Nephite fathers. In the mouths of these three witnesses, the Nephite traditions of Christ were firmly established. Though they were labeled as "foolish" or "silly" traditions by pagan Nephites, they provided an unteachable foundation for those who were sensitive to the Voice of the Spirit.

## JESUS CHRIST–THE CENTRAL AND KEY SUBJECT OF THE BOOK OF MORMON

The prophet Mormon was foreordained to fulfill the pivotal and monumental task of abridging and organizing the history of the Nephites from the large plates of Nephi. Masterfully, and by inspiration, he structured it into a work of art, which is focused upon Jesus Christ, the Savior of the world. Naturally, the appearance of Christ in the Americas and the prophecies and events that preceded His visitation were more integral to the portrayal of Christ than those which followed. The prophecies of the coming Christ, which comprise a large portion of the Book of Mormon, endow the story with power.

It was in looking forward to the coming of the Lord in the face of death that the Nephites demonstrated their greatest faith. It provides us with inspiration to do the same, as we look forward to the Second Coming of the Lord. That part of the Book of Mormon which contains the greatest detail is the Nephite period which parallels our own period, as pertaining to the coming of Christ. Today, the current period is one which ultimately will be filled with great tribulation and suffering, as mankind spirals downward once more in decadence to a crash landing at the Savior's Second Coming.

The destruction of the wicked in connection with the Savior's AD 34 appearance to the Nephites provides an amazing parallel to the prophecies related to the Second Coming of Jesus Christ. Today, Christians of all faiths believe that we are in the final period of earth history, which will end with the Lord's return in power and great glory. Christians believe that His righteous followers will be changed at that time to endure His presence, but the wicked will be destroyed.[986]

## FINAL THOUGHTS

Joseph Smith declared that the "Book of Mormon is the most correct of any book on earth."[987] Surely that is because it thoroughly defines the vital role of Jesus Christ as the Savior of the entire world and clearly reveals that Nephite prophets knew and prophesied of His coming long before he arrived. His power and control over the entire universe is poignantly demonstrated in the description of many heavenly signs that accompanied His birth and His crucifixion, for the heavens boldly proclaimed the earthshaking importance of His life to the inhabitants of the earth. The Book of Mormon, however, does not stop with the coming of the Lord at the meridian of time.

During His appearance to the Nephites, the Savior delineated the continuance of His great work, which will not end until His Second Coming. The book of 3 Nephi contains His personal prophecies of the great falling away of the Nephites from the faith, the disappearance of Christianity from the Western Hemisphere, a worldwide drought of the word of God, the restoration of the Gospel in the last days, and the gathering of Israel before He would come again the second time. Important saving principles of the gospel were laid out with great care.

If we glean from the Book of Mormon only the information relating to the history of the Nephites, or the geography and archaeology of the New World, then we are missing the Lord's great purpose in bringing forth the Book of Mormon to the inhabitants of the earth during these latter days. If we ignore its spiritual purpose, and focus only upon the historical or physical veracity of the record, then we have wasted our time in reading from its sacred pages.

May the Lord's holy scripture serve to draw each of us to Christ as our personal Savior. May it lift us up and fill us with greater love for the Lord and for our fellowman. May it help us to improve our lives according to the Lord's Standard. Let us pray always that we may seek to utilize His holy word—His great gift of knowledge to all mankind—to draw near to Him in obedience, through faith in Jesus Christ, Who holds the keys of our salvation in the kingdom of God.

# PART 5

# NEPHITE GEOGRAPHY DURING THE PERIOD OF THE GADIANTON ROBBERS (55 BC–AD 34)

# INTRODUCTION

In 55 BC, only four years before the rise of the robbers, the first Nephite migrations into the land northward began. During this final pre-Christ period, a large number of Nephites would migrate northward.[988] Still, the perspective of the Book of Mormon throughout the following eighty-nine–year period remains exclusively within the land southward. The land northward would remain far removed from the center of Nephite activity in Zarahemla, where the Nephite record-keepers lived. Thus, the land northward was a land set apart—both geographically, and with respect to the Book of Mormon account.

From the time of their establishment in 51 BC, the robbers and other dissenters plagued the Nephites within the land southward until they were completely destroyed in the Great Storm, which took place on the fourth day of AD 34. The Savior's appearance on day four would also take place within the land southward—at "the temple which was in the land Bountiful."[989] The geography of the land southward, as recorded during that final pre-Christ period, is considered in Part 5.

## NEPHITE GEOGRAPHY THROUGHOUT THE PRE-CHRIST ERA

Chapter 5.1 reviews Nephite geography from Lehi's landing through the initial settlement of Jershon. Chapter 5.2 summarizes the settlement of the four regional lands of Zarahemla. The war which occurred during the first period of the robbers will then be depicted in Chapter 5.3.

In AD 17, during the second period of the robbers, the Nephites gathered from across the land southward into a core region to defend against them. [990] The geography associated with that gathering is explored in Chapter 5.4. The location of the mountains and wilderness occupied by the robbers during the same period are considered in Chapters 5.5 and 5.6. Finally, the key features of the proposed geography of the land southward, as identified today, are presented in Chapter 5.7.

CHAPTER 5.1

# A SUMMARY OF BOOK OF MORMON GEOGRAPHY FROM 600 TO 78 BC

THE PEOPLE OF LEHI departed from Jerusalem in 600 BC. During the next few years they migrated slowly southward along the Red Sea until they reached a place called Nahom.[991] Upon their departure from Nahom, they headed eastward. In time, they arrived at a place called Bountiful, [992] which was located by the Waters of Irreantum—the Indian Ocean, as it is known today.

Upon their arrival at Bountiful, they had wandered through the wilderness for a period of eight years, following their departure from Judah. After many additional days, during which an ocean-worthy vessel was constructed according to explicit instructions from the Lord to the prophet Nephi,[993] they set out into the sea. They sailed for many days,[994] whereupon they arrived in the "promised land."[995] According to statements made by previous leaders of the Church of Jesus Christ of Latter-day Saints, the location of their landing was the west coast of South America near the present-day city of Valparaiso, Chile. See Map 1.0.

**MAP 1.0: Valparaiso, Chile—** the Location of Lehi's Landing (as identified by various apostles of The Church of Jesus Christ of Latter-day Saints)

## THE PLACE OF LEHI'S LANDING

A number of apostles and three presidents of the Church have espoused a hemispheric geography for Book of Mormon cultures. All have referred to a South American landing for Lehi and company, for the most part on the coast of Chile. The only statement that does not refer explicitly to Chile was one that placed it "a little to the south of the Isthmus of Darien," which though non-specific still places it within South America.

## FREDERICK G. WILLIAMS

Frederick G. Williams was a member of the First Presidency of the Church under the Prophet Joseph Smith from 1833 to 1837, though he was never an apostle. According to Nancy Williams, the wife of his grandson, Elder Williams attended the dedication of the Kirtland Temple on March 27, 1836.[996] During the course of the meeting, he penciled the following words, a revelation which he later transcribed in ink on another sheet of paper: "The course that Lehi traveled from the city of Jerusalem to the place where he and his family took ship: they traveled nearly a south, southeast direction until they came to the nineteenth degree of North Latitude, then, nearly east to the Sea of Arabia then sailed in a southeast direction and landed on the continent of South America in Chili [Chile] thirty degrees south latitude."[997]

## ORSON PRATT

The apostle Orson Pratt identified Valparaiso, Chile, as the landing place of Lehi's party. Elder Pratt was an apostle from 1835 to 1881. The following is recorded in the *Journal of Discourses* within a discourse Elder Pratt delivered on February 11, 1872: "As near as we can judge from the description of the country contained in this record the first landing place was in Chile, not far from where the city of Valparaiso now stands."[998]

## GEORGE Q. CANNON

The apostle George Q. Cannon was born in Liverpool, England, on January 11, 1827. He was converted to the gospel in 1840. He left England and came to the United States, arriving in Nauvoo in 1843 at age sixteen—one year before the martyrdom of Joseph and Hyrum Smith. He was ordained as an apostle in 1860 and served until his death on April 12, 1901. During that period, he served in the First Presidency under four successive presidents of the Church: Brigham Young, John Taylor, Wilford Woodruff, and Lorenzo Snow.

Concerning the place of Lehi's landing, Elder Cannon said the following in 1883: "The Prophet Joseph, in speaking of their place of landing, said it was on the coast of the country now known as Chile."[999]

His statement thus identifies Joseph Smith as the source of this important information. He also stated the following: "It is also known that the landing place of Lehi and his family was near what is now known as the city of Valparaiso, in the republic of Chili [Chile]. The book itself does not give us this information, but there is not doubt of its correctness."

## JAMES E. TALMAGE

According to the apostle James E. Talmage, who served in the Quorum of the Twelve from 1911 to 1933, the Book of Mormon gives an account of the voyage of Lehi and company. He said: "The book tells of the journeyings across the water in vessels constructed according to revealed plan, of the peoples' landing on the western shores of South America probably somewhere in Chile...Continually advancing northward, these people in time occupied the greater part of the valleys of the Orinoco, the Amazon, and the Magdalena."

## THE PROPHET JOSEPH FIELDING SMITH

In 1954, the Prophet Joseph Fielding Smith wrote the following:

> When the Lord began to lead the family of Lehi to this land, he said to them: "And inasmuch as ye shall keep my commandments, ye shall prosper, and shall be led to a land of promise; yea, even a land which I have prepared for you; yea a land which is choice above all other lands." It is generally understood that they landed in South America, and that their nations, the Nephites and Lamanites, dwelt in South and Central America during the greater part of their sojourn here. At any rate, the time of their civilization was principally spent in the south and not in the region now comprising the United States. This proves beyond the possibility of doubt that the choice land was South as well as North America, and while the City New Jerusalem, which the Book of Mormon tells us is to be built on this land that is choice above all other lands, will be in Jackson

> County, nevertheless, if one accepts the Book of Mormon, one must accept the whole hemisphere as the land of Zion.[1000]

## THE PROPHET SPENCER W. KIMBALL

The confidence, as well as the revelatory tone of President Smith's statement, was continued by others which followed him, though not in any official quotes. Spencer W. Kimball, the twelfth president of The Church of Jesus Christ of Latter-day Saints, led the Church from 1973 to 1985. According to a friend of the author—a former missionary from Modesto, California, who served a mission in Bolivia during the late eighties—members of the Church in Bolivia claim that Spencer W. Kimball told them that "Lamanites of purest descent" live in that country. More recently, a former missionary to Ecuador states that the Saints in that country make the same claim with respect to a similar statement President Kimball made to them.

Both countries lie between Valparaiso, Chile, and the hydrographic divide, which separates the waters of the Magdalena and Orinoco rivers from the tributaries of the Amazon. According to Book of Mormon geography, as set forth in this book (and as projected by President Talmage above), the lands of Zarahemla and Nephi were located within the region drained by those three river systems. See Map 9.0 in following Chapter 5.2.

## BRUCE R. MCCONKIE

A former missionary to Chile recorded the following: "I served my mission in Chile (1979–81). While I was there, Bruce R. McConkie (an apostle) came to organize a few stakes. While speaking to us missionaries in a closed meeting he told us that while he was in Valparaiso, a city on the central coast of Chile, he was walking along the shore with several local church leaders. He stopped suddenly and turned to the sea. After a long moment without speaking, he turned to the local church leaders and proclaimed, 'Brethren, the soil upon which we walk is holy ground.' 'Why is that?' they asked. Elder McConkie responded confidently, 'This is where Lehi landed.'"

## LET US HAVE FAITH IN THE PROPHETS AND APOSTLES

Many former leaders of the Church thus viewed Book of Mormon geography as being hemispheric in scope. However, the 1980s brought a barrage of limited geographical models, which rested not upon revelation but upon conventional archaeology and conventional dating, or in other words, upon the theories of men. Afterward, church leaders have become silent in their public views of Book of Mormon geography.

The views espoused in this book and the previous book by this author *(The War Against Christianity)* are in harmony with the above views of former apostles and prophets, as relating to a hemispheric Book of Mormon geography. All held the holy priesthood of God and were ordained as prophets, seers, and revelators. No church leaders have expressed an alternate view. Their words should thus form the foundation of any study of Book of Mormon geography.

The wisdom of man should never be allowed to take precedence over the words of the prophets. Man's philosophies are merely opinions that often vary sharply from man to man. On the other hand, the above prophets of the past never varied significantly from one another.

Given a landing on the coast of Chile and a final destruction at the Hill Cumorah in New York, the Nephite/Lamanite cultures were truly hemispheric in scope. It is therefore projected that the peoples of the Book of Mormon represent the major cultures of the Western Hemisphere. Otherwise, the great cultures, such as the classic Maya and the Toltec cultures, as well as the Inca, would have been identified in the Book of Mormon as separate cultures. They would have significantly affected Nephite history, like the nations surrounding Israel in the Bible. Only by proceeding from a scriptural foundation will the archaeological cultures of both North and South America ever be correctly identified and placed within the proper periods of time.

## DEPARTURE OF THE PEOPLE OF NEPHI INTO THE WILDERNESS

The prophet Lehi died not long after his party arrived in the Western Hemisphere. Almost immediately, his two eldest sons, Laman and Lemuel, and the sons of Ishmael began plotting to take Nephi's life. Soon, it became necessary for Nephi to flee with his followers into the wilderness.

After many days of travel, they arrived at a location high in the Andes Mountains, as known today. They called it the land of Nephi, after their leader, who was Lehi's fourth son. They immediately established a city, also named Nephi. The people of Nephi would inhabit the highlands of Nephi for almost 400 years. Throughout most of that period, they were frequently attacked by the Lamanites.[1001] See Map 2.0 on the next page.

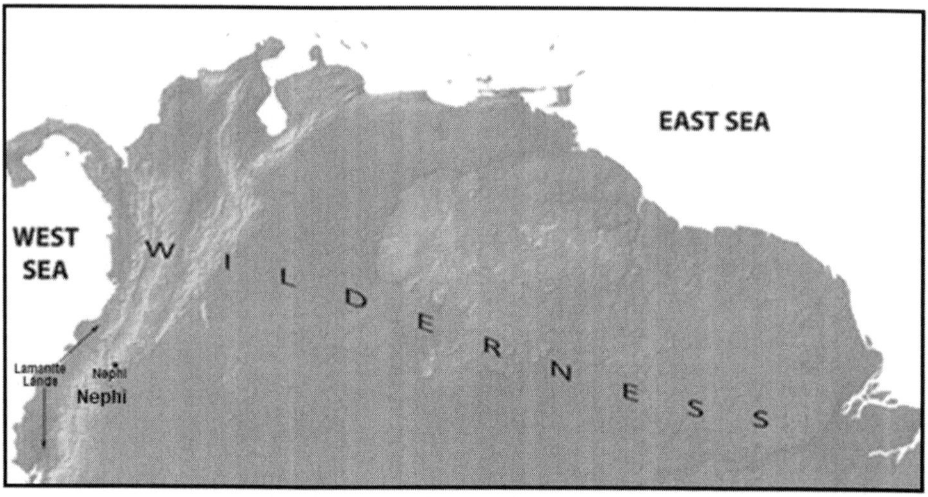


MAP 2.0: The Nephites Occupy the Land of Nephi from ca. 589 to ca. 200 BC

## THE PEOPLE OF MOSIAH

In *ca.* 200 BC, the Lord commanded the Nephites, through revelation given to their ruler, King Mosiah I, to flee out of the land of Nephi into the wilderness.[1002] Like the prophet Nephi 400 years earlier,[1003] the purpose of their flight was to escape the violent aggression of the Lamanites, who were descendants of Laman, Lemuel, and the sons of Ishmael.[1004]

They plunged into the heart of the vast wilderness which throughout their history had prevented any expansion of the northern and eastern boundaries of Nephi. Following their departure, the Lamanites immediately took possession of the land of Nephi, adding it to the lands already under their control along the western seaboard.

As the people of Mosiah migrated through the wilderness, they were directed by God, likely by means of the Liahona.[1005] After many days of travel, they arrived at the Sidon River (See Map 3.0 on the following page). According to the proposed geography, as first presented in *The War Against Christianity*, the Sidon River is identified today as the Orinoco River in northern South America. At the Sidon, they discovered the people of Zarahemla,[1006] many of whom were direct descendants of Mulek, the youngest son of King Zedekiah, the last king of Judah prior to the Babylonian Captivity.[1007] The Mulekite settlement was confined exclusively to the Sidon River Valley.

## RETURN OF THE PEOPLE OF ZENIFF TO THE LAND OF NEPHI

Shortly after the Nephites arrived in Zarahemla, a man named Zeniff persuaded a number of them to return to the land of Nephi. They completed the return journey only by wandering determinedly through the great body of wilderness.[1008] Upon their arrival back in the land of Nephi, Zeniff obtained permission from the Lamanite king to resettle the same land that had been deserted by the people of Mosiah. The people of Zeniff were allowed to occupy the cities of Nephi and Shilom.[1009]

The wilderness was located only a short distance from the two cities.[1010] It is therefore concluded that the city of Nephi had originally been established at the borders of the wilderness.[1011] Furthermore, the

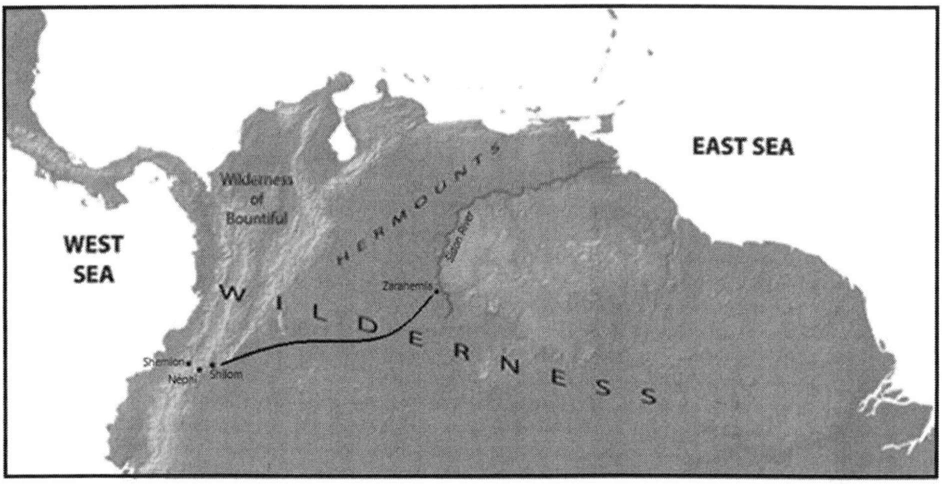


**MAP 3.0: King Mosiah Leads the Nephites from Nephi to Zarahemla**

borders of the land of Nephi had not moved outward on the wilderness side throughout the entire period of Nephite habitation there. Neither would they move during the subsequent period of Lamanite control while the people of Zeniff lived there. The delimiting factor throughout both periods was the simple fact that the keys to navigation of the wilderness remained completely unknown to both Nephites and Lamanites. Those entering into its dense forests invariably became lost.

The people of Mosiah had migrated into the very heart of this great wilderness. At that time, Zeniff passed through the wilderness between the cities of Nephi and Zarahemla four times—to include the first time, with Mosiah at the helm.[1012] Notwithstanding the size and density of its forests, he therefore possessed at least a cursory knowledge of the wilderness, and a general understanding of the geographical relationship between the two lands. He did not transfer such information to his descendants.

As a result, the people of Zeniff and the people of Mosiah became completely isolated from one another. In fact, even the general directional relationship between the lands of Nephi and Zarahemla—perhaps known only to Zeniff and others who made the final three journeys with him—was completely lost to the following generation. This fact is revealed when Zeniff's grandson, Limhi, sent forty-three men in search of Zarahemla.[1013] The search party became lost and completely disorientated. Instead of moving eastward toward Nephite lands along the Sidon River, they wandered northward through the narrow neck of land into the land northward.[1014] See Map 4.0 below.

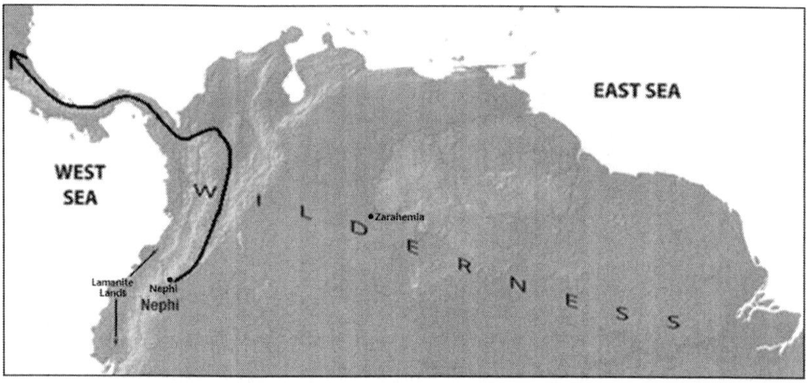


MAP 4.0: Potential Route of Limhi's Search Party of 43 Men

## NAVIGATION OF THE WILDERNESS

Alma the Elder, initially a priest of Zeniff's wicked son, King Noah, was the first Nephite to understand and navigate the only precise and identifiable route between the city of Zarahemla and the city of Nephi, which was a narrow strip of wilderness extending from the West Sea to the East Sea.[1015] In *ca.* 145 BC, the necessary geographical keys were given to Alma through direct revelation from God as he led his people from the Waters of Mormon to the land of Helam.[1016] In 120 BC, he again utilized the same keys to follow the previously unidentified narrow strip of wilderness eastward from the land of Helam to the headwaters of the Sidon River. See Map 5.0 below.

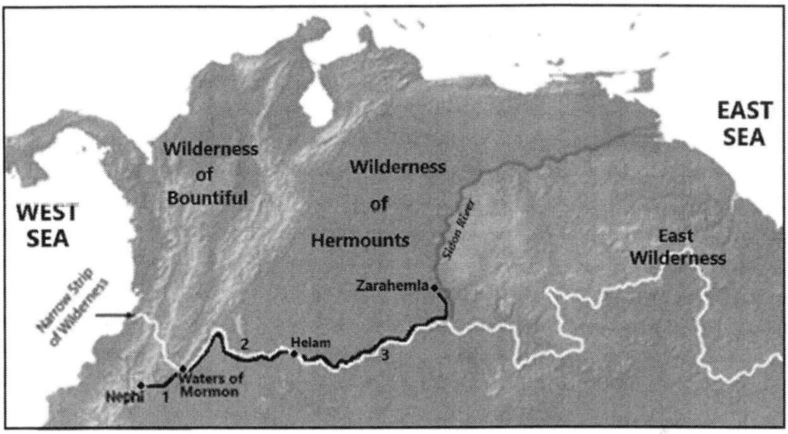


**MAP 5.0: The Three Segments of Alma's Journey from Nephi to Zarahemla (147–121 BC)**

1. Alma—Flees from Noah's Court to Waters of Mormon
2. People of Alma—Flee from Waters of Mormon to Helam
3. People of Alma—Flee from Helam to Zarahemla

## THE GEOGRAPHIC RELATIONSHIP BETWEEN NEPHI AND ZARAHEMLA

It is noted that throughout the Book of Mormon, the geographic relationship between Nephi and Zarahemla is always described as "up to Nephi" and "down to Zarahemla."[1017] This relationship between the two lands does not appear to be a reference to the north and south compass directions, but as first projected in *The War Against Christianity* (page 17), more likely refers to highlands versus lowlands.

## GEOGRAPHIC KEYS GIVEN TO THE LAMANITES

In *ca.* 120 BC, shortly before Alma departed with his people from Helam, he informed the Lamanites— under duress—of the geographic keys.[1018] From that time forth, the Lamanites utilized those keys to navigate the wilderness. As a result, when the Sons of Mosiah served their mission among the Lamanites from 91 to 77 BC, the precise configuration of the wilderness and the geographic relationship between the lands of Nephi and Zarahemla were well known to the Lamanites.

It is likely that a Lamanite army used this geographic understanding in 87 BC (while the Sons of Mosiah were serving their mission in Nephi) to journey to Zarahemla where they assisted the Amlicites in their war against the Nephites.[1019] See Map 6.0.

In 81 BC, the same geographic understanding enabled the Lamanites and Amalekites to journey along the narrow strip of wilderness from Nephi to the western border of Zarahemla, as configured at that time. At that point they headed northward along the western boundary

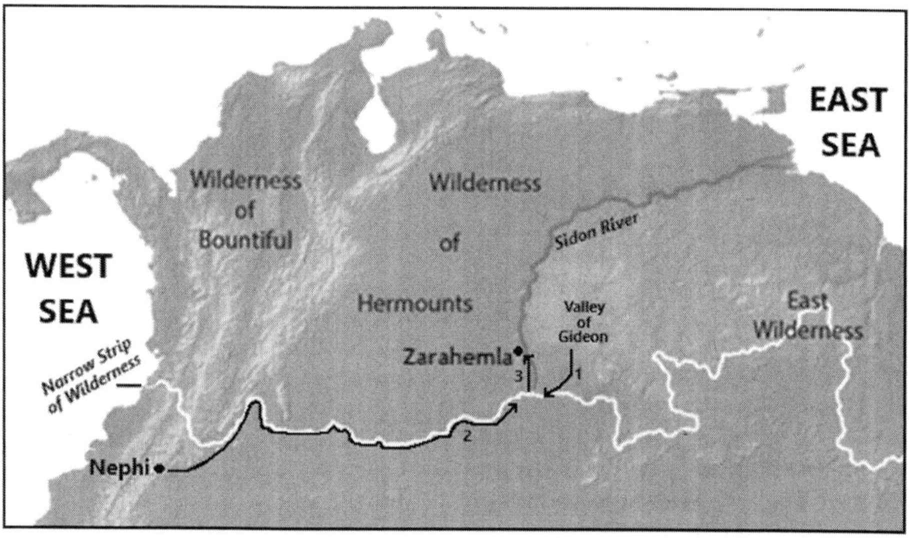


**MAP 6.0: 87 BC—The Lamanites Assist the Amlicites in their War Against the Nephites**

1. Amlicites flee from the Nephite army.
2. Lamanites arrive from the land of Nephi.
3. Combined Lamanite/Amlicite Army attacks the city of Zarahemla.

of Zarahemla to the city of Ammonihah,[1020] which they completely destroyed.

Afterward, they returned southward to the narrow strip of wilderness, whereupon instead of turning westward toward the city of Nephi, they turned eastward toward the east wilderness (see Map 7.0 below). Upon their encounter with the Nephite armies, they fled deep into the wilderness. At that time, prior to the settlement of the people of Anti-Nephi-Lehi in Jershon, the east wilderness extended all the way to the East Sea, both north and south of the narrow strip of wilderness. The Lamanites remained in that wilderness for three years, utilizing it as a base camp for waging war against the Nephites. They departed from the east wilderness and returned to highland Nephi in 78 BC.[1021]

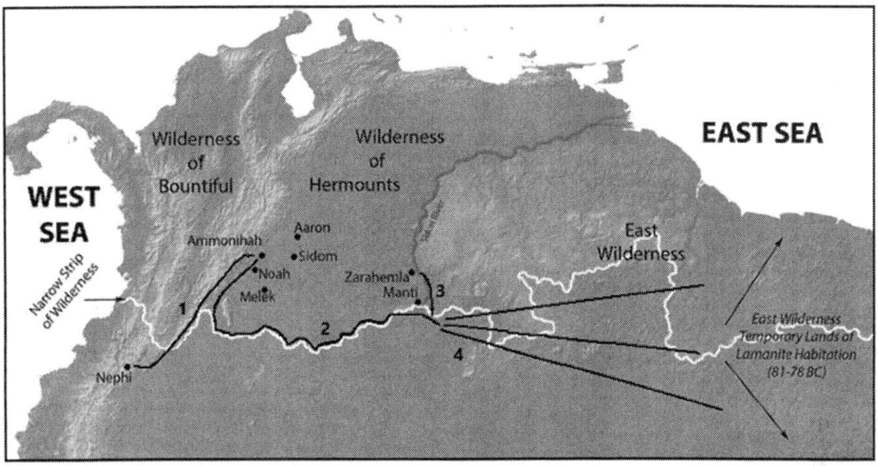


**MAP 7.0: 81 BC—The Lamanites Destroy Ammonihah and Flee into the Wilderness**

During the following year (77 BC), the people of Anti-Nephi-Lehi fled with the sons of Mosiah from the land of Nephi to the land of Zarahemla. The Nephites allowed them to settle the land of Jershon, which bordered along the east coast.[1022] They established a city by the name of Aaron. See Map 8.0 on the next page. The Lamanites and Amalekites, whose hostilities had driven them out of the land, gathered an army and soon pursued after them. At that time, these marauders moved permanently into the east wilderness. There, they could maintain their war with the people of Anti-Nephi-Lehi—and with the Nephites who protected them.

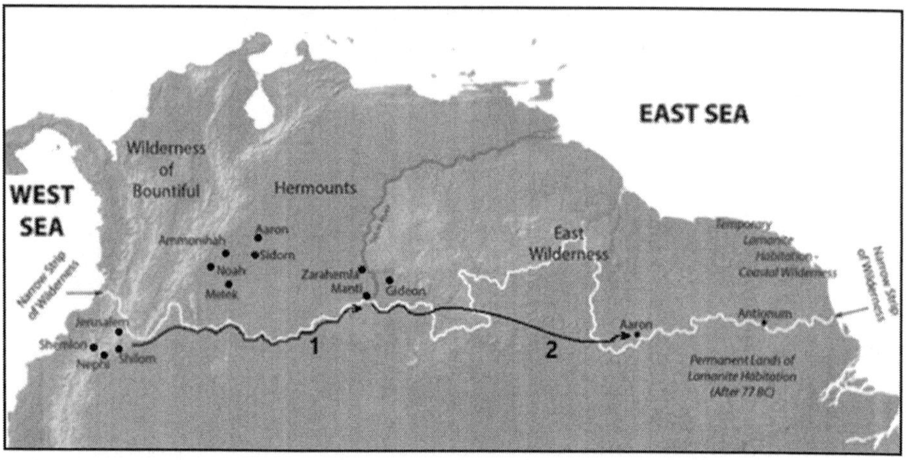


**MAP 8.0: 77 BC—The Sons of Mosiah Escort the People of Anti-Nephi-Lehi to Zarahemla**

1. Journey from the Land of Nephi through the wilderness to Manti
2. The Nephites allow the people of Anti-Nephi-Lehi to settle in Jershon

## NEPHITE DISINTEREST IN THE GEOGRAPHY CONNECTING ZARAHEMLA TO NEPHI

As noted above, the precise route between the highlands of Nephi and the headwaters of the Sidon River was known explicitly to Alma the Elder. Following his arrival in Zarahemla, however, such knowledge was not utilized by the Nephites throughout the following thirty–year period to travel to the land of Nephi—with the exception of dissenters, who, like the Lamanites, carefully preserved it thereafter. The Lamanites revealed it to the sons of Mosiah during their mission from 91–77 BC.[1023] Only after the return of Mosiah's sons to Zarahemla did it become generally known among the Nephites for the first time.[1024]

## CHAPTER 5.2

# THE SETTLEMENT OF THE FOUR LANDS OF ZARAHEMLA

In *ca.* 200 BC, when the Nephites first encountered the people of Zarahemla on the banks of the Sidon River, they were in the midst of a virtual sea of wilderness, extending hundreds of miles from east to west. For more than 100 years, they remained tightly clustered along the Sidon River, relishing the relative safety provided by the dense wilderness that surrounded them. When they finally began to spread outward, however, settlement of the entire wilderness from the east sea to the west sea took place within less than forty years, as summarized below. Please refer to Map 9.0 at the end of this chapter.

### ELIMINATING THE WILDERNESS

The idea of a diminishing wilderness across the entire land of Zarahemla from sea to sea during the pre-Christ period was considered in *The War Against Christianity*.[1025] Beginning shortly after 87 BC, when Nephites first began moving outward from the Sidon River Valley, it was largely a natural result of population growth and dispersion.[1026] In two instances, however, such outward movement was the product of cultural and religious animosity, which resulted in the establishment of the city of Ammonihah, a city of the Nehors, sometime before 82 BC,[1027] and the Zoramite city of Antionum just prior to 74 BC.[1028]

In 72 BC, the rate at which the wilderness was eliminated suddenly increased exponentially through the settlement of uninhabited wilderness regions as a defensive strategy. At that time, Chief Captain Moroni drove the Lamanites out of all Nephite wilderness lands, both eastward and westward of the heartland region. He then placed a total of eight fortified cities along Zarahemla's southern border from the sea east to the sea west, three of which lay along the southern border of the land of Jershon. Five additional cities were established along the east coast of Jershon, and another city was placed in the land of Bountiful, next to its border with Jershon.

One of Moroni's primary purposes for such fortifications was to encourage the people to move to remote locations outside the heartland region along the Sidon.[1029] Each fortified city provided a sense of security for the Nephite families that settled nearby, which in return provided support for the army stationed therein. Not until the fortified cities were in place did large numbers of Nephites begin to occupy many unidentified towns, villages, and hamlets in remote regions across the entire face of the land from the sea east to the sea west.

## THE SETTLEMENT OF THE WILDERNESS—TWO PIVOTAL YEARS

Considering the overwhelming dominance of the wilderness, which completely surrounded the heartland region on all sides from *ca.* 200 BC to 87 BC, it was never fully understood by the Nephites throughout that entire period. However, 87 BC was the first of two pivotal years, the second being the year 72 BC. Both years represented the beginning of sharply transitional periods of growth and development across the land of Zarahemla.

During the Amlicite War of 87 BC, the wilderness of Hermounts bordered the city of Zarahemla on the north and on the west.[1030] Following the war, the region very quickly evolved from a wilderness filled with carnivorous beasts of every kind into the most capital parts of the land less than forty years later.[1031] This may have been the initial stimulus for which may have been the animosity that resulted from the war. Moroni's placement of fortified cities around the perimeter of Nephite lands in 72 BC immediately brought about the settlement of the lands of Bountiful and Jershon. This sea to sea settlement of the wilderness regions surrounding the land of Zarahemla, which began with Hermounts, is summarized below.

## THE WILDERNESS OF HERMOUNTS

At the time of the Amlicite War, the wilderness of Hermounts bordered the land of Zarahemla "on the west, and on the north."[1032] It was "infested with wild and ravenous beasts." Hermounts thus comprised the eastern portion of a large wilderness region that extended from the River Sidon all the way to the west sea.

By 72 BC, the Nephites had settled the wilderness of Hermounts, and cities dotted the region. While it remained wilderness, Hermounts was clearly distinguished from the remainder of the west wilderness. In that line of reasoning, following the settlement of Hermounts, the remainder of the west wilderness is never again referred to as Hermounts. Furthermore, the two were never identified as a single body of wilderness.

In this book, the wilderness of Hermounts, following settlement, is identified as the "land of Hermounts," which assumes the boundaries of the settled land and the previous wilderness were the same. However, the Book of Mormon does not identify it as the land of Hermounts but as "the land between Zarahemla and Bountiful,"[1033] or "the land which was near the land Bountiful."[1034]

## THE HEARTLAND REGION—THE CENTER OF THE LAND

Rapid growth and development within the heartland region began shortly after the Amlicite War.[1035] In 51 BC, when Coriantumr headed northward toward the city of Bountiful after attacking the city of Zarahemla,[1036] he did not encounter the wilderness of Hermounts, which had blanketed the region in 87 BC.[1037] Instead, he passed "through the most capital parts of the land,"[1038] which signifies a tremendous amount of growth during the intervening thirty-six years. In a very short period of time, the central region had thus been transformed from uninhabited wilderness (Hermounts) into a land filled with cities, towns, and communities.

The rapid growth was not limited exclusively to northward expansion from the city of Zarahemla in the direction of the city of Bountiful. There was also substantial development to the west of the city, considering the number of cities identified in the account of Alma's 82 BC mission to the region. Alma's mission had taken place only five years after the Amlicite War.[1039] Melek and Ammonihah were established at an unknown time between 87 and 82 BC.[1040] Noah was likely established at the same time, though it was not mentioned in the Book of Alma until the following year—81 BC.[1041] In 72 BC, the three cities lay at the east boundary of the west wilderness. On the opposite side of the Sidon, the city of Gideon, located a short distance to the east of the city of Zarahemla, was established between 87 and 83 BC.[1042]

## THE EAST WILDERNESS—THE LAND OF JERSHON

The entire east wilderness, which lay eastward of the city and land of Gideon, and which extended all the way to the east sea, was completely uninhabited by either Nephites or Lamanites prior to 81 BC. The region was first occupied by the Lamanites during that year, following the attack on the city of Ammonihah,[1043] though only for approximately three years. They departed the east wilderness in *ca.* 78 BC and returned to the land of Nephi.[1044] In 77 BC, they returned to the east region in pursuit of the people of Anti-Nephi-Lehi.[1045] In the subsequent battle, they were defeated by the Nephite armies, and scattered throughout the east wilderness.[1046]

At that time, the Nephites allowed the people of Anti-Nephi-Lehi to settle in the land of Jershon.[1047] They became known to the Nephites as the people of Ammon.[1048] From that time forth, Lamanites inhabited the east region, due primarily to the settlement of the people of Ammon there. Initially, they were distributed throughout the region, on both sides of the narrow strip of wilderness—on the south in the land of Nephi, and on the north along the east coast in Jershon.

Five years later in 72 BC, Moroni expelled all Lamanites from Jershon, driving them southward across the narrow strip of wilderness into the land of Nephi.[1049] He then established and fortified the cities of Moroni and Nephihah and fortified the pre-existing city of Aaron along Jershon's southern border to prevent their return, which can be concluded from Alma 50:13–14. As first projected in *The War Against Christianity*, Chapter 3.4, Aaron (likely named after Mosiah's eldest son) had been previously established in 77 BC, when the people of Ammon first arrived in Jershon. [1050]

In addition to the three cities along the southern border of Jershon, other fortified cities were also established to the north of Moroni along the eastern seaboard, including Lehi, Morianton, Omner, Gid, and Mulek.[1051] Such protective measures were followed by Moroni's appeal to Nephites in Zarahemla to inhabit the region for defensive purposes.[1052] Thereafter, the Nephites permanently inhabited the land of Jershon, from the border of Nephi on the south to the border of Bountiful on the north.[1053] See Map 9.0 on page 251.

## THE WEST WILDERNESS—THE LAND OF BOUNTIFUL

At the beginning of 72 BC, the cities of Melek, Ammonihah, and Noah marked the western border of Nephite inhabited lands. At that time, the west wilderness region extended westward from the three cities all the way to the west sea. This would soon change, however. Later during the same year, Nephites began migrating westward to settle the west wilderness,[1054] which in time would be completely eliminated. As a result of Moroni's defensive cities along the southern border that year, and the resulting settlement of the west region, the entire region would quickly become a southern extension of the land of Bountiful.[1055] Eventually, Nephites would spread throughout the entire region.

As recorded in Alma 22:33, Bountiful extended "from the east to the west sea." That statement refers exclusively to the region immediately surrounding the narrow neck at Desolation. It was given purely in reference to hemming "in the Lamanites on the south, that thereby they should have no more possession on the north, that they might not overrun the land northward."

Prior to 72 BC, it seems that habitation of Bountiful was largely limited to its northern portion from the narrow neck of land to the northwest border of Jershon. Whether correct or not, this assumption is supported by the fact that all references to Bountiful involve either the region immediately surrounding the narrow neck of land, or the city of Bountiful which bordered upon Jershon.[1056] It is further projected that the southern portion of Bountiful, extending southward along the west coast to the narrow strip of wilderness, was not inhabited until after 72 BC. This southern portion did not extend from the west sea to the east sea, for it was bordered on the east by Hermounts ("the land between Zarahemla and Bountiful").[1057]

By the time of Alma's mission in 82 BC, cities had begun to dot the landscape of Hermounts. Uninhabited wilderness extended only from Melek, Ammonihah, and Noah westward.[1058] That portion of the western wilderness bordering upon Melek is first mentioned during Alma's mission to the city during that year.[1059] The same wilderness is referenced once again in the following year (81 BC), when the Lamanites attacked the city of Ammonihah from the wilderness side and completely destroyed it.[1060] In these events of 82 and 81 BC, the wilderness of Bountiful is not referenced at any time, and it seems the west wilderness was not considered at that time to be an extension of Bountiful.

Nine years later, in 72 BC, the Lamanite army sent by Amalickiah to attack the rebuilt city of Ammonihah also journeyed through the west wilderness.[1061] Later in the same year, however, Moroni established fortified cities along the southern boundary of Nephite lands (the narrow strip of wilderness) from the Sidon River to the west sea.[1062] Afterward, the Nephites would begin to settle the entire west wilderness all the way to the west sea,[1063] which was an essential element in

Moroni's defensive plan. From that time forward, the region would no longer be identified as wilderness.

## THE EXPANSION OF BOUNTIFUL

It was only after Bountiful transitioned from wilderness to one of the four regional lands of Zarahemla that its borders were expanded southward all the way to the narrow strip of wilderness. Until then, based on the descriptions given and the events that took place in Bountiful,[1064] it can only be perceived as a wilderness region extending along the east coast from the narrow neck of land to the northern border of Jershon. From 72 BC forward, however, it is projected that the land of Bountiful would encompass the entire region extending westward from Ammonihah and Noah to the west sea and southward from the narrow neck of land/east sea to the narrow strip of wilderness. Following the placement of the fortified cities and the structured settlement of the west region which followed, the land of Bountiful was not considered by the Nephites to be a wilderness region.

## LAMANITE HABITATION WITHIN THE LAND OF BOUNTIFUL

Given the open borders between Zarahemla and Nephi after 30 BC,[1065] many Lamanites likely moved northward into Bountiful from the highly populated highland region surrounding the cities of Nephi, Shilom, Shemlon, and Jerusalem. Significant Lamanite occupation of the region during that period would have further eliminated any remaining wilderness zones in Bountiful.

## SUMMARY

The transition of Zarahemla from an extensive wilderness to four lands of habitation took place during a period of less than thirty years. Following the Amlicite War in 87 BC, the Nephites began to move outward from the core region along the Sidon River. Between 87 and 72 BC, the wilderness of Hermounts became the first wilderness region to be settled.

Then, beginning in 72 BC, under Moroni's direction, they began settling the east and west wildernesses, which would enable them to better defend the land against invasion. At that time, as the Nephites spread across the entire face of the land from sea to sea, an even greater level of growth was taking place in the center of the land. By 12 BC, when the

Zoramites re-established the Secret Society of Gadianton, there were no remaining wilderness regions within the entire land of Zarahemla.

## CITIES ACROSS THE GREATER LAND OF ZARAHEMLA IN THE PRE-CHRIST ERA

The following map (9.0) was first presented in *The War Against Christianity* as Map A-6.[1066] It depicts the land of Zarahemla, as fully developed in the pre-Christ era. Table 12.0 was also included in the previous book as Appendix B. They are presented again for the reader's convenience.

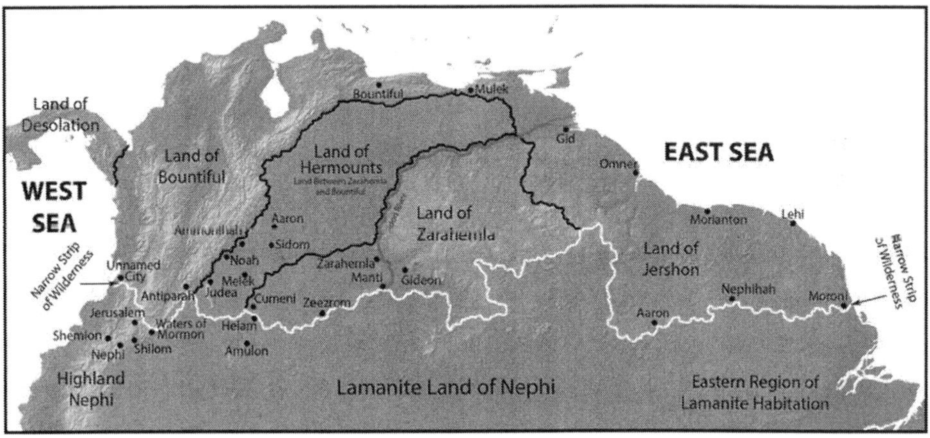


**Map 9.0: The Geography of the Land Southward as Developed by 51 BC**

### *TABLE 12.0*

## A QUICK-REFERENCE SCRIPTURAL GUIDE TO THE PLACEMENT OF CITIES ON MAP 9.0

| City | Location | Scripture |
|---|---|---|
| Aaron (southeast) | Southern Border of Jershon, the third fortified city from the East Sea. | Alma 43:25; 50:13–14 |
| Aaron (*War* west) | Near Ammonihah | Alma 8:13 |
| Ammonihah | West of the city of Zarahemla, three days north of Melek. | Alma 8:3, 6 |

| | | |
|---|---|---|
| Amulon | In the wilderness between the cities of Nephi and Zarahemla. | Mosiah 23:30–31 |
| Antionum | Southern border of Jershon. | Alma 31:3 |
| Antiparah | Southern border of Zarahemla between Cumeni and the unnamed city along the narrow strip of wilderness. | Alma 50:11; 56:13–14, 30–31, 57:1–7 |
| Bountiful | North of city of Zarahemla, bordered on East Sea. | Alma 51:22–32; 52:16–17, Helaman 1:23 |
| Cumeni | Southern border of Zarahemla between Antiparah and Zeezrom along the narrow strip of wilderness. | Alma 50:11, 56:13–14 |
| Desolation | Fortifications only, not a city during the pre-Christ period. Located on the Narrow neck of land, at the northern border of Bountiful. | Alma 22:31–32, 50:33–34; Helaman 4:4–7 |
| Gid | Located on the East Coast between Omner and Mulek. | Alma 51:26 |
| Gideon | Less than one day east of city of Zarahemla. | Alma 2:15–20, 6:7 |
| Helam | Eight days eastward from the Waters of Mormon along the narrow strip of wilderness and twelve days westward of Manti. | Mosiah 18:30–34, 23:1–5, 20, 24:20–25 |
| Jerusalem | Near the Waters of Mormon. | Alma 21:1 |
| Judea | Northward of Antiparah toward the city of Zarahemla. | Alma 50:11, 56:9, 13–15, 1–32 |
| Lehi | Located between Morianton and Moroni on the borders of the East Sea. | Alma 50:13–14, 25, 51:22–32, 52:16–17 |
| Omner | Between Gid and Morianton on the borders of the East Sea. | Alma 50:13–14, 25; 51:22–32 |
| Manti | Located at the headwaters of the Sidon River, less than 1 day south of the city of Zarahemla. | Alma 16:6–7; 22:27, 43:22, 50:11, 56:13–14, 57:4–12 |
| Melek | Located westward from the city of Zarahemla and three days south of Ammonihah. | Alma 8:3–6 |

| | | |
|---|---|---|
| Morianton | Between Omner and Lehi on the borders of the East Sea. | Alma 50:13–14, 25; 51:22–32; 52:16–17 |
| Moroni | At the southeast corner of Jershon on the borders of the East Sea. | Alma 50:13–14, 51:22–26 |
| Mulek | Between Bountiful and Gid on the borders of the East Sea. | Alma 50:13–14, 51:22–32, 52:16–17 |
| Nephi | Highland Nephi south of the Waters of Mormon. | Mosiah 9:8, 10:7–8, 11:12–13 |
| Nephihah | On the narrow strip of wilderness between Aaron and Moroni. | Alma 50:11, 13–14; 51:24–25 |
| Shilom | Bordered on the city of Nephi in the land of Nephi | Mosiah 9:8, 10:7–8, 11:12–13 |
| Shemlon | Located near the cities of Nephi and Shilom in the land of Nephi. | Mosiah 9:8, 10:7–8, 11:12–13 |
| Sidom | Located near the city of Ammonihah. | Alma 15:1 |
| Unnamed City | At the southwest corner of the greater land of Zarahemla on the borders of the West Sea. | Alma 50:11, 56:30–33 |
| Waters of Mormon | North of the city of Nephi in the borders of the land [of Nephi]. | Mosiah 18:1–5, 16; 30–31 |
| Zarahemla | In the center of Nephite lands after 200 BC, located on the west side of the Sidon River. | Omni 1:12–13; Alma 2:21–26; Alma 17:1 |

# CHAPTER 5.3

# THE FIRST PERIOD OF THE ROBBERS

### *52 BC*

As considered in Chapter 2.1, the first period of the robbers began in the city of Zarahemla.[1067] The rise of the robbers was a natural result of the secrecy surrounding the assassination of Chief Judge Pahoran II by Kishkumen. The coup then continued with the attack in the center of the land by Coriantumr, who was sent by Tubaloth from the land of Nephi in support of the robbers.

Map 10.0 depicts Coriantumr's attack of the city of Zarahemla, in which he bypassed the fortified perimeter cities at the

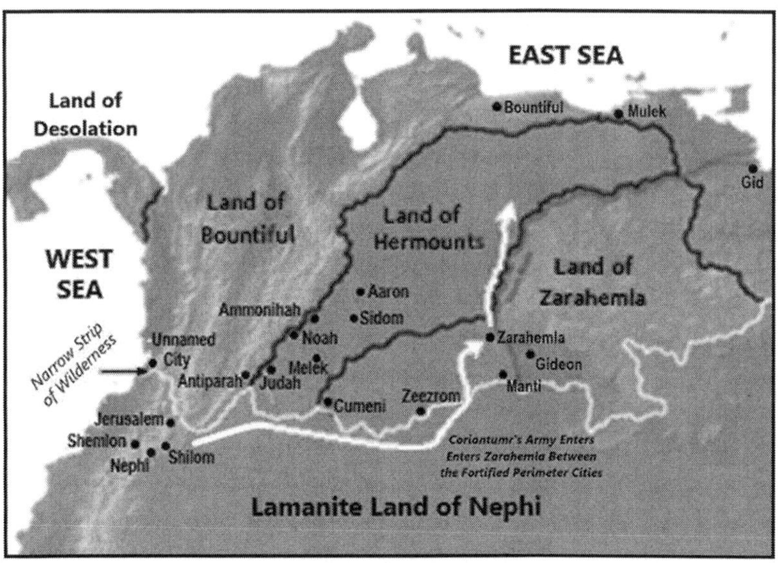


Map 10.0: Coriantumr's 51 BC Attack in the
Center of the Land of Zarahemla

southern border of the land. Setting a direct course for the city of Zarahemla, he skirted all interior cities along the way, which would delay his timing. After seizing the city, he continued his march northward through the heartland region toward the city of Bountiful,[1068] "taking possession of many cities and of many strongholds" along the way.[1069]

### *35–32 BC*[1070]

### THE FIRST NEPHITE MILITARY DEFEAT—DRIVEN FROM THE LAND SOUTHWARD

Map 11.0 depicts the Lamanite offensive against the land of Zarahemla, in which the Nephites were driven northward to the southern border of Desolation. In 35 BC, during the fifth year of Nephi's reign, dissenters (Gadianton robbers) joined with the Lamanites and invaded the land of Zarahemla.[1071] Over the following three years, the Nephites were driven from their homes and cities. Never before had they been driven from the entire land southward. In fact, it was the first time since their arrival in Zarahemla in which they were driven from their capital city.

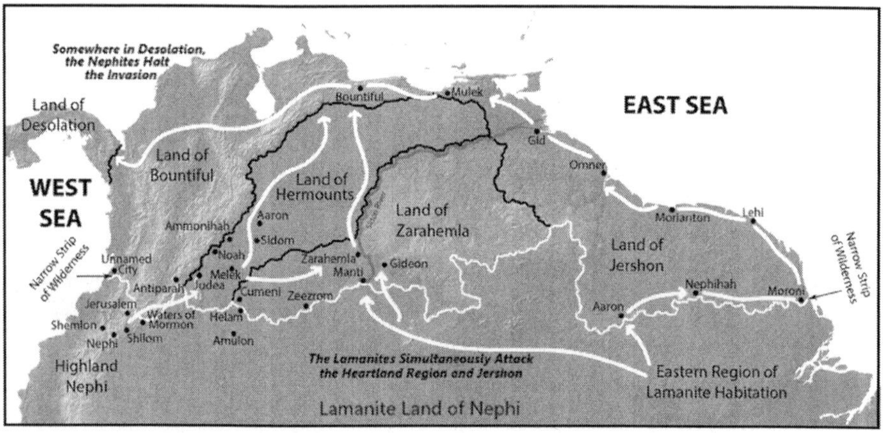


**MAP 11.0: Lamanite Invasion of 35 BC—Nephites Driven from the Land Southward**

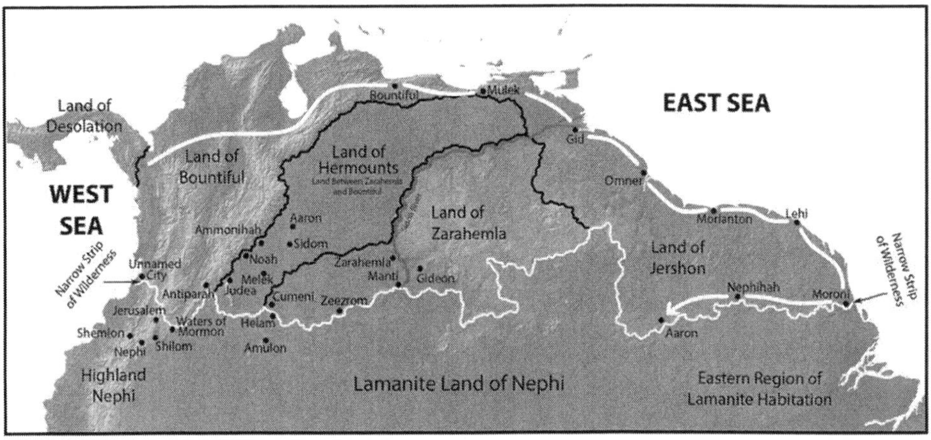


**MAP 12.0: Moronihah Leads the Nephites to Retake Half of their Lands**

*31–30 BC*[1072]

## MORONIHAH LEADS THE NEPHITE ARMIES TO RECLAIM HALF OF THEIR LANDS

Map 12.0 illustrates the route taken by Moronihah's armies[1073] to recapture one-half of Nephite lands. The actual path they took to reclaim their lands (the city of Bountiful and the coastal cities of Jershon) is not described until Helaman 5:14–16, which outlines the preaching of Nephi and Lehi to the Nephites within the recovered lands. Afterward, the two missionaries went to the lands of Zarahemla and Hermounts, which were still under the control of the Lamanites (verses 16–19).

Only through the missionary efforts of Nephi and Lehi would the heartland region be returned to the Nephites.[1074] Such a feat, undertaken in the midst of the war, required that they go forth with the power and protection of the Lord.[1075] Through their efforts, 8,000 Lamanites in Zarahemla were baptized. They then journeyed up to the land of Nephi and resumed their mission, whereby "the more part of" the Lamanites were converted to the gospel. Not until then was the heartland region returned to the Nephites (verse 52). Map 13.0 on the next page depicts the journey undertaken by Nephi and Lehi.

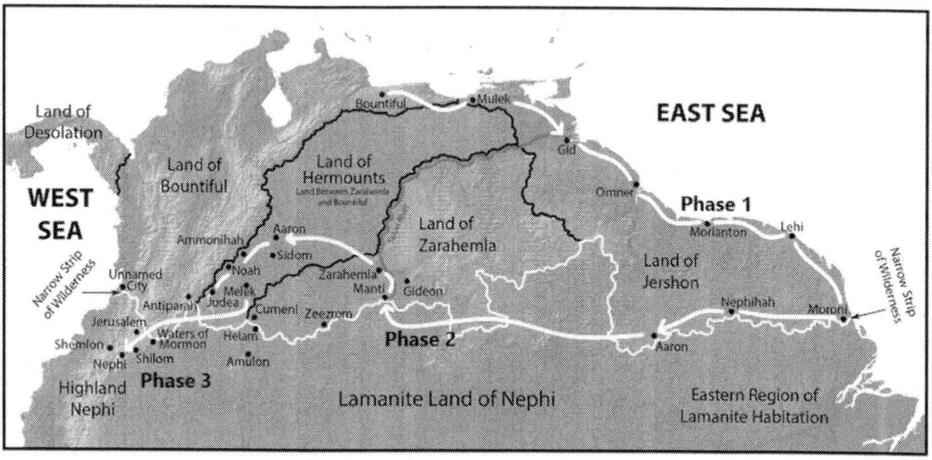


**MAP 13.0: The Missionary Journey of Nephi and Lehi—Three Phases**
Phase 1: To the Nephites in Jershon, which Moronihah had retaken
Phase 2: To the Heartland Region—The Lamanites were still in control
Phase 3: To the Land of Nephi, the Lamanite Center of Government

CHAPTER 5.4

# THE SECOND PERIOD OF THE ROBBERS—THE NEPHITE REGION OF GATHERING

## *AD 17*

Geography comprised a substantial and crucial element in the war between the Nephites and the Zoramite-led robbers. In response to the "proclamation of Lachoneus,"[1076] Nephites throughout the greater land of Zarahemla and from the land northward gathered to the "appointed" land within the land southward.[1077] Lamanites gathered from the land of Nephi into the chosen region—having been "numbered among the Nephites" and "called Nephites" for the previous four years.[1078] Joining together within a relatively small, well-fortified region in Zarahemla was vital to a Nephite victory.

Perhaps the most remarkable thing about the circumstances requiring the Nephite gathering was the brevity of time during which the robbers had grown to such great numbers that they could threaten the very existence of the Nephite nation and the Christian religion. Following the 17 BC extinction of the robbers,[1079] five years had passed before the Zoramites recovered the secret plans of destruction in 12 BC and reestablished the robbers within an uninhabited mountain and wilderness region.[1080] Only twenty-eight years later, Giddianhi, the leader of the robbers, sent an epistle to Lachoneus, demanding the surrender of all Nephite lands and cities to the robbers, and vowing to destroy them if they did not comply.

Lachoneus was fully aware of the large and growing number of robbers, and of their willingness to spread death and destruction throughout the land. Therefore, his proclamation was sent across the entire face of the land, both in the land southward and in the land northward, calling the people to join together in the land southward. Their response to his decree is recorded as follows: "And it came to pass in the seventeenth year, in the latter end of the year, the proclamation of Lachoneus had gone forth throughout all the face of the land, and they had taken their horses, and their chariots, and their cattle, and all their flocks, and their herds, and their grain, and all their substance, and did march forth by thousands and by tens of thousands, until they had all gone forth to the place which had been appointed that they should gather themselves together, to defend themselves against their enemies."[1081]

The region to which the Nephites gathered is then described: "And the land which was appointed was the land of Zarahemla, and the land which was between the land Zarahemla and the land Bountiful, yea, to the line which was between the land Bountiful and the land Desolation."[1082]

As described in verse 23, the region of gathering fully encompassed three lands: Zarahemla, Bountiful, and the land which was sandwiched in between the two lands.[1083] According to this verse, the region thus extended northward from the southern boundary of the regional land of Zarahemla to the northern boundary of the land of Bountiful at Desolation on the narrow neck of land. The land of Jershon was the only land not included. Map 14.0 depicts the outer boundary of this composite region of gathering according to this description.

## A CLOSER LOOK AT THE SOUTHERN BORDER OF THE REGION OF GATHERING

The precise location of the southern border of the appointed region is not identified in the above description. It is reasonable to assume, however, that, as depicted on Map 14.0, it was the narrow strip of wilderness, which lined the entire southern border of the greater land of Zarahemla. The Nephites could then take advantage of defensive cities along that border, which had been established by Chief Captain Moroni between 72 and 67 BC.[1084] These cities had been fortified specifically to defend against frequent Lamanite attacks. Therefore, by making the narrow strip of wilderness the southern border of the region of gathering, the preparations required for defense against the robbers would be considerably reduced.

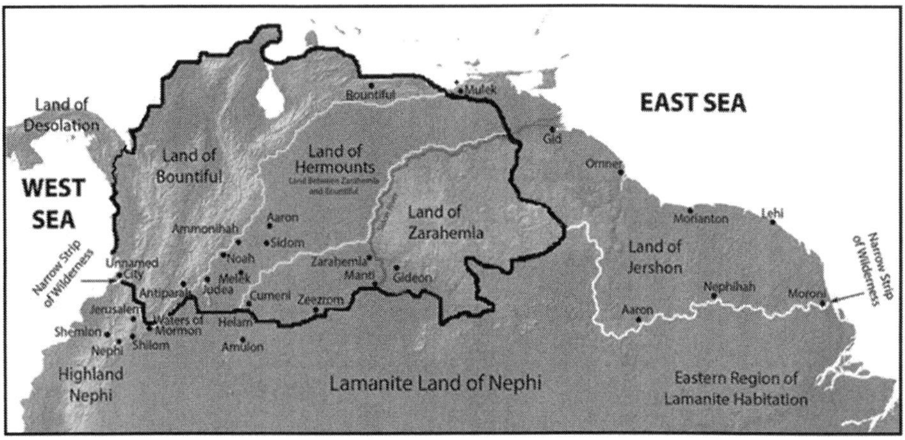


**MAP 14.0: Mormon's Description of the AD 17 Region of Gathering** (Note: The Region of Gathering encompasses the lands of Zarahemla, Hermounts, and Bountiful)

## A REASSESSMENT OF THE NORTHERN BORDER OF THE REGION OF GATHERING

With respect to Mormon's identification of the northern border of the region of gathering, it does not become evident until 3 Nephi 4:23–25 that the region could not have extended northward to the southern border of Desolation on the narrow neck of land. Until that passage, the student of the Book of Mormon is operating under the impression given in 3 Nephi 3:23. In the latter passage, however, it suddenly becomes obvious that the land of gathering did not obstruct the narrow neck of land, because Gidgiddoni had to send out the Nephite armies to intercept Zemnarihah's band of robbers to prevent them from fleeing into the land northward.[1085] Furthermore, it could not have extended across the land of Bountiful from the east sea to the west sea at any location.

Any geographical statement at this point in the Book of Mormon, which concerns the narrow neck of land, must be consistent with the abundant and precise geographical information, which has been set forth previously. It must also be consistent with previous historical events. Consider the following:

The geographical configuration of the narrow neck of land, which connected the land northward to the land southward, was addressed in

*The War Against Christianity.*[1086] Alma 22:32 and 50:34 clearly describe the narrow neck of land as an isthmus, surrounded by ocean on both sides.

Furthermore, according to the statement contained in Alma 22:33, Nephite habitation of the land of Bountiful "from the east unto the west sea . . . with their guards and their armies . . . had hemmed in the Lamanites on the south, that thereby they should have no more possession on the north, that they might not overrun the land northward." The reverse of this statement is also true. The placement of armies across Bountiful from the east sea to the west sea would prevent robbers in the land northward from joining with the robbers in the land southward.

The same is true of Nephite control of any location, either on or leading to the narrow neck of land, which would eliminate movement between the land southward and the land northward. This had previously occurred during the War of 35 BC.[1087] At that time the Nephites could not stop the advancing Lamanite forces until they reached the choke point of the narrow neck.

If the land to which the Nephites gathered in response to Lachoneus' proclamation had actually extended all the way "to the line which was between the land Bountiful and the land Desolation,"[1088] the following would have resulted:

1. The land northward would have been completely sealed off from the land southward.
2. When the Nephites gathered to the appointed location, the robbers would not have been able to freely take possession of the deserted lands, "both which were in the land south and which were in the land north."[1089]
3. At the end of the war, there would have been no available escape route to enable Zemnarihah to flee with the robbers from the land southward into the land northward.[1090]
4. It would have been unnecessary for Gidgiddoni to "send out his armies in the night-time "[to] cut off the way of their retreat,"[1091] for they would have already been in position.

If the Nephites had occupied the "line which was between the land Bountiful and the land Desolation" throughout the time of gathering, they would have prevented all movement in either direction—from the beginning to the end of the war. Robbers attacking from the land northward would have had little or no success in breaking through the fortifications at the southern boundary of Desolation. As a result, they could not have participated in the war in any significant way.

If they were unable to move past the line between Bountiful and Desolation, however, they could have fled back into the land northward at any time. At the end of the war within the land southward, they would have remained a threat to the Nephites. It was therefore crucial to leave the passage open, allowing them to move past the constriction into the land southward, which ultimately became a trap. Additionally, western Bountiful must also be left open for the same purpose, to enable them to move across the land southward from the constriction at Desolation to join with the robbers in the uninhabited mountain and wilderness region within the land of Nephi.[1092]

Considering the location of the robber lands as considered in Chapter 5.6 (Map 18.0), it would have been necessary for the Nephites to vacate a large portion of Bountiful, extending from the narrow neck of land southward to highland Nephi, and from the west coast to the borders of Hermounts.[1093] All robbers would then be able to participate in the conflict. They could migrate freely from the land northward across the deserted portion of Bountiful, then through the deserted land of Nephi to join the robbers in the wilderness, which lay eastward from highland Nephi. Map 15.0 depicts the reduced area of the region of gathering, as necessitated by 3 Nephi 4:23–25.

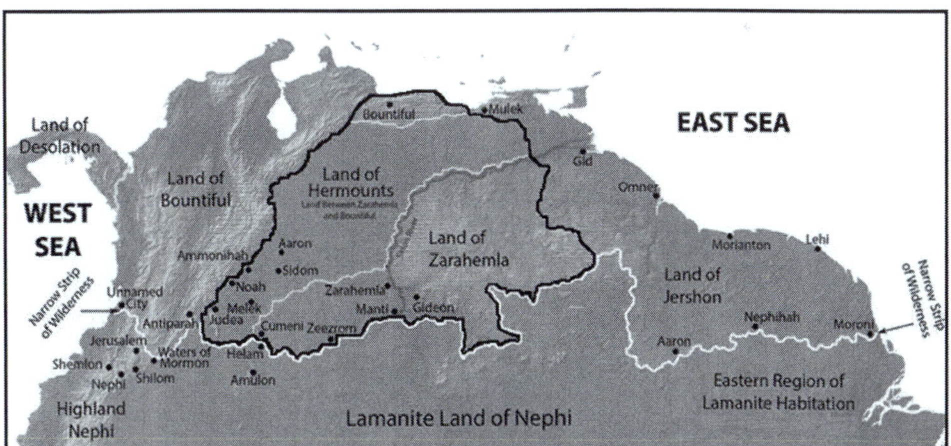


**Map 15.0: Most of the Land of Bountiful is eliminated from the Region of Gathering** (Compare with Map 14.0)

## A FURTHER REDUCTION OF THE REGION OF GATHERING

Without the scenario in 3 Nephi 4 surrounding Zemnarihah's attempted flight into the land northward,[1094] an adjustment to the boundaries of the region of gathering would have never been considered, or perhaps even perceived. However, the requirement for making such an adjustment has triggered a much closer examination of 3 Nephi 3:12–25. The following is concluded from statements made in the passage:

It was a matter of critical importance to limit the area of gathering to a single homogeneous region, uninterrupted by intervening wilderness and/or mountainous regions, and completely surrounded by fortified cities. This is the apparent message contained in the third chapter of 3 Nephi: "Now Lachoneus did cause that they should gather themselves together in the land southward."[1095] "And the land which was appointed was the land of Zarahemla, and the land which was between the land Zarahemla and the land Bountiful . . . to the line which was between the land Bountiful and the land Desolation."[1096] "And they did dwell in one land and in one body."[1097] "And [Lachoneus] caused that fortifications should be built round about them."[1098]

The land to which the Nephites congregated was not a single land in the political sense. Rather, as described in 3 Nephi 3:23, it extended across three of the four regional lands of Zarahemla. Hence, the description in 3 Nephi 3:25 apparently refers to "one land," in the perspective that every location was contiguous, or adjoining with the rest, with no intervening mountains, and surrounded by fortifications. Only then could the people "dwell . . . in one body" while occupying the three lands.

In consideration of these aspects, it is apparent that the mountainous portion of Bountiful was not included in the region of gathering, which leaves only the northeastern coastal portion where the city of Bountiful was located. This small portion of Bountiful lay to the north of the city of Zarahemla[1099] and bordered on the "Land Between" (Hermounts). Its eastern boundary touched the northwest border of the land of Jershon.[1100] With respect to the regional land of Zarahemla, the eastern mountainous region (as projected in this book), must also be removed from the region of gathering.

It is only through these projected adjustments to the region of gathering that all of the stated characteristics are satisfied:

1. All three lands—Zarahemla, Bountiful, and the Land Between—were included (to varying degrees) within the region of gathering.
2. The people gathered "in one land, and in one body"—impossible in an expansive, sprawling region with interlying mountains.
3. They were surrounded by fortifications, many of which were already in place.

## OTHER CONSIDERATIONS

### *THE LAND SOUTHWARD*

It seems apparent that there were additional reasons Lachoneus selected the land southward as the place of gathering. Though the curse upon the land northward[1101] was sufficient to eliminate it from consideration, there were other advantages that would compel Lachoneus to choose the land southward. It had long been the heartland of the Nephite and Lamanite cultures. Highland Nephi and the adjacent western coastal region had been inhabited by either Nephites or Lamanites for 605 years (589 BC-AD 16). The land of Zarahemla had been inhabited by the Nephites for approximately 216 years. In comparison, Nephite habitation of the land northward was of recent origin, having been initiated only 71 years earlier—in 55 BC.

Without doubt, the population within the land southward was much greater than in the land northward. Convenience for the great majority of the people would surely have been a significant factor to greatly reduce the time required for gathering. Additionally, the governing organizations that supported Lachoneus would not be displaced.

### *THE REGION OF GATHERING: "THE CENTER OF OUR LANDS"*

There is another indication that the Nephites did indeed gather exclusively within the central heartland region of Zarahemla extending northward from the city of Manti to the city of Bountiful. It lies simply in the terminology used to describe the region of gathering. Lachoneus referred to the region as "the center of our lands."[1102] In the first chapter of the book of Helaman, the same terminology had been used to describe the heartland region during Coriantumr's 51 BC attack on the city of Zarahemla.

In the account of Coriantumr's swift march into the Sidon River Valley to capture the capital city, the region was identified as "the heart of their lands."[1103] When he then headed northward out of the city toward the city of Bountiful,[1104] he marched through the "center of the land."[1105] It was also referred to as "the most capital parts of the land,"[1106] or in other words, the most densely populated (and most developed) region within the greater land of Zarahemla.

### *THE MOST FORTIFIED REGION*

As a result of more than 100 years of defensive posturing to repel repeated Lamanite and dissenter attacks, it was also the most fortified region. Unlike the land of Nephi, the heartland region along the Sidon River had been defended against attack almost continuously since 87 BC. For that reason, it was extensively fortified long before the current war began, which of itself would be of great benefit in the preparations for defense.

## THE BOUNDARIES OF THE REGION OF GATHERING

The Nephites arrived in the land of Zarahemla from highland Nephi in about 200 BC. Throughout the first century of habitation in Zarahemla, they occupied a small, compact location centered around the city of Zarahemla on the north-flowing Sidon River.[1107] It was not until around 100 BC during the reign of Mosiah II that they began to move outward from the core area in all compass directions, "building large cities and villages in all quarters of the land."[1108]

The cities visited by Alma the Younger approximately fifteen years later in 84 and 83 BC[1109] were some of the earliest cities established outside the core area along the Sidon River. When fully expanded, the boundaries of this heartland region extended eastward to the city of Gideon, and westward to the cities of Ammonihah, Noah, and Melek. In 72 BC, at Chief Captain Moroni's direction, the region of habitation was extended southward to the cities of Manti, Zeezrom and Cumeni along the narrow strip of wilderness and northward to the coastal city of Bountiful. See Map 16.0 on page 268.

In terms of present-day geography, the cities of Ammonihah, Noah, and Melek are projected to have been located along the western edge of the Sidon (Orinoco) watershed, bordering on the Andes Mountains, which initially were identified simply as the west wilderness,[1110] or wilderness.[1111] This west wilderness, which ultimately became a southern extension of the land of Bountiful, extended across the east, central, and west Andes of present-day Colombia to the west sea (Pacific Ocean). It is further projected that the city of Gideon, which was located on or near the eastern edge of the region, bordered on the mountainous region known today as the Guiana Highlands.

The cities of Manti, Zeezrom, and Cumeni marked the southern boundary of the region. The three cities lay along the southern boundary of the Sidon (Orinoco) River watershed, described in the Book of Mormon as the narrow strip of wilderness. At that time, other cities were established to the north of the city of Zarahemla along the Sidon, ultimately spreading northward all the way to the coastal city of Bountiful. It is concluded that this entire region was the location to which the Nephites gathered in AD 16.

## MULTIPLE ADVANTAGES WITHIN THE CENTRAL REGION

There were a number of inherent advantages in gathering within a homogeneous, non-mountainous, highly populated, and highly developed region with an extensive history of defense against the Lamanites:

1. Defensive cities were already in place, many if not all having been previously fortified to defend against frequent Lamanite attacks.
2. A network of well-developed roads and relatively flat terrain would make troop movements feasible from one side to another as necessary to defend against robber attacks at any location on the perimeter.
3. No internal wilderness or mountainous regions harboring robbers would exist to breach the security of the perimeter fortifications, or to provide a pathway for robber infiltration.

Such a geographical configuration would enable a relative ease of defense and provide a similar level of security for everyone.

## THE NEPHITE GATHERING IN SUMMARY

The gathering of the Christian Nephites according to the proclamation of Lachoneus entailed the exodus of all Christian Nephites from the land northward. In the land southward, it required the evacuation of Lamanites from the entire land of Nephi, that is, from the western region extending from highland Nephi to the west sea, and from the eastern region located to the south of Jershon. It required the evacuation of Nephites from the mountainous portion of the land of Bountiful, which extended from the cities of Ammonihah, Noah, and Melek to the west sea. Finally, it required the abandonment of the entire land of Jershon. See Hypothesis 7.0 in Appendix A.

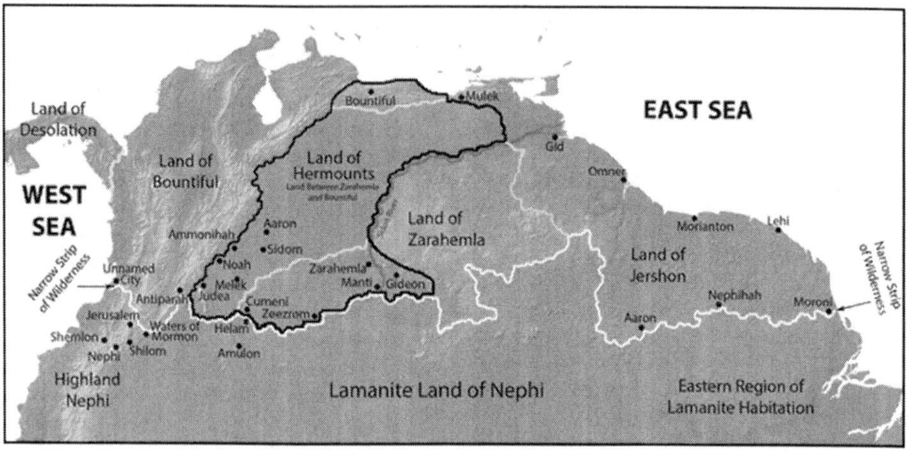


**MAP 16.0: The Highland Region of Zarahemla is eliminated from the Region of Gathering** (Compare with Map 15.0)

# CHAPTER 5.5

# SEARCHING ZARAHEMLA FOR THE WILDERNESS LANDS OF THE ROBBERS

The Book of Mormon was neither written[1112] nor abridged[1113] as a geographical discourse. However, no historical account is complete without its geographical setting, and the keepers of the Nephite record did not withhold such information. The majority of Book of Mormon accounts identify the geographical location of the events taking place therein—both prior to Lehi's departure from the Old World and following the arrival in the New World.

This is especially true of Mormon's abridgment, which, following the loss of the 116 pages,[1114] begins with Words of Mormon.[1115] Though Mormon's account contains generally concise and occasionally vague descriptions of Book of Mormon lands, a great deal of information has been provided. Furthermore, such descriptions can be significantly expanded and clarified through the examination of all geographic statements as a single body of interrelated information.

Though explicit and detailed geographic statements are provided in some instances, brief and more or less implicit geographical information is supplied in most cases. Such information is included in the accounts of missions, migrations, flights, wars, and preparations for war. Each account contributes in one way or another to the understanding of Book of Mormon geography.

The majority of the geographic regions extending across the lands of Nephi and Zarahemla were examined in *The War Against Christianity*. This body of geographical information will now be consulted in a different way. The process of elimination will be utilized to identify the only regions never explicitly described in any previous account. They are the only regions which remained uninhabited wilderness, notwithstanding the settlement of both Nephite and Lamanite lands from sea to sea. For that reason, they were the only geographical regions available to the Gadianton robbers in 12 BC, which can indeed be perceived through study of the Book of Mormon text—not according to what is provided, but rather, what is not provided.

## THE SECOND PERIOD OF THE GADIANTON ROBBERS—NEW LEADERSHIP

As previously observed in Part 3 of this book, the second period of the robbers was masterminded by a well-known group of dissenters who had lived in the land of Nephi since 74 BC.[1116] The Book of Mormon identifies them in 12 BC when they re-established Gadianton's murder cult, though not by name.[1117] It was not until fourteen years later in describing the sudden Gadianton advances of AD 3 that they are specifically identified as the Zoramites.[1118] The Zoramite identity, as outlined in the books of Alma, Helaman, and 3 Nephi, is provided in Chapter 3.5. The account of the second period of the robbers under their direction and control begins in Helaman 11:24.

The reorganization of the robbers transferred the leadership from Gadianton[1119] to the Zoramites. The transfer was only symbolic, however, because the robbers had been completely disbanded for five years when the reorganization took place. Therefore, the Zoramites simply established a new secret combination. The primary connection to Gadianton's band of robbers lay exclusively in the fact that they utilized Gadianton's plans of secret murder and robbery as their standard[1120] and proudly claimed the Gadianton name.[1121] Still, it is likely that a large percentage of the individuals who then united with them had been a part of the robber organization five years previously, at the time they disbanded.

A number of scriptural references reveal the presence and influence of the Zoramites in the land of Nephi throughout the period from 74 BC to AD 16. As noted in Chapter 3.6, their position at the head of the Gadianton robbers is one of many indications that the robbers were simply an extension of the pagan dissenters. Accordingly, the period of the robbers can be defined basically as a late pre-Christ phase of the pagan conspiracy to destroy the Christian Nephite culture. Combining this idea with other elements, which were addressed in previous chapters, the following scenario can be identified:

1. The Lamanites were the resource of choice for pagan Nephite dissenters until the conversion of largely the entire Lamanite

nation in 30 BC. Not only did the Lamanites become completely unreceptive to the arguments of the dissenters following their conversion, but they would no longer allow them to operate in their midst.[1122] The antidote for a bad case of the robbers was thus rooted in the Christian religion.

The Lamanite conversion to Christianity destroyed the robbers' influence and control among the Lamanites in two ways. First, their conversion to the gospel removed them from the insidious pagan religion upon which the robber organization rested. Second, the gospel message taught them the principles of faith in God and love for their fellow man.

2. The robbers were not all converted to the gospel through the preaching of the Lamanites. Neither did they become extinct. They merely fled into an uninhabited wilderness region of the land southward, where they could operate covertly. From their hiding places, they secretly recruited from among the rising generation of Nephites and Lamanites.

   Due to their pagan (Zoramite) leadership after 12 BC, the robbers resisted the gospel, in spite of frequent miracles of healing, fulfillment of prophecy, heavenly manifestations, and calamity. They became more and more enraged at each obstacle that delayed their rise to absolute power. Their rage was likely focused primarily upon the Christians, whose elimination they felt was completely necessary to enable them to achieve their goal.

3. Following the reorganization of the robbers in 12 BC, they had no choice but to separate themselves completely from both the Lamanites and the Nephites. In 24 BC, they had been "destroyed from among the Lamanites."[1123] In 17 BC, they were "swept away . . . from amongst" the Nephites.[1124] It was therefore out of necessity that the new Gadianton lands of habitation must be located in unsettled wilderness lands.

## GADIANTON ROBBERS—DISTINCT AND SEPARATE LANDS OF HABITATION

For the next twenty-eight years leading to Giddianhi's epistle to Lachoneus, the robbers would inhabit highland and lowland wilderness lands, which were separate and distinct from both Nephite and Lamanite lands of habitation, yet near enough to enable frequent attacks. These wilderness lands were likely undesirable for habitation prior to 12 BC. This is concluded from the fact that they remained wilderness, notwithstanding the fact that the Lamanites and the Nephites had spread across the entire face of the lands of Nephi and Zarahemla from sea to sea.

Considering the apparent proximity of these wilderness lands to both Nephite and Lamanite lands, if habitable, they would surely have been inhabited by that time. Lamanite eastward expansion out of the Lamanite heartland region in highland Nephi had been underway for seventy years. They had taken control of territory all the way to the east sea.[1125] For the Nephites, outward expansion from the Nephite heartland region surrounding the Sidon River Valley had begun sixty years earlier with Moroni's sea to sea fortification of perimeter cities.[1126]

As previously considered in Chapter 3.1, the Book of Mormon divides these wilderness regions into two subsets, denoted by the terms "mountains" and "wilderness." The distinction is first made in the 11th chapter of Helaman. Three verses in the book of Helaman and two in 3 Nephi provide five references to these mountain and wilderness regions as being distinct from one another.[1127] The two regions may have been contiguous with one another, or in other words, a single region containing both highland and lowland portions. They may also have been considered as separate, but bordering regions.

The reference provided in 3 Nephi 3:20 describes the robber lands in connection with sending an army to attack them in the wilderness. It was the people's desire to "go up upon the mountains and into the wilderness" to "destroy them in their own lands." From this description, it is concluded that "mountains" referred to precipitous mountain regions, and "wilderness" referred to dense forest lowland regions, neither of which had ever been settled by Nephites or Lamanites.

## THE CRITICAL IMPORTANCE OF COMPLEMENTARY DATA

Geographical concepts and relationships, which are observed or identified in one account within the Book of Mormon, should generally agree with similar data contained in other accounts pertaining to the same region. An idea or impression perceived through the reading of one account will in many cases be reinforced, refined, or augmented by a second account. As multiple descriptions for a region are merged into one, the one or two-dimensional image is transformed into a multifaceted image. The new perspective may then become beneficial in the understanding of yet other related geographical relationships. Occasionally, however, the initial impression is nullified, or must be revised because of conflicting information contained in the second account.

## DEALING WITH CONFLICTING GEOGRAPHICAL INFORMATION

In the event of conflicting geographic statements—which seldom occurs—the text must be scrutinized carefully to choose which statement is more compatible with other related information. A simple example of this is found in Alma 51:25–26, with respect to the city of Nephihah. It concerns conflicting statements surrounding Lamanite troop movements after Amalickiah's army attacked and took possession of the city of Moroni. Verse 25 states that they did not attack Nephihah at that time, whereas verse 26 states that they did attack. The correct answer may appear to be obvious, but there are two opposing statements, and a choice must be made, unless additional information is provided later in the account. In this specific case, the correct answer is indeed verified later in the account of the war—Amalickiah did not attack Nephihah at that time.[1128]

As deliberated in the previous chapter, the phenomenon of additional information, which sometimes calls for a revision of the initial statement, is observed in the account of the second period of the robbers. In that account, which begins in 3 Nephi 3:23, the geographical boundaries of the region of Nephite gathering to defend against the robbers are initially set forth. The boundaries defined in that verse must then be reduced, as required by later events, which took place during the course of the war, and according to specific statements made in the account.

## THE REGION OCCUPIED BY THE ROBBERS—PROBLEMS GENERATED BY THE ABSENCE OF GEOGRAPHICAL INFORMATION

The Book of Mormon provides no specific geographical location for the wilderness region(s) inhabited by the robbers during the second period, which began in 12 BC. A relative location within, or adjacent to known regions is not given—like the one provided for the Nephite region of gathering in AD 17.[1129] Neither is a specific location within the land of Zarahemla or Nephi provided, as in the geographical description of Jershon "on the east by the sea" and "on the south of the land Bountiful."[1130] In the absence of such geographical information, a more extensive process must be utilized to identify the location of their highland and lowland wilderness lands.

## NO IDENTIFIED WILDERNESS WITHIN THE LAND OF ZARAHEMLA

As considered in Chapter 5.2 above, Alma 50 describes a period of accelerated growth and development across the land of Zarahemla. It began in 72 BC as an essential element in Chief Captain Moroni's defensive plan. The direct result of such phenomenal growth was the elimination of virtually all wilderness from the greater land of Zarahemla during the following sixty–year period. On the basis of such remarkable and purposeful expansion, it is unlikely that any significant bodies of wilderness were available for habitation by the robbers within the land of Zarahemla between 12 BC and AD 25—with the possible exception of the Guiana Highlands, as they are known today.

This high level of development across the land of Zarahemla is further corroborated by the statement in 3 Nephi 4:2 that "there were no wild beasts nor game in those lands which had been deserted by the Nephites."[1131] It is concluded that in 12 BC when the robbers first began to occupy the wilderness, there was no wilderness anywhere within the greater land of Zarahemla, again with one possible exception.

## THE MOUNTAIN WILDERNESS OCCUPIED BY THE ROBBERS

According to the Book of Mormon, the land of Zarahemla extended across the northern portion of the land southward, from the narrow strip of wilderness northward to the narrow neck of land, and from the west sea to the east sea. Every significant geographical component within the proposed region as known today should be taken into account. One such component is the Guiana Highlands, which today extends across largely the entire state of Bolivar in Venezuela. It is a large mountainous region, comprising approximately a fourth of Venezuela, much of which is difficult to traverse. A portion of this region at the southeast corner of the state is known as Gran Sabana. There, the Pacaraima mountain range, which extends into southwestern Guyana and northern Brazil, is punctuated by 115 tepuis, which jut upward like "islands in the sea," ranging in height from 3,000 to more than 9,000 feet above sea level. Gran Sabana contains the greatest concentration of tepuis within the entire highland region.

A tepui—also referred to as a mesa—is a tabletop mountain with vertical sidewalls. The tepuis vary greatly in size. The largest, Auyan Tepui, from which Angel Falls plummet from an elevation of 8,040 feet, has a surface area of 270 square miles. In comparison, the tallest tepui, Cerro Roraima, rises to 9,220 feet above sea level, but has a surface area of only twelve square miles. It might well be concluded that the structure of the tepuis, which are capped by extensive plateaus, embody the very essence of the description given in 3 Nephi 3:20: "Now the people said unto Gidgiddoni: Pray unto the Lord, and let us go up upon the mountains . . . that we may fall upon the robbers and destroy them in their own lands."

There is no earlier reference in the Book of Mormon to a mountainous region between Jershon and the Sidon River—likely because the region was not directly involved in any event prior to the Gadianton Robber War. If the proposed geography is correct, however, then it was a part of the Nephite world. The many tepuis in Gran Sabana, and other prominent features, such as Angel Falls, would have certainly been observed by Nephites, Lamanites, and robbers as they passed by.

Due to the precipitous nature of the region, it would have posed a barrier to passage. Generally, the rivers are not navigable, due to the many waterfalls. The region would have provided many places of refuge, including a large number of cave systems, some of which are networks that meander for thousands of feet with multiple intersections.

Today, there are few roads across the Guiana Highlands. Fortified cities were likely not required along that interval of the Narrow Strip of Wilderness. According to the projected geography, this highland region lies immediately to the north of the narrow strip of wilderness between the city of Aaron in the land of Jershon and the city of Manti at the headwaters of the Sidon River. It is a viable candidate for the mountainous region occupied by the robbers. See Map 17.0 on the following page.

## CONCLUSIONS

The western edge of the highlands of Nephi were initially considered to be the location of the robbers' mountain sanctuary, notwithstanding the following reservations:

1. The Andes, which comprise the inhabited region of highland Nephi, have a linear configuration.

2. No discrete body of mountains is set apart or distinguishable from highland Nephi.
3. The Andes are remote from the projected region of gathering along the Orinoco River.

Ultimately, the Guiana Highlands were chosen according to the following factors:

1. No reference to the region is otherwise provided in the Book of Mormon.
2. The region borders on the projected region of gathering.
3. The highlands of Guiana are well-known today for the impediment they pose to passage.
4. The tepuis are riddled with caves.

Given the above considerations, it is concluded that the mountain wilderness inhabited by the robbers between 12 BC and AD 25 was the Guiana Highlands, or a portion thereof.

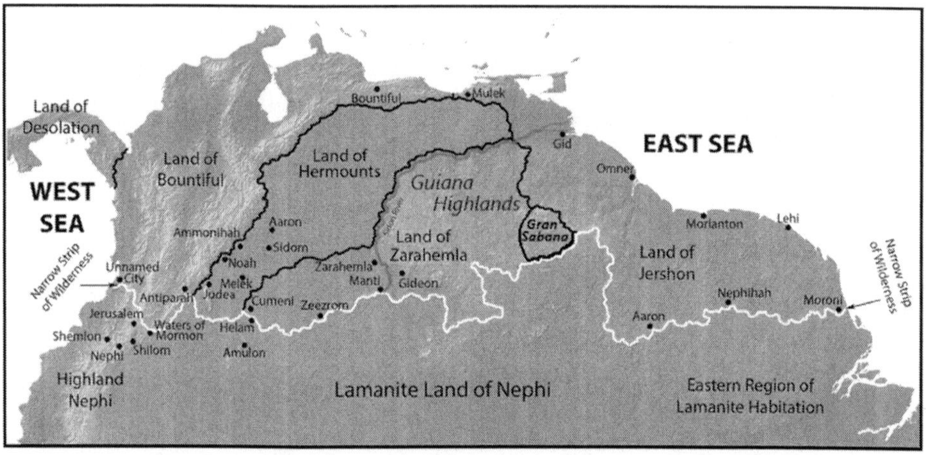


**MAP 17.0: The Guiana Highlands—**
**The Mountain Wilderness Inhabited by the Gadianton Robbers**

# CHAPTER 5.6

# SEARCHING FOR ROBBER LANDS WITHIN THE LAND OF NEPHI

IN THIS CHAPTER, ALL geographic data for the various lands of Lamanite habitation are considered. As in the previous chapter with respect to the Nephites, each will be examined for the purpose of identifying any significant regions to the south of the narrow strip of wilderness that were never inhabited by the Lamanites. Again, the process of elimination will be utilized to identify any wilderness region, which may have been available for habitation by the robbers.

## LAMANITE LANDS OF HABITATION

The geographical description in Alma 22:27–29 provides essential information pertaining to three geographic regions occupied by the Lamanites. Verse 27 describes the lands ruled by the father of Lamoni and Anti-Nephi-Lehi[1132] in a sea to sea configuration. If correct, then with respect to the east wilderness, it is a reference to lands claimed, but not yet possessed—a logical assumption according to the following reasoning:

The narrow strip of wilderness was described in the above passage as dividing the land of Nephi from the land of Zarahemla. Verse 27 refers to the king sending "a proclamation throughout all the land, amongst all his people who were in all his land, who were in all the regions round about, which was bordering even to the sea, on the east and on the west." It might thus be concluded that the Lamanites had explored the full extent of the narrow strip of wilderness, for they knew it extended from sea to sea. However, the initial, three-year period of Lamanite occupation of the east wilderness did not begin until 81 BC[1133]—following the death of the king.[1134] Thus, they considered the entire region from sea to sea to belong to them, though they had not yet taken possession of the east wilderness.

Another possibility for this reference to Lamanite habitation from sea to sea prior to 81 BC may lie in the intertwining of two accounts—the account of Alma preaching the word of God across the land of Zarahemla[1135] and the account of the sons of Mosiah preaching to the Lamanites in the land of Nephi.[1136] Mormon had written about the 81 BC destruction of Ammonihah and the flight of the Lamanites into the east wilderness in Alma 16. The description of the king's lands in Alma 22 is in essence a flashback and may therefore simply reflect Mormon's understanding of Lamanite lands after they were fully expanded. It is completely understandable, because he was working on both sides of the expansion, This idea was initially addressed in *The War Against Christianity*.[1137]

## PERMANENT HABITATION OF THE EAST WILDERNESS

Permanent Lamanite habitation in the eastern portion of Nephi did not take place until 77 BC.[1138] Not until after the permanent settlement of the east wilderness did Lamanite lands of habitation extend all the way to the east sea to include the eastern region located to the south of Jershon. Truly, this was a time of great geographical transformation —in Nephi as well as Zarahemla.

Alma 22:27 considers the overall relationship between Lamanite and Nephite lands. Most significantly, it describes the "narrow strip of wilderness," which divided the two nations, and "which ran from the sea east even to the sea west." Verse 28 then outlines the distribution of the Lamanites in the western region during the reign of the Lamanite king, identifying specific wilderness regions surrounding highland Nephi, which were inhabited by "the more idle part of the Lamanites" at that time.

In Alma 23, highland Nephi, the center of Lamanite government, is identified, not as wilderness, but as a metropolitan region containing a number of cities. The cities of the heartland region included seven cities inhabited by those Lamanites "who were converted to the Lord." [1139] Also included within the region are other largely unnamed cities and villages inhabited by Lamanites under the influence of the Amalekites and Amulonites.[1140]

As described in Alma 22 and 23, Lamanite lands of habitation within the land of Nephi included the following two regions prior to 77 BC:

1. Traditional coastal wilderness lands extending both northward and southward from the narrow strip of wilderness, from the location of Lehi's landing on the south to an unknown point on the north.
2. Highland Nephi, where the Nephites had lived from *ca.* 589 to *ca.* 200 BC. In 81 BC, the Lamanites temporally occupied the region eastward of Manti, and in 77 BC, the following third region of habitation was permanently added:
3. Eastern Lamanite lands of habitation bordering Jershon on the south, which included the coastal lands along the east sea. From that time forward, the borders of Nephi extended all the way to the east sea.

## THE WILDERNESS ON THE NORTH BY THE LAND OF ZARAHEMLA

After eliminating the three regions of Lamanite habitation from consideration, there remains a large geographical region located between the east and west regions, which is never identified as a region of habitation in the Book of Mormon. In fact, it can only be identified through this process of elimination, for it is not the focus of any account. It is briefly mentioned only twice prior to the Gadianton Robber War, both times in a very ambiguous and unrevealing way.

The only account that directly involves the region is found in Alma 16. In that account, which takes place in 81 BC, a Lamanite army destroyed the city of Ammonihah and fled southward with captives taken from the neighboring land of Noah. When they reached the narrow strip of wilderness, they turned toward the east wilderness, instead of returning to highland Nephi.[1141]

Giving heed to a revelation from the prophet Alma the Younger, Chief Captain Zoram and his sons marched with their armies into the "south wilderness." There, they intercepted the Lamanite army, rescued the captives, and drove the Lamanites deep into the east wilderness. This account does not provide enough information to identify the "south wilderness" as a discrete body of wilderness, separate and distinct from other wilderness regions, such as the east wilderness, or the "wilderness of Hermounts."[1142] The term "south wilderness" could have been a reference simply to its location, in relation to the limited configuration of Zarahemla, as settled at that time. It could have been a reference to the narrow strip of wilderness, which lined the southern border of Manti.

For this reason, Alma 22:27–29 once again provides unique and crucial information that cannot be found elsewhere in the Book of Mormon. Two geographical statements in the passage explicitly describe the "south wilderness" in two different perspectives:

1. Verse 27 refers to it in a Lamanite perspective as "the wilderness which was on the north by the land of Zarahemla." At that time, Zarahemla was limited to the region immediately surrounding the Sidon River Valley. The boundaries would not be extended to the east and west seas until 72 BC, when Moroni established fortified cities along the borders of Zarahemla.
2. Verse 29 then describes the south wilderness in a Nephite perspective: "nevertheless, the Nephites had taken possession of all the northern parts of the land bordering on the wilderness, at the head of the river Sidon." This statement reveals the relative location of the south wilderness, but gives no indication of its dimensions or boundaries, especially considering Zarahemla's limited dimensions prior to the expansion of 81 and 72 BC.

It is concluded that the south wilderness, as identified in these verses, lay to the south of the narrow strip of wilderness at Manti by the headwaters of the Sidon River. From there, it is projected to have extended westward toward the borders of highland Nephi possibly as far as the cities of Amulon and Helam or beyond, and eastward to the eastern lands of Lamanite habitation.

## FINAL CONCLUSIONS

Throughout Nephite history, this central region within the land of Nephi remained a large, uninhabited wilderness stretching westward from the east region all the way to highland Nephi. To most travelers who passed by in the narrow strip of wilderness, it was like a row of unread and virtually incomprehensible books, sandwiched between the two bookends of Lamanite habitation. The region thus constituted a great void in the geographical center of Nephi, certainly for the reader of the Book of Mormon.

If the robber lands were indeed located within this central wilderness of Nephi, they would have bordered the highlands of Nephi on the east, the eastern lands of Lamanite habitation on the west, and the Nephite cities of Manti, Zeezrom, and possibly Cumeni on the south. This central location would have made it convenient for the robbers to conduct frequent raids against both Lamanite and Nephite cities, towns, and villages. See Map 18.0 below.

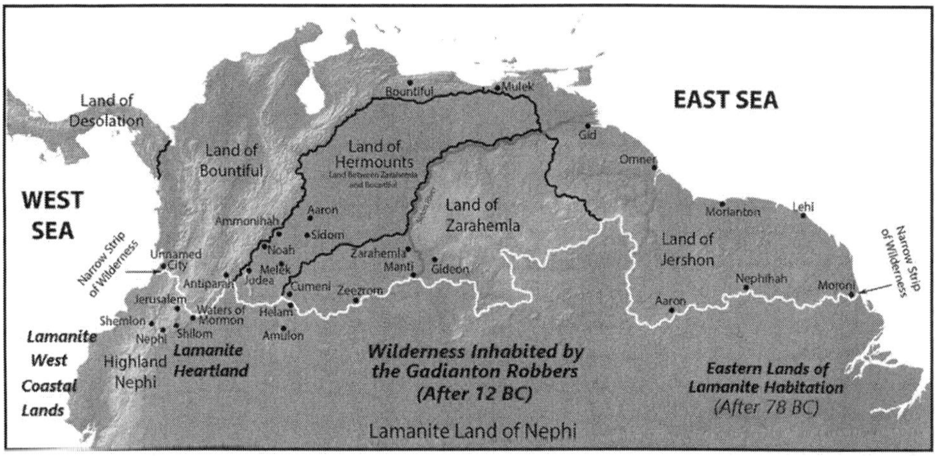


MAP 18.0: The Lowland Wilderness Inhabited by the Robbers

CHAPTER 5.7

# KEY FEATURES OF THE PROPOSED GEOGRAPHICAL MODEL—AS IDENTIFIED IN THE PRESENT DAY

THROUGHOUT THE FIRST 634 years of their history in the Western Hemisphere, the Nephites sequentially occupied two geographical regions within the land southward. During the first approximately 400–year period, their lands of habitation were limited to highland Nephi. Then, in *ca.* 200 BC, the people of Mosiah departed from the land of Nephi[1143] and made their way through the great wilderness to the Sidon River Valley, where they discovered the people of Zarahemla.

After they settled in the land of Zarahemla, it was only a matter of time until the region they claimed would be greatly expanded under the direction of Moroni, the head of the Nephite military.[1144] Ultimately, Zarahemla would extend from the east sea to the west sea, and from the narrow strip of wilderness on the south[1145] to the narrow neck of land on the north,[1146] all of which was confined within the land southward. In 55 BC, the first migrations into the land northward took place, though the Book of Mormon account remained focused exclusively within the land southward.

## THE GEOGRAPHICAL LOCATION OF THE LANDS OF ZARAHEMLA AND NEPHI

In 1976, twenty-five years before *The War Against Christianity* and *The Gadianton Robbers* were conceived, the greater land of Zarahemla was first considered by this author to occupy the entire northern portion of South America. The narrow neck of land bordering Zarahemla on the north was believed to be the Isthmus of Panama. The southern boundary of the region—the narrow strip of wilderness—was later identified as a composite hydrographic divide, which for the most part marks the northern perimeter of the Amazon River drainage basin. See Map 19.0 at the end of this chapter. According to the proposed geography, highland Nephi was located on the west in the present-day Andes Mountains, immediately to the south of the same hydrographic divide. See Map 18.0 at the end of the previous chapter. Following the *ca.* 200 BC departure of the Nephites into the wilderness, the Lamanites took control of the land of Nephi. Afterward, they did not change the name of Nephi, but likely maintained the name to commemorate their success in driving the Nephites out of the land.

Nephi's boundaries were expanded from sea to sea to facilitate the Lamanite wars against the Nephites. Afterward, the newly claimed region is projected to have encompassed the entire Amazon drainage basin, extending all the way to the river's mouth at the east sea. The new Lamanite holdings, which included highland Nephi, were thus added to their original west coastal lands. From that time forth, Lamanite lands would extend from sea to sea. Following the subsequent expansion of Zarahemla, the border between the two lands also extended from sea to sea.

Focusing upon this entire region as it is known today, a number of major geographic features are considered below. Their location and physical characteristics correspond remarkably well with the proposed geography. Readers may determine for themselves if the features provide any degree of confirmation for the proposed geography.

## SPECIFIC COMPONENTS OF NEPHITE GEOGRAPHY

The continent of South America and the Isthmus of Panama are the most conspicuous geographic features of the region, as addressed previously in this book and in *The War Against Christianity*. In combination with the North American continent, as described in Alma 22:32, they provide the necessary components for a hemispheric geography. Due to the fundamental nature of these three primary constituents and their familiarity among Latter-day Saints, they are not included in this chapter.

It is noted that the first three features presented below—the hydrographic divide, the Orinoco (Sidon) River, and the Llanos—were first considered in *The War Against Christianity*. They are included here for the purpose of listing all of the geographic features that correlate so well with the geography of the land southward.

## HYDROGRAPHIC DIVIDE

The narrow strip of wilderness[1147] was identified In *The War Against Christianity* as the hydrographic divide, from which the Orinoco flows. The divide forms the northern boundary of the Amazon River drainage basin. It could be utilized "to move along a tangible and discernible pathway through the wilderness,"[1148] notwithstanding the density of the rainforest between highland Nephi and the city of Zarahemla. Adjustments to the course of travel could be made any time a stream was encountered by simply moving upstream to the stream's headwaters, then continuing on in the initial direction of travel, whether eastward toward the headwaters of the Sidon, or westward toward the highlands of Nephi.

Knowledgeable travel between the city of Nephi and the city of Zarahemla was made possible only by following the one visible and unchanging geographic feature in an otherwise incomprehensible region. Prior to Alma the Elder's identification of the keys necessary for travel along the narrow strip of wilderness, the wilderness could be traversed only by wandering determinedly for many days without any definite sense of direction, other than that which was provided by the sun. For the Lamanites, their wilderness illiteracy ended with the acquisition of Alma's geographic knowledge in 121 BC.[1149] For the Nephites, it did not end until 77 BC, when Mosiah's Sons returned to Zarahemla from their mission to the Lamanites.[1150]

## THE ORINOCO RIVER

As considered in *The War Against Christianity*, the Orinoco River is identified as the Sidon River, according to the proposed geography. It lay at the center of the greater land of Zarahemla and largely defined the border between the land of Zarahemla and the land of Hermounts. See Map 19.0 on page 288.

## THE LLANOS

The Llanos is a tropical grassland region extending across large portions of Colombia and Venezuela today. Bordering on the East Andes mountains, it is identified as the wilderness of Hermounts, which in the Book of Mormon account was located to the north and west of the city of Zarahemla.[1151] Considering the geographic placement of the city of Zarahemla on the banks of the Orinoco River, the Llanos region corresponds precisely with the wilderness of Hermounts. The Llanos extends northward from the northern edge of the Amazon Basin to within a few miles of the Caribbean coast, much of it bordering along the Orinoco on the west and north. (See Map 19.0.)

## THE AMAZON RAINFOREST

The lowland wilderness region inhabited by the robbers was identified in the previous chapter through a process of elimination. The region is located eastward from highland Nephi, southward from the headwaters of the Sidon River, and westward from the eastern Lamanite lands of habitation. (See Map 19.0.) Though the Nephites and Lamanites had spread across the entire face of the lands of Zarahemla and Nephi from the west sea to the east sea, these lands remained wilderness. Because of their nutrient deficiency with respect to the growing of crops, they remained available to the robbers at that time, notwithstanding their proximity to the heartland regions.

According to the proposed geographic model, this region is known today as the rainforest region drained by the Rio Negro, a tributary of the Amazon River. The river runs black in color, a result of abundant plant tannin, which is constantly produced by the tropical rainforest. The soils of the region are infertile, having been depleted by natural rainforest growth processes. According to one source, "The nutrient deficiency of the soils along the shores of the Rio Negro makes the river known by Indians as the River of Hunger."[1152] The conditions found in the region today correlate well with the barren condition of the wilderness inhabited by the robbers between 12 BC and AD 25, as considered in the previous chapter.[1153]

## THE GUIANA HIGHLANDS

The highland wilderness region inhabited by the robbers is projected to have been primarily that portion of the Guiana Highlands which is located within the country of Venezuela. As considered previously in Chapter 5.5, the flat-topped mountains of this region, which are located primarily in Gran Sabana, are considered most likely to have been the mountain wilderness occupied by the robbers.

The region lies to the north of the hydrographic divide separating the Amazon watershed from the rivers to the north. Some of its rivers flow northward into the Orinoco River. Others flow eastward to empty directly into the Atlantic Ocean at various points between the Orinoco and the Amazon.

In the perspective of travelers, however, this mountainous rainforest region is a continuation of the lowland Amazon rainforest. The two regions blend into one another, and at their common border look essentially the same. Similar to the Rio Negro, most of the rivers of this highland region have dark, tea colored waters, due to the tannin from the luxuriant tropical foliage.

## THE MARONI AND COURANTYNE RIVERS

Bordering the country of Suriname on the east and on the west, there are two rivers, which are known today as the Maroni and the Courantyne. Considering the uniqueness of the two names, especially in combination,[1154] it is obvious the rivers were named by the native cultures, which inhabited the Americas before the AD 1492 arrival of the Europeans. The location of the rivers in northeastern South America places them within the Nephite land of Jershon, according to this geographic model. It is proposed that the rivers received their names from the Nephites during the developmental period of the land Jershon, which is recorded in detail in the Book of Mormon.[1155]

Thus is provided a logical explanation for the fact that the two rivers bear the names of Chief Captain Moroni and Alma's youngest son, Corianton. As recorded in the book of Alma, the two men were directly involved in the early events in Jershon.[1156] The morphology of the two names at the time of the European arrival was essentially unchanged from the Book of Mormon account. It is concluded that the rivers were named at that time, and that subsequent to the fall of the Nephites, the names were passed down from generation to generation until the arrival of the Europeans.

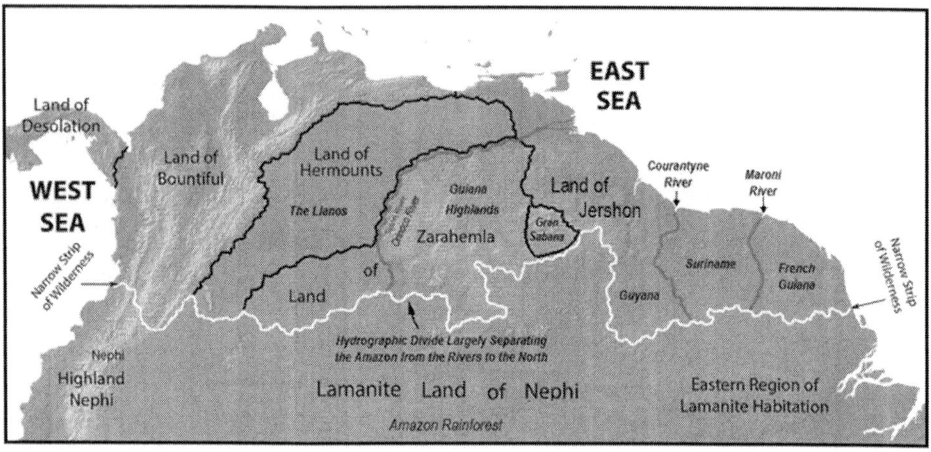


**MAP 19.0: Present-Day Rivers, Landforms and Biomes in the Land Southward**

1. Hydrographic Divide Separating Major River Systems
2. Orinoco River
3. Llanos of Venezuela and Colombia
4. Guiana Highlands
5. Amazon Rainforest
6. Maroni and Courantyne Rivers

APPENDIX A

# HYPOTHESES PROPOSED IN THIS BOOK

FIVE HYPOTHESES WERE ADVANCED in *The War Against Christianity*,[1157] which are reviewed as follows: Hypothesis 1 theorizes the time and the scope of the Nephite "transgression," as referenced in 3 Nephi 5:12. Hypothesis 2 postulates a Jaredite origin for the Order of Nehor. Hypotheses 3 and 4 propose the means by which the cult was transferred from the Jaredites to the Nephites, and from the Nephites to the Lamanites. Hypothesis 5 sets forth the idea that the narrow strip of wilderness was a hydrographic divide separating river drainage basins.

## THREE ADDITIONAL HYPOTHESES

Three hypotheses are submitted in this book:

1. The location of the wilderness lands occupied by the second generation of Gadianton robbers.
2. The location of the region of gathering according to the Proclamation of Lachoneus.
3. Concerns the names given to two rivers in northeastern South America.

## HYPOTHESIS 6: THE LOCATION OF GADIANTON ROBBER LANDS

*(PART 3, CHAPTER 3.1 AND PART 5, CHAPTERS 5.5 AND 5.6)*

### *THE HIGHLAND WILDERNESS REGION*

During the second Gadianton robber period (12 BC–AD 25), the robbers inhabited a perpetual wilderness region. It was a large mountain and lowland wilderness region which extended across portions of Zarahemla and Nephi. The mountain wilderness region was located immediately north of the narrow strip of wilderness. It was positioned between the Sidon River and the land of Jershon. See Map 17.0 at the end of Chapter 5.5. This highland wilderness is never referred to in the Book of Mormon, except as the mountains inhabited by the robbers.

*THE LOWLAND WILDERNESS REGION*

Lying immediately to the south of the narrow strip of wilderness, the lowland wilderness region extended eastward from near the highlands of Nephi to an unknown point near the eastern region of Lamanite habitation.[1158] See Map 18.0 at the end of Chapter 5.6. Though it bordered upon the headwaters of the Sidon River, it was never inhabited by the Lamanites during the entire Zarahemla period.

In the Nephite perspective, this lowlying body of wilderness bordered the narrow strip of wilderness on the south—from near the city of Cumeni on the west to the borders of Jershon on the east (Map 17.0). Notwithstanding its strategic location, it remained uninhabited wilderness in AD 16, because it was a non-arable land—unfit for farming. It was sufficient for the needs of the robbers as long as they could obtain their food by attacking and pillaging cities lying to the north in Zarahemla, and cities in Nephi lying to the west and east.

## HYPOTHESIS 7: THE LOCATION OF THE NEPHITE REGION OF GATHERING

*(PART 3, CHAPTER 3.7 AND PART 5, CHAPTER 5.4)*

During the Gadianton Robber War (AD 16–25), the Nephites gathered into the Nephite heartland to defend against the Gadianton robbers. The region of gathering extended from the cities of Manti, Zeezrom, Cumeni, and near Antiparah on the south to the city of Bountiful on the north. It extended from the city of Gideon on the east to the cities of Ammonihah, Noah, and Melek on the west. It therefore encompassed the greater part of Hermounts and relatively small portions of Bountiful and Zarahemla. See Map 16.0 in Chapter 5.4.

The projected configuration was determined by the following line of reasoning: As described in 3 Nephi 3:23, the region of gathering encompassed the entirety of the lands of Zarahemla and Bountiful, and the land which lay between them. The configuration of this region is then reduced significantly, by the information contained in 3 Nephi 4:23–25.

By subsequently considering additional information supplied in the account of the war, as well as that provided in the accounts of previous wars throughout the period of the judges, the boundaries of the region are reduced even more—to encompass only the heartland region of Zarahemla. As with every other element in the geography of the Book of Mormon, the boundaries of the region are dictated exclusively by the configurations of each projected land as they exist today. Obviously, all such configurations rest entirely upon the hemispheric geography proposed by this author.

## HYPOTHESIS 8: THE NAMING OF THE MARONI AND COURANTYNE RIVERS

*(PART 5, CHAPTER 5.7)*

The Maroni and Courantyne Rivers frame the country of Suriname, on the east and on the west. Suriname is situated along the east coast of South America between the countries of Guyana and French Guiana. Not only do the two rivers bear Book of Mormon names, but names directly related to the land of Jershon. They were named by the Nephites, likely between 75 BC, when Corianton accompanied his father Alma on a mission to the Zoramites,[1159] and 67 BC, when Moroni established the fortified cities along the coast of Jershon. The names were preserved through generation after generation until the discovery of the Americas by Christopher Columbus. Today, the names remain the same—a testament to the reality of the Nephite culture and the truthfulness of the Book of Mormon.

# BIBLIOGRAPHY

1. Aesop (1867) *Aesop's Fables*, "The Fox and the Lion."
2. Ballard, M. Russell. "The Law of Sacrifice" *Liahona*, March 2002.
3. Butler, Rhett. "The Forest River—River Types," Mongabay.com. Last updated July 31, 2012.
4. Dennis, Jerry. *The Living Great Lakes, Searching for the Heart of the Inland Seas*, 2003, St Martin's Press, New York, NY.
5. Doctrine and Covenants, published by The Church of Jesus Christ of LDS
6. *Encyclopedia of Mormonism*; Twentieth Century Mormon Publications, Harold B. Lee Library, Brigham Young University; Copyright 1992 Macmillan Publishing Company [Purchased by Gale Group in 1999]; Copyright 2001 Brigham Young University [copyright transferred to BYU in 2001].
7. Holy Bible, King James Version, (1979). Published by The Church of Jesus Christ of Latter-day Saints, Salt Lake City, Utah.
8. *Journal of Discourses*, November 24, 2011.
9. Knabb, Richard D., Rhome, Jamie R., and Brown, Daniel P., Tropical Cyclone Report, Hurricane Katrina, 23–30 August 2005, National Hurricane Center, 20 December 2005.
10. Ludlow, Daniel H, ed. (1992), *Encyclopedia of Mormonism*. New York: Macmillan Publishing, ISBN 0–02–879602–0, OCLC 24502140.
11. Noah Webster's dictionary, copyright 1828
12. Pearl of Great Price, the book of Moses, (1979), published by The Church of Jesus Christ of Latter-day Saints, Salt Lake City, Utah.
13. The Book of Mormon, translated by Joseph Smith. Published by The Church of Jesus Christ of Latter-day Saints, Salt Lake City, Utah.

14. Turner, Frederick Jackson. "The Significance of the Frontier in American History," 1893.

15. Webster's Deluxe Unabridged Dictionary, copyright 1979 by Simon and Schuster.

# ENDNOTES

1 Helaman 11
2 Frederick Jackson Turner, "The Significance of the Frontier in American History," 1893. Note: This theory is one-dimensional. It does not consider other factors, such as the freedom under which the people of the United States have operated throughout their history. It does not consider the hand of God in the process.
3 Enos 1:1–3
4 Mosiah 27:1–5
5 Mosiah 27:6
6 Ibid.
7 Alma 6:7
8 See Alma 8:3, 6, 13; 15:1–3; 16:2–3.
9 The land of Manti is first mentioned in 81 BC (see Alma 16:6–7).
10 Alma 48:8; 49:3–4, 13–14
11 50:6–15
12 Alma 43:16–17
13 Alma 8
14 Alma 31
15 Alma 15:15; 16:11
16 Alma 31:3
17 See *The War Against Christianity*, Part 2, Chapters 2.3 and 2.4.
18 Helaman 1:27–29
19 Mosiah 27:6.
20 Helaman 1:23, 27
21 Mormon 1:7
22 See *The War Against Christianity*, Chapter 2.5, Amalickiah—A New Model for Deception, 105.
23 Alma 50:9–11
24 Alma 22:34
25 Mosiah 9:6–10
26 Mosiah 22:10–16

27 Ether 10:21
28 Ether Chapter 15
29 Ether 7:6; 14:6
30 Omni 1:21
31 Ether 14:22–23
32 Alma 22:31
33 Ibid.
34 Ether 9:31, 32
35 Helaman 3:5
36 Ether 11:4–7
37 Omni 1:21
38 Alma 63:4
39 The book of Ether; Alma 22:30–31.
40 Alma 22:29, 33; 50:32
41 Alma 50–51
42 Alma 52:9
43 Alma 50:28–29
44 Alma 52:9
45 Alma 52:2
46 Alma 50:7
47 Alma 50:29
48 Alma 50:33–35
49 Alma 51:30
50 See Chapter 2.3, The First Nephite Military Defeat.
51 Helaman 4:1–7
52 Mormon 3:5–6
53 Mosiah 8:6–12; 21:25–27
54 Ether 1:2; 15:33
55 See Mosiah 8:8.
56 Mosiah 8:7
57 Alma 62:45
58 Alma 63:4
59 Alma 63:5
60 Alma 63:9
61 Alma 63:10; Helaman 3:3–14
62 Helaman 3:3
63 Alma 63:8
64 3 Nephi 7:9–13, 9:9

65 The only information available concerning the existence or destruction of Jacobugath was provided by the Savior during His communication with the Nephites in the aftermath of the Great Storm of AD 34 (3 Nephi 9). The violent but just conclusion to Jacob's reign of evil is thus revealed, which otherwise is not referenced in the Book of Mormon.
66 Helaman 3:7–11
67 Helaman 6:6
68 Helaman 7:2–3
69 Ibid.
70 Helaman 5
71 Helaman 1:16
72 Alma 62:36
73 Helaman 1:15
74 Helaman 1:27
75 Helaman 1:27–31
76 Helaman 1:33
77 Omni 1:12–13
78 See *The War Against Christianity*, p. 57, paragraph 2.
79 Omni 1:14
80 Omni 1:17
81 Mosiah 3:8
82 See *The War Against Christianity*, Chapter 2.3, The Order of the Nehors.
83 Alma 1:1–6; 2:1; 14:16–18; 15:15, 16:11
84 Alma 21:4; also see *The War Against Christianity*, Chapter 2.3, p. 67.
85 Alma Chapter 43; 3 Nephi 1:29
86 3 Nephi 11:1
87 3 Nephi Chapter 8
88 Helaman Chapters 1–2
89 Helaman 6:17–31
90 Romans 6:23
91 Helaman 1
92 Alma 51:5
93 Alma 51:2
94 Alma 51:3
95 Alma 51:7
96 Helaman 1:5
97 Alma 2:1–10
98 Alma 46:4–10

99 Alma 46:1–3

100 Alma 51:13

101 Alma 61:8; Alma 62:6–9

102 See *The War Against Christianity*, p. 65, "Political Freedom—New Opportunities for Pagan Leaders."

103 See Alma 2:1–7 (Amlici), 46:1–6 (Amalickiah), 51:2–5 (king-men).

104 Alma 46:4

105 Alma 51:21; 62:9–10.

106 Infiltrating the government through Paanchi was the only legal option to gaining control of the government, though the power of a chief judge was not nearly as great as the absolute power of a king. A chief judge could be overruled by the voice of the people.

107 Not until AD 30 would anyone attempt to seize power as king. See 3 Nephi 7:9–13.

108 Alma 62:9–10: "And whosoever was found *denying their freedom* was speedily executed according to the law" (italics added).

109 See *The War Against Christianity*, Chapter 2.5.

110 Mosiah 29

111 By 30 BC, this new mindset would lead to the election of Zoramites, who apparently were not Christian. See "A Constitutional Crisis" in Chapter 1.4, "Nephi Relinquishes the Judgment Seat."

112 Mosiah 29:1–36

113 Helaman 1:8

114 A similar incident occurred at the time of Solomon's ascension to the throne. See 1 Kings 2:13–25.

115 Helaman 1:12

116 Helaman 1:9

117 Helaman 1:21

118 Helaman 2:2–7

119 See Helaman 2:3–5.

120 Helaman 2:1–9

121 Helaman 1:11

122 Helaman 2:3–5

123 Helaman 6:26

124 Helaman 1:11

125 Helaman 6:25–29

126 Helaman 6:28

127 Moses 5:49–51; 8:29–30

128 Alma 37:22, 26–29
129 Ether 8:9
130 Ether 8:17
131 Ether 9:26
132 Ether 10:34
133 Omni 1:17
134 Alma 22:30
135 Ether 7:6
136 Ether 14:6
137 Alma 37:21–32
138 Alma 37:27–29; Helaman 6:25
139 Alma 51:8
140 Helaman 3:23
141 Helaman 6:24
142 Ibid.
143 Helaman 1:4
144 Helaman 2:1
145 Helaman 2:2
146 Alma 63:13
147 Alma 63:2
148 Alma 4:15–18
149 Helaman 2:3–5
150 See Helaman 2:10
151 Helaman 2:7
152 Had Kishkumen been successful, he would have returned quickly, for he was very swift of foot (see Helaman 1:10).
153 Helaman 2:11
154 Helaman 3:20
155 Helaman 3:1–3
156 Helaman 3:17
157 Helaman 3:23
158 3 Nephi, Chapter 3
159 3 Nephi 3:24
160 See 3 Nephi 1:28–30. Though this verse refers to tactics used by the robbers to regain control after the prophesied sign at the birth of Christ had caused a great reduction of their power and influence, it likely gives insights into the methods used from the beginning of dissent, which were further developed and fine-tuned after the establishment of the robbers.

161 3 Nephi 3
162 Helaman 3:24
163 Helaman 3:26
164 Helaman 3:33
165 Helaman 3:21
166 Helaman 5:5–14. The emphasis on repentance was likely a response to the continual pagan cry that a person need not fear the justice and the judgments of God regardless of the life they lived.
167 Helaman 3:37
168 Helaman 3:37
169 Helaman 4:1
170 Alma 2:2
171 Alma 51:5
172 Alma 51:1–5
173 Alma 45:23–46:10
174 Alma 2:4. See also Alma 43:45–47.
175 Alma 46:1–7
176 Helaman 4:1
177 Helaman 4:2. This Lamanite king is not identified. It had been sixteen years since Tubaloth the son of Ammoron had sent Coriantumr against the Nephites. However, there is no way to tell if Tubaloth or his descendant was still in power.
178 Alma Chapter 47
179 Helaman 4:3
180 Helaman 4:4
181 Helaman 4:5
182 Helaman 4:5–7
183 Mosiah 26:1–5 (see verse 5).
184 Mosiah 27:1–2
185 Alma 16
186 Alma 28:1–2
187 See *The War Against Christianity*, Chapter 2.3, The Order of the Nehors.
188 Words of Mormon 1:12, 15–16
189 See *The War Against Christianity*, Appendix C, Hypothesis 4.
190 Alma 1:15; 2:2
191 Alma 2:1
192 Alma 2:4
193 Alma 2:2–7

194 Alma 2:18, 31
195 Alma 43:19–21
196 Alma 49:2–8, 14
197 Alma 46:28–29; 50:12
198 Alma 51:19
199 Alma 51:8, 17, 18, 21. "[Moroni] put an end to the stubbornness and the pride of those people who professed the blood of nobility."
200 Alma 51:20
201 Alma 62
202 Alma 59–62
203 Alma 51:6–7
204 The Sons of Helaman (see Alma 53:14–18).
205 Helaman 1:27–32
206 Helaman 1:28
207 AD 327–363 (thirty-six years) and AD 378–385 (seven years). See Mormon 2:1–2; 3:10–11; 5:1; 6:5–10.
208 Alma 16:5–8
209 See *The War Against Christianity*, p. 98.
210 Alma 49:16–17
211 Alma 61:14–21
212 Alma 2:18, 31; Alma 14:26; 17:36; 18:3; 43:50; 44:5; 49:20, 23; 51:31; 56:56; Helaman 4:13; 3 Nephi 4:10
213 Helaman 4:24–26
214 Helaman 4:13
215 Amlicite War: Alma 2:27–28; Zoramite War: Alma 43:21, 51; Amalickiah and Ammoron War: Alma 51:27; Alma 57:2, 8
216 See Helaman 4.
217 Identified in the Book of Mormon as "the land which was between the land Zarahemla and the land Bountiful" (3 Nephi 3:23), but see *The War Against Christianity*, Chapter 3.5.
218 See "Nephite Control of the Narrow Neck of Land" in Part 1, Chapter 1.4, Nephite Migrations into the Land Northward.
219 Alma 50:25–36
220 Helaman 4:7
221 As referenced in the previous section, the idea that the lands southward and northward were separated by a narrow pass, which bordered on the West Sea and an unmentioned mountain range on the east is dismissed

by Alma 50:34, which clearly states that sea bordered the narrow neck of land on both sides—"on the west and on the east."

222 Helaman 4:11–12

223 Helaman 3:33–34

224 Alma 63:4–10; Helaman 3:1–12

225 Alma 51:31; 56:56

226 Helaman 4:13

227 Alma 61:4–5, 8

228 Alma 62:6–8

229 Helaman 1:18–30

230 Helaman 4:5–7

231 Helaman 4:9–10, 14–17

232 Helaman 1:14–34

233 Alma 51:12, 23–30

234 See *The War Against Christianity*, Chapter 2.5, Amalickiah—A New Model for Deception (p. 105) and Appendix D: The Amalickiah and Ammoron Offensive—A Year by Year Account (p. 216).

235 Alma 56:31

236 Alma 52:12–13

237 Helaman 4:2

238 Helaman 4:4

239 Helaman 4:14

240 Helaman 4:15–16

241 Helaman 4:18–20

242 Helaman 4:16, 19

243 The order listed for the retaking of the cities of Gid and Mulek is not correct, based on the earlier detailed account of the Amalickiah and Ammoron War (Alma 51:26–37; 52:1–2; 53:1–6; 55:1–23). According to the account of the previous war, Mulek bordered on Bountiful. Verse 15 should therefore read, "And from thenceforth to the city Mulek; and from the city of Mulek to the city of Gid."

244 Helaman 5:14–16

245 The unnamed land lying immediately to the north of Zarahemla was identified in the previous book (*The War Against Christianity)* as "Hermounts."

246 Helaman 4:18–20

247 See *The War Against Christianity,* Chapters 2.5 and 2.6

248 Helaman 4:5

249 Helaman 5:19–21

250 Helaman 1:12

251 Helaman 4:1–4

252 The prime example of pagans joining forces to destroy a common enemy, afterwards focusing their hostility toward one another in the pursuit of total power, took place with respect to the final Nephite battle at Cumorah (see Moroni 1:2).

253 See the introduction to Part 2.

254 Alma 51:17–19

255 Alma 62:9–10

256 Helaman 7:10

257 An abridgment of Nephi's record is found in Helaman 4–16.

258 Alma 4:19

259 Helaman 4:16; 5:16

260 Helaman 5:14

261 Helaman 4:22—The reference to Lamanite wickedness was given immediately prior to their conversion to Christ.

262 Helaman 5:4

263 Helaman 5:3

264 Helaman 4:22

265 Helaman 1:2

266 Alma 2:1–7

267 Alma 51:1–7

268 Alma 51:3

269 Helaman 5:4

270 Helaman 5:2

271 The law that only descendants of Nephi were entitled to rule over the Nephites was apparently a carryover from the system of monarchy, in which "the kingdom [could be] conferred upon none but those who were descendants of Nephi." See Mosiah 25:13.

272 Alma 51:3,4

273 The Christian Nephites believed that Mosiah enacted laws through inspiration from God.

274 Helaman 5:2

275 Mosiah 25:13

276 Abraham 3:22–26; Moses 4:1–4

277 Abraham 3:27–28

278 Jeremiah 1:5

279 D&C 138:53–56

280 Helaman 5:14—This is perhaps the most important clue to suggest that the seat of government was in the city of Bountiful at that time when the Nephites had been displaced from the land of Zarahemla. Thus, Nephi resigned his post as chief judge and commenced his missionary work in the same city, rather than journeying to another starting point.

281 Helaman 5:16

282 Helaman 5:17

283 Helaman 5:19

284 Mosiah 9:6

285 Mosiah 7:6–7

286 Helaman 5:24

287 Helaman 5:24–25

288 Helaman 5:29

289 Helaman 5:31

290 Helaman 5:33

291 (Helaman 5:36–52)

292 See *The War Against Christianity*, Chapter 2.3.

293 Helaman 5:52

294 Helaman Chapter 6

295 Enos 1:20

296 The Amulonites taught the Lamanites to read and write the Nephite language. See Mosiah 24:3–7.

297 Alma 17–26

298 See *The War Against Christianity*, Chapter 2.3, "The Order of Nehors."

299 Helaman 4:8

300 Helaman 4:7

301 See Helaman 6:6 and 7:1–3

302 Alma 63:4–10

303 Alma 22:33–34; 50:32; 52:9

304 Helaman 7:1–3

305 Helaman 5:49

306 Helaman 6:1

307 Helaman 5:21–22

308 Helaman 5:35

309 Alma 31:1–7

310 Alma 15:12

311 Alma 45:18–19

312 Alma 43:4

313 Helaman 5:50

314 The platform of the robbers was a pagan religion with a hidden agenda. Like the people in the city of Ammonihah, on the surface the robbers were advancing the cause of their religion, but secretly they sought to "destroy the liberty of the Nephites" (Alma 8:17).

315 Mosiah 10:12–17

316 Helaman 11:24–25

317 Helaman 6:18

318 Helaman 6:37

319 During the post-Christ era, following the 160–year period of love and peace (see 4 Nephi 1:20–49), dissent would have yet another dynamic character, focused upon a foundation of Lamanite dissent, as in the very beginning of Nephite history (see 4 Nephi 1:20, 38).

320 See Alma 47:2; Helaman 4:3.

321 Helaman 1:9–12

322 Helaman 5:1–3

323 Helaman 6:29–31

324 Alma 54:23

325 Jacob 1:13; Mormon 1:8; 4 Nephi 1:36–37

326 Helaman 6:15

327 Helaman 1:13. See also Alma 50:37–40.

328 Helaman 8:27

329 Helaman 6:6

330 Helaman 7:3–8

331 Helaman 1:9–13; 2:1–3

332 Helaman 2

333 Helaman 3:23

334 Helaman 6:15, 18–19

335 Helaman 7:4; 9:23

336 Helaman 8:27–28; 9:25–38

337 Helaman 7:3

338 Helaman 7:4

339 Helaman 7:7

340 Helaman 7:10

341 Helaman 7:11

342 Helaman 7:13

343 Helaman 7:15–19

344 Helaman 7:20–28

345 Helaman 8:4
346 Helaman 8:2
347 Helaman 8:3. See Helaman 5:2.
348 Helaman 8:5
349 Helaman 8:6
350 Helaman 8:7
351 Helaman 8:10–11
352 Helaman 8:12
353 Helaman 8:13
354 Helaman 8:17
355 Helaman 8:20
356 Helaman 8:25
357 Helaman 8:26
358 Helaman 8:27–28
359 Helaman 9:2
360 Helaman 9:5
361 Helaman 9:12
362 Helaman 9:26–38
363 Helaman 5:18
364 Helaman 6:22, 24
365 Helaman 7:25
366 Helaman 8:13–20
367 Helaman 8:20
368 See *The War Against Christianity*, Chapter 1.1, p. 11, "Nephite Revelations Verified: Discovery of the People of Zarahemla."
369 Helaman 9:40
370 Helaman 9:41
371 Helaman 10:1
372 Helaman 10:4–7
373 Helaman 10:12
374 Helaman 10:17
375 Helaman 10:18
376 Helaman 11:1
377 Helaman 11:2
378 Helaman 11:6
379 Helaman 11:4
380 Helaman 11:5
381 Helaman 11:6

382 Helaman 11:6
383 Helaman 11:8
384 Helaman 11:9
385 Helaman 11:10
386 Helaman 11:10–16
387 Helaman 11:17
388 Helaman 11:21
389 Helaman 11:23
390 Helaman 11:10
391 Helaman 11:17
392 Helaman 11:24
393 See Chapter 3.5: "The Identity of the New Robber Leadership is Revealed."
394 Words of Mormon 1:12–16—This first instance of dissenters inciting the Lamanites to violence against the Nephites took place during the reign of King Benjamin.
395 Alma 24:1; 27:2; 43:6–8; 47:1; 48:1–3; Helaman 1:16–17
396 Helaman 11:24, 25
397 Helaman 11:28
398 Helaman 11:33
399 Helaman 11:21–25
400 Helaman 11:15
401 Helaman 11:34–37
402 Helaman 11:34
403 Helaman 11:36
404 Helaman 11:37
405 Helaman 11:25
406 3 Nephi 4:3, 19
407 Helaman 11:25
408 Helaman 2:11
409 3 Nephi 4:19–21
410 Omni 1:12–14
411 Alma 31:3; 39:3
412 Helaman 11:24–32
413 Helaman 13:2
414 Helaman 13:3
415 The entrance to the city of Zarahemla was guarded. See Helaman 1:20

416 Helaman 13:10. Samuel's actual words were that the people would be smitten less than four hundred years later (13:9) during the subsequent fourth generation (13:10). The year he was speaking of was 385 AD, which was approximately 390 years away.

417 Helaman 13:9–10

418 Helaman 13:14

419 Helaman 13:17

420 Helaman 13:30

421 Helaman 12:26

422 Helaman 13:27

423 Helaman 13:1

424 See Helaman 5:20–52.

425 1 Nephi 5:9

426 1 Nephi 4:15–16

427 2 Nephi 25:24–25

428 See Helaman 8:13–16.

429 Mosiah 2:1–3

430 Alma 25:15–16

431 Moses 5:4–7

432 (Leviticus 1–7; Mosiah 13:30

433 Ludlow, Daniel H., ed. (1992), Encyclopedia of Mormonism, New York: Macmillan Publishing, 1249. Note: Richard D. Draper made the above quote within a section of the referenced book entitled *Sacrifice in Biblical Times.*

434 Helaman 14

435 Alma 34:14

436 Alma 34:13

437 Helaman 14:11–12

438 Alma 14:5; 21:7–8; 30:13–14; 31:16;

439 Helaman 14:2–7

440 Helaman 14:20–27

441 Helaman 14:25

442 See Helaman 14:3–5.

443 Helaman 15:3, 17

444 It would also bring destruction to many that would wake up and turn to Christ, then according to the predominant cycle, yield once again to the enticements of the evil one.

445 Helaman 9:40–41; 11:18

446 Helaman 16:4
447 Helaman 10:14
448 Helaman 16:6
449 Helaman 16:5
450 Helaman 16 :6
451 Helaman 16:7
452 Helaman 16:13
453 Helaman 16:14; Luke 2:10
454 Helaman 16:15
455 Helaman 16:19–20
456 Helaman 16:23
457 Helaman 13:1–2
458 Helaman 14:2
459 Helaman 16:13, 14:6
460 3 Nephi 1:2
461 Alma 45:18 19
462 3 Nephi 1:3
463 3 Nephi 1:4
464 Helaman 16:13
465 3 Nephi 1:9
466 3 Nephi 1:1
467 Alma 45:23–46:11
468 3 Nephi 1:11
469 3 Nephi 1:13
470 Helaman 8:18–20
471 D&C 39:21
472 1 Nephi 10:4–6
473 3 Nephi 1:16
474 3 Nephi 1:17–18
475 3 Nephi 1:22
476 *I*bid.
477 3 Nephi 1:23
478 Jarom 1:13; Mosiah 29:46
479 See also Jacob 1:1; Enos 1:25; Jarom 1:5, 13; Omni 1:3–5; Mosiah 6:4
480 3 Nephi 2:8
481 3 Nephi 1:24
482 3 Nephi 1:25

483 Helaman 2:1–11. The term "Secret Society of Gadianton" is used only once in the Book of Mormon, as their leader Giddianhi referred to them in his AD 16 communication with Lachoneus (see 3 Nephi 3:9).
484 Helaman 11:24–26
485 Alma 47
486 This twofold plan of attack had first been utilized in Zarahemla during King Benjamin's reign (see Words of Mormon 1:12–18). It was also attempted by Amlici in 87 BC (see Alma 2).
487 The loss of the first 116 pages of Mormon's abridgment resulted in a limited view of Nephite history in the land of Nephi.
488 Words of Mormon 1:12, 16
489 Words of Mormon 1:16
490 Alma Chapter 2
491 Alma 2:2–7
492 Alma 2:24–27
493 Alma Chapter 62
494 3 Nephi 1:28
495 Helaman 7–9
496 Helaman 11:5–6
497 Helaman 11:10
498 Helaman 11:24
499 Helaman 11:26
500 Helaman 11:5–10
501 3 Nephi 1:26
502 3 Nephi 1:22
503 3 Nephi 1:27
504 3 Nephi 1:28
505 3 Nephi 1:30
506 Aesop (1867) Aesop's Fables, "The Fox and the Lion."
507 Mosiah 26:1–4
508 Alma 21:2–3; 43:4–6; 46:28
509 Helaman 4:1–4..
510 3 Nephi 1:28
511 See *The War Against Christianity*, Part 2, Chapter 2.4, The Zoramites.
512 Alma 43:4
513 Helaman 6:37
514 Helaman 11:24–26
515 See *The War Against Christianity*, Chapter 2.3, The Order of Nehors.

516 See Alma 1 through 28:1–10. The Amlicite War (87 BC) and the Nehor War (83–77 BC) are collectively referred to as the Nehor Wars in the previous book by this author, *The War Against Christianity*, because each was provoked by the Order of Nehor.

517 Alma 31:12

518 Alma 1:1

519 See *The War Against Christianity*, Part 2, Chapter 2.3, "The Order of the Nehors."

520 Alma 30:59; 31:3

521 Alma 31:1; see Chapter 2.7.

522 Alma 43:5–8

523 Alma 48:5; 52:20, 22, 33–35; Helaman 5:35–41; 11:24; 3 Nephi 1:29

524 Helaman 11:24–26

525 The first era of the robbers occurred in the period leading to the appearance of Christ to the Nephites.

526 Helaman 2:11

527 Helaman 11:6

528 Helaman 2:5–11

529 Helaman 3:23

530 Helaman Chapters 7–9

531 Helaman 10:18

532 Helaman 11:1–2

533 A similar series of events occurred in Ether 13:13–16.

534 Helaman 11:10

535 Helaman 11:24–26. It is not clear whether the secret plans were retrieved from the place of burial, or were obtained from other sources—the latter would seem to be the more likely scenario.

536 3 Nephi Chapter 5

537 3 Nephi 1:22

538 Helaman 5:35–52. See Part 2, Chapter 2.5. Also see *The War Against Christianity*, Chapter 2.4.

539 3 Nephi 1:28

540 3 Nephi 1:30

541 3 Nephi 2:2. The term "foolish traditions" was used frequently by pagans in describing Christian doctrine. See the last paragraph of Chapter 3.10.

542 Compare with the great falling away during the reign of Mosiah II (see Mosiah 26:1–4).

543 3 Nephi 2:11

544 Helaman 5:2

545 See Helaman 6:15–19. Seezoram's name is not provided until Helaman 9:23.

546 Helaman 6:7–9

547 Helaman 11:24–25

548 3 Nephi 1:28

549 3 Nephi 2:13

550 3 Nephi 2:14

551 See *The War Against Christianity*, Chapter 1.1 under the heading, "Nephites, Lamanites, and Mulekites," p. 13.

552 See Alma 54:23–24

553 3 Nephi 2:16

554 3 Nephi 2:12. See also Alma 2:4 (the dissenter Amlici's intent to destroy the Church) and Alma 44:2 (the anger of the Zoramite dissenters because of the Christian religion of the Nephites).

555 The implication of these verses was previously considered on the first page of Chapter 3.4.

556 Alma 43:3–4

557 Helaman 6:37

558 Helaman 3:23

559 Helaman 11:10

560 Helaman 6:37

561 Helaman 6:15

562 See 3 Nephi 1:5–9

563 Helaman 11:10

564 3 Nephi 1:28

565 3 Nephi 1:29–30

566 3 Nephi 3:1

567 Helaman 11:24–25

568 3 Nephi 2:16

569 3 Nephi 2:18

570 3 Nephi 3:8

571 Ammoron made a similar statement in his epistle to Moroni (Alma 54:21–22).

572 3 Nephi 3:9

573 Helaman 2:1–4

574 Helaman 6:26–30

575 Alma 30:53

576 Helaman 2:4
577 Helaman 6:26
578 3 Nephi 3:9
579 Genesis Chapters 9–10
580 Genesis 10:6–10. See also Joshua 24:15.
581 Genesis 10:10
582 Genesis 11:4; See verses 1–9.
583 Ether 1:33
584 Ether 1:5, 33–43
585 Ether 1:33–36
586 See *The War Against Christianity*, Chapter 2.4, The Zoramites.
587 Helaman 11:24–26
588 3 Nephi 3:10. Ethnic flattery generally revolved around the right-to-rule. Among the Lamanites it revolved around the rights of Laman as Lehi's eldest son, whereas the Mulekites were of the kingly tribe of Judah.
589 3 Nephi 3:3
590 3 Nephi 3:10
591 Genesis 49:8–10
592 3 Nephi 3:12
593 Alma 60:27; Helaman 7:4
594 3 Nephi 2:18
595 3 Nephi 3:23
596 3 Nephi 3:24
597 3 Nephi 6:2
598 Helaman 7:2–3
599 3 Nephi 3:24
600 3 Nephi 3:14
601 3 Nephi 3:15–16
602 3 Nephi 3:18
603 3 Nephi 3:19
604 3 Nephi 3:17
605 3 Nephi 1:1
606 3 Nephi 6:4–19
607 Helaman 16:10–15
608 Helaman 16:12
609 Helaman 6:15–19
610 Helaman 11:10
611 Helaman 11:17

612 Helaman 11:21
613 Helaman 11:22
614 Helaman 11:23–24
615 Helaman 11:34
616 Helaman 11:24–26
617 Helaman 11:24–35
618 Helaman 11:36
619 3 Nephi 2:18–19
620 3 Nephi 3:10; Alma 51:8; Mosiah 10:15–17
621 Israel's frequent incontinence is revealed in the Old Testament books of 1 and 2 Samuel, 1 and 2 Kings, and 1 and 2 Chronicles.
622 Helaman 15:3
623 The Order of Nehor and the Zoramite cult
624 Helaman 12:1
625 Helaman 12:4–5
626 Helaman 12:3
627 3 Nephi 3:16
628 3 Nephi 3:20
629 Ether 1:34
630 The Book of Exodus
631 2 Nephi Chapter 5
632 Omni 1:12–13
633 Mosiah 5:1–4.
634 Mosiah 23:26–29
635 Alma 16:5–6; 43:23–24
636 Alma 27:4–15
637 Helaman 11:8
638 Mormon 5:1
639 3 Nephi 3:21
640 Mormon 3:9–11
641 Mormon 4
642 3 Nephi 2:11
643 3 Nephi 2:12
644 3 Nephi 2:16
645 3 Nephi 2:12
646 3 Nephi 2:17–19
647 3 Nephi 3:1–8
648 3 Nephi 3:13–16, 22–23

649 3 Nephi 3:3
650 3 Nephi 4:1
651 3 Nephi 4:3
652 3 Nephi 4:2
653 Ibid.
654 3 Nephi 4:6
655 3 Nephi 4:6
656 3 Nephi 4:13
657 3 Nephi 4:14
658 3 Nephi 4:17
659 3 Nephi 3:20–21
660 3 Nephi 4:6
661 See "Apparent Infertility of the Wilderness" at the end of Chapter 3.1.
662 3 Nephi 4:16
663 3 Nephi 4:18
664 3 Nephi 4:4
665 3 Nephi 4:16–28
666 Alma 51:9 through 62:39
667 3 Nephi 4:23
668 3 Nephi 4:24
669 3 Nephi 4:26
670 This idea is further considered in Ether 8:20–26.
671 3 Nephi 4:29
672 3 Nephi 5:4–5
673 3 Nephi 6:3
674 3 Nephi 6:2
675 3 Nephi 11
676 Helaman 11:24–26
677 Helaman 11:31
678 3 Nephi 3:20–21
679 3 Nephi 4:13
680 3 Nephi 6:3
681 3 Nephi 3:8
682 Moses 7:7
683 Ether 15:29–32
684 3 Nephi 5:6–7
685 4 Nephi 1:42,44; Mormon 1:18; Mormon 2:27–28
686 Alma 45:10–11

687 Helaman 13:9–11
688 Mormon 2:10–27
689 Genesis 4:1–16
690 Moses 8:28–30
691 Genesis 4:2
692 Genesis 4:3–4
693 Genesis. 4:5
694 Hebrews 11:4
695 Moses 5:29–30
696 Genesis 4:8
697 Genesis 4:10–12; 3 Nephi 4:6. The Gadianton robbers, whose power rested upon the principle of secret murder, could not enjoy the strength of the earth and were forced to go against the Nephites in battle.
698 Genesis 4:10–12
699 Genesis 4:15
700 Alma 42:17–18
701 Alma 42:24
702 Helaman 6:26–27
703 3 Nephi 4:4
704 The curse of secret combinations, which brought about the extinction of the Nephites and eliminated Christianity from the Western Hemisphere, will be considered in a future publication.
705 See *The War Against Christianity*, Chapters 2.3 and 2.4.
706 Omni 1:14–15; Helaman 6:10
707 Omni 1:12–13; Alma 2:15
708 Omni 1:20–21
709 Mosiah 27:8
710 Mosiah 27:8–24; Acts 9:1–18
711 Mosiah Chapter 23; 24:8
712 Ether 1:12, 28
713 Mosiah 27:8
714 Mosiah 27:10
715 Alma 24:28
716 Alma 28:1–7
717 Alma Chapter 31
718 See Alma Chapters 43 and 44.
719 Helaman 2:11; 6:18
720 Helaman 11:24–25

721 Alma 48:5; 52:20. See Alma 43:6–8.

722 Alma 54:23: Amalickiah's brother, Ammoron was a descendant of Zoram.

723 Alma Chapter 49

724 See "The West Wilderness" in *The War Against Christianity*—p. 171.

725 Alma 48:9; 49:3–4, 14

726 Alma 43:4–6

727 Helaman 5:17–52

728 Alma 31:6, 32

729 Alma 45:17–19

730 Helaman 11:24–26

731 3 Nephi 1:28

732 3 Nephi 1:29

733 3 Nephi 5:6–7

734 Alma 43:6; Amalekites were of the Order of Nehor (Alma 21:4).

735 Alma 3:11

736 Alma 21:8

737 Alma 8:11

738 Alma 30:14, 16, 23, 27, 31

739 Alma 31:17

740 Compare with Amalickiah and Ammoron's 13 year period of aggression from the beginning of 73 BC (see Alma 46:1) until the end of 61 BC (see Alma 62:39).

741 3 Nephi 2:11–13

742 3 Nephi 5:6–7

743 Alma 46:1

744 Alma 62:39

745 3 Nephi 4:33

746 3 Nephi 6:2.

747 3 Nephi 6:8

748 3 Nephi 6:5

749 Proverbs 16:18

750 3 Nephi 6:12

751 3 Nephi 6:2

752 3 Nephi 3:13

753 3 Nephi 6:12

754 3 Nephi 6:10

755 Mosiah 4:21–26

756 3 Nephi 6:13
757 3 Nephi 6:15
758 3 Nephi 6:14
759 3 Nephi 5:3
760 Mosiah 25
761 Mosiah 26
762 Mosiah 26:6
763 Alma 27:1–2
764 See Helaman 12:1–2
765 2 Peter 2:22
766 Omni 1:12
767 Mosiah 18:7–17
768 Mosiah 25:14–19
769 Mosiah 25:21
770 Mosiah 5:7
771 Moses 5:6–7
772 Mosiah 2:3. According to M. Russell Ballard of the Quorum of the Twelve Apostles, under the law of Moses "there was an expansion in the number and variety of offerings under the law of sacrifice," though "everything about Mosaic sacrifice [still] focused on Christ." See "The law of sacrifice" by Elder M. Russell Ballard, *Liahona*, March 2002.
773 Mosiah 8:13–17
774 Omni 1:20
775 Omni 1:21–22
776 Ammon was the leader of the sixteen strong men, which were sent into the wilderness in search of the people of Zeniff. See Mosiah 7:2–3.
777 Mosiah 8:13–18
778 Mosiah 5:7
779 Mosiah 3:13; 4:3, 11, 12, and 20
780 Mormon 7:10;
781 Mosiah 7:13 Nephi 30:2
782 Mosiah 24:17
783 Mosiah 5:7
784 Mosiah 1:11–12; 5:7–15.
785 Alma 46:13–15
786 Mosiah Chapter 26, 27:1–2
787 Mosiah 26:4
788 Alma 1:32

789 Mosiah 26:11–12
790 Helaman 5:1–3
791 Mosiah 26:12
792 Mosiah 26:33–34
793 Mosiah 26:32
794 Mosiah 26:29–30
795 Mosiah 26:32
796 See 3 Nephi 6:14. The church was broken up in AD 30 because of "inequality," which directly violated this law of Mosiah.
797 Mosiah 27:1–3
798 Alma 1:14
799 Alma 6:1–4
800 Alma 30—note the direct involvement of the chief judge Nephihah in the protection of the Church (verse 57).
801 Alma 45:20–22
802 Alma 45:23–24
803 Alma 46:1–3
804 Alma 46:11–41
805 Nephi, the son of Helaman
806 Helaman 4:1
807 Helaman 4:1–2
808 Helaman 6:15–19; 7:4
809 Helaman 11:1–21
810 See Chapter 4.3.
811 Compare with the Lamanite conversion, which was both real and permanent.
812 Alma 4:4–5
813 Alma 3:25–4:4
814 Alma 4:6–10; Alma 1:21
815 Alma 4:4
816 Alma 4:3
817 Alma 4:19
818 Alma 7:5–6
819 This was during the period in which the Gadianton Robbers went about secretly in the land of Zarahemla. See Helaman 2.
820 Helaman 3:24–26
821 Helaman 3:33–36
822 Helaman 4:1

823 Helaman 4:1–3
824 Helaman 4:4
825 Helaman 4:5–8
826 Helaman 11:17–25
827 See Chapter 2.6 above: "A Major Shift in the Dynamics of Dissent."
828 Helaman 11:21
829 Helaman 11:22
830 Helaman 11:23
831 3 Nephi 5:1
832 3 Nephi 5:3
833 3 Nephi 3:16
834 3 Nephi 4:30–33
835 See Mormon's lamentations on this subject in Helaman 12:1–6.
836 3 Nephi 6:10–14
837 (3 Nephi 6:19)
838 See "The Reign of the Judges" in *The War Against Christianity*—pp. 63–65.
839 See 3 Nephi 6:1–4.
840 3 Nephi 6:4,9
841 3 Nephi 6:10
842 3 Nephi 6:14
843 In Chapter 3.7, see "The Previous Election of Chief Judge Lachoneus" and "A Second Possible Election Year."
844 Alma 2:1–8; 51:5–7
845 Mosiah 27:1–2
846 1 Nephi 1:18–20
847 3 Nephi 6:20
848 3 Nephi 6:24
849 3 Nephi 6:26
850 3 Nephi 6:28
851 Helaman 6:24
852 3 Nephi 7:1
853 3 Nephi 6:29
854 3 Nephi 6:30
855 3 Nephi 6:29
856 3 Nephi 6:13–14
857 3 Nephi 6:20–23
858 Helaman 1–2

859 Helaman 1:9–21

860 Helaman 2:7–11

861 The first secret combination (the Gadianton robbers) was established in 52 BC.

862 3 Nephi 6:26–30. See also 7:1–14. None of the tribes mentioned in this entire account are identified by name, that is, as descendants of the original fathers: Nephi, Jacob, Joseph, Laman, Lemuel, Zoram, Ishmael, or Mulek.

863 Helaman 2:4

864 3 Nephi 6:23–26

865 3 Nephi 2:12

866 3 Nephi 3:14

867 3 Nephi 2:14

868 3 Nephi 8–30

869 3 Nephi 7:1

870 3 Nephi 6:30

871 Alma 46:4; 47:35; 52:3

872 3 Nephi 7:11

873 3 Nephi 7:12–13

874 3 Nephi 8:12; 9:9

875 3 Nephi 6:10

876 3 Nephi 6:14

877 3 Nephi 6:20–23

878 3 Nephi 7:1

879 3 Nephi 7:2

880 3 Nephi 6:10–13

881 3 Nephi 6:14

882 3 Nephi 6:20–23

883 3 Nephi 7:1–4

884 3 Nephi 6:30

885 3 Nephi 6:13–14

886 Examples: Antionum and Ammonihah. Also see Alma 51:20.

887 Mosiah 25:4

888 Lamanites against Nephites, Zoramites against Nephites

889 3 Nephi 5:6, 7; 6:1

890 4 Nephi 1:41

891 4 Nephi 1:42

892 Helaman 11:6–10 and 24–26

893 3 Nephi 5:6–7; 6:27–28
894 Helaman 11:26
895 3 Nephi 7:6
896 Alma Chapter 51
897 (3 Nephi 3:10)
898 Alma 51:8,17; 3 Nephi 3:10; 3 Nephi 6:13, 7:9
899 Alma 46:1–7; 60:16–17; 61:4; 3 Nephi 7:12
900 Mosiah 25:2; Helaman 6:10, 8:21
901 Alma 31:1–3
902 Alma 54:23
903 1 Nephi Chapter 4
904 Alma 46:1–4
905 Alma 54:23–24
906 3 Nephi 7:14
907 It can only be assumed that Seezoram ascended to the judgment seat upon the death of Cezoram—not stated.
908 It is not directly stated that Lachoneus I ruled until AD 30. From 3 Nephi 6:1–14, it is concluded that he could have stepped down at any time from AD 26 through AD 28 (verses 4, 9), but not in AD 29 (verses 10–14).
909 3 Nephi 5 20
910 3 Nephi 5:21
911 Mormon 1:3
912 Mosiah 18:18
913 Mormon 5:12
914 Helaman 14:20–28
915 3 Nephi 6:14
916 3 Nephi 6:20–21
917 3 Nephi 7:14
918 3 Nephi 7:20
919 3 Nephi 7:21
920 Ibid.
921 Helaman 13:12–14
922 3 Nephi 7:14
923 3 Nephi 8:12
924 3 Nephi 7:14
925 3 Nephi 6:14
926 3 Nephi 7:15–26

927 3 Nephi 7:15–16

928 3 Nephi 7:19

929 3 Nephi 8:2

930 3 Nephi 8:3

931 See Webster's Dictionary, 1828 edition.

932 3 Nephi 8:6

933 3 Nephi 8:16

934 3 Nephi 8:12, 17

935 Tornados are commonly formed inside hurricanes. See Tropical Cyclone Report, Hurricane Katrina, 23–30 August 2005, by Richard D. Knabb, Jamie R. Rhome, and Daniel P. Brown, National Hurricane Center, 20 December 2005

936 Earthquakes are not accompanied by wind, lightning, and thunder.

937 3 Nephi 9:3, 9, 10

938 3 Nephi 9:4, 7

939 3 Nephi 9:5–6, 8

940 Helaman 14:23

941 Helaman 14:21–22

942 3 Nephi 8:18

943 Helaman 14:24

944 Some thought the storm lasted longer than three hours (see 3 Nephi 8:19).

945 3 Nephi 8:12

946 3 Nephi 9:5–12

947 3 Nephi 9:9

948 3 Nephi 8:11–12

949 Helaman 6:6

950 Helaman 7:1–3

951 3 Nephi 9:9. See 3 Nephi 7:9–13.

952 3 Nephi 8:22

953 3 Nephi 8:23–25

954 3 Nephi 9:2–13

955 3 Nephi 9:13–15

956 3 Nephi 9:16

957 Luke 4:17–21

958 Luke 4:28–30

959 3 Nephi 9:17

960 3 Nephi 9:19

961 3 Nephi 9:20–21
962 Matthew 26:26–28; 1 Corinthians 10:16–17
963 3 Nephi 10:2
964 3 Nephi 10:4–7
965 3 Nephi 10:8–9
966 Acts 2:22
967 See D&C 121:34–37, 40–42.
968 See the Book of Mormon, Title Page: "And now, if there are faults they are the mistakes of men; wherefore condemn not the things of God, that ye may be found spotless at the judgment-seat of God."
969 See Luke 3:21–23.
970 Luke 4:1–13; Matthew 4:1–11
971 1) John 2:13, 2) John 6:4, and 3) John 11:55
972 John 11:55; 12:1; 13:1; 18:28, 39; 19:14
973 Exodus Chapter 12
974 Helaman 14:-4
975 *Encyclopedia of Mormonism*, Twentieth Century Mormon Publications, 61–62. Harold B. Lee Library, Brigham Young University; Copyright 1992 Macmillan Publishing Company [Purchased by Gale Group in 1999]; Copyright 2001 Brigham Young University [copyright transferred to BYU in 2001]
976 Easter falls on the first Sunday following "the first full moon" after the vernal (spring) equinox.
977 Exodus 12
978 3 Nephi 7:14: "And they did stone the prophets and did cast them out from among them" (3 Nephi 7:25–26).
979 3 Nephi 11:1–10
980 2 Nephi 3:11–12
981 2 Corinthians 13:1
982 Matthew 24:14
983 1 Nephi 8–10
984 1 Nephi 11:3–33
985 2 Nephi 2:1–4; 10:1–4; 11:1–3
986 1 Corinthians 15:52; Philippians 3:20–21
987 Introduction to the Book of Mormon
988 Alma 63, Helaman 3:1–11
989 3 Nephi 11:1
990 3 Nephi 3:12–13

991 1 Nephi 16:34
992 1 Nephi 17:4–5
993 1 Nephi 17:8; 18:1–2
994 1 Nephi 18:3–23
995 1 Nephi 17:13, 18:22–23
996 The first temple of this dispensation
997 *Journal of Discourses*—Vol. 14, p. 325
998 Ibid.
999 George Q. Cannon, *The Life of Nephi, the Son of Lehi* (Salt Lake City: The Contributor Company, 1883).
1000 *Doctrines of Salvation*, Vol. 3, pp. 73–74
1001 See *The War Against Christianity*, Chapter 1.2, Nephite History in the Land of Nephi.
1002 Omni 1:12–13
1003 2 Nephi 5:1–6
1004 Mormon 1:9
1005 1 Nephi 16:10–16; Alma 37:38–39
1006 Omni 1:12–13
1007 Mosiah 25:2;
1008 Mosiah 9:4
1009 Mosiah 7:21
1010 Mosiah 22:11
1011 2 Nephi 5:7–8
1012 Omni 1:12–13
1013 Mosiah 8:7–12
1014 Ether 1:1–2
1015 See *The War Against Christianity*, Part 3, Chapter 3.3, "The Wilder ness Regions of the Land Southward," p. 153.
1016 See *The War Against Christianity*, Part 3, Chapter 3.2, "Alma Teaches the Geography of the Wilderness to the Lamanites," p. 149.
1017 See Omni 1:13; Mosiah 7:1, 2, 9, 13; 8:2; 9:3; 28:1, 5, 9; Helaman 4:4–5.
1018 Mosiah 23:36–38
1019 Alma 2
1020 Alma 16:2
1021 Alma 25:13
1022 See Map 9.0 at the end of Chapter 5.2.
1023 Alma 17

1024 Alma 22:27

1025 See *The War Against Christianity*, Part 3, Chapter 3.3, p. 169.

1026 Mosiah 27:6

1027 Alma 8:7–17

1028 Alma 31:1–4. No city is directly mentioned or referenced in the account of the Zoramites, but it is assumed the synagogues, houses, and streets in the land of Antionum (Alma 32:1) were located within a city.

1029 Alma 50:9–12

1030 Alma 2:36–38

1031 Helaman 1:27

1032 Alma 2:37

1033 3 Nephi 3:23

1034 Helaman 4:5

1035 Alma Chapter 2

1036 Helaman 1:23

1037 Alma 2:37

1038 Helaman 1:27

1039 Alma 8–15

1040 Alma 8:6 records the first reference to the city of Ammonihah in 82 BC.

1041 Alma 16:3; see also Alma 49:12–15

1042 Alma 2:20; 6:7

1043 Alma 16:1–8

1044 Alma 27:1

1045 Alma 28:1–2

1046 See Map 7.0 in the previous chapter.

1047 Alma 27:21–22

1048 Alma 43:11

1049 Alma 50:7

1050 Alma 28:1

1051 Alma 50:15, 25–36; 51:26–30;

1052 Alma 50:9

1053 Alma 27:22; 52:15–17

1054 Alma 50:10–11

1055 Bountiful was one of the four regional Nephite lands in the greater land of Zarahemla.

1056 Alma 22:29–33; 27:22; 50:32

1057 3 Nephi 3:23

1058 Alma 49:11–12: “Therefore (the Lamanites) retreated (from Ammonihah) into the wilderness.”

1059 Alma 8:3, 5

1060 Alma 16:1–10

1061 Alma 48:6; 49:12, 25

1062 Alma 50

1063 Alma 50:11

1064 Alma 22:29–33; 27:22; 50:32; 51:28, 30–32; 52:9, 15, 18, 39; 63:5

1065 Helaman 6:1–9

1066 See *The War Against Christianity*, Appendix A, Map A-6 (p. 205).

1067 Helaman 1–2

1068 See Helaman 1:19–23

1069 Helaman 1:27

1070 Helaman 4:5–8

1071 See Helaman 4.

1072 Helaman 4:9–10

1073 Helaman 4:14–16

1074 Helaman 5:52

1075 See Helaman 5

1076 3 Nephi 3:22

1077 3 Nephi 3:23

1078 3 Nephi 2:14–16

1079 Helaman 11:10

1080 Helaman 11:24–26

1081 3 Nephi 3:22

1082 3 Nephi 3:23

1083 In *The War Against Christianity*, Chapter 3.5, this land is identified as Hermounts, which was initially described as the wilderness of Hermounts when the Nephites arrived in the land of Zarahemla (see Alma 2:37).

1084 Alma 50:10–11

1085 See “The Robbers Attempt to Flee Northward in Chapter 3.8.

1086 See *The War Against Christianity*, Chapter 3.3, “The Narrow Neck of Land” (p. 184).

1087 Helaman 4:6–7; also see Part 1, Chapter 1.3.

1088 3 Nephi 3:23

1089 3 Nephi 4:1

1090 3 Nephi 4:22–23

1091 3 Nephi 4:24

1092 Helaman 11:25. See Part 5, Chapter 5.6. See also Part 3, Chapter 3.1.

1093 See *The War Against Christianity*, Chapter 3.5.

1094 3 Nephi 4:22–25

1095 3 Nephi 3:24

1096 3 Nephi 3:23

1097 3 Nephi 3:25

1098 3 Nephi 3:14

1099 Helaman 1:23, 28–29

1100 The boundaries of the four lands were set forth in *The War Against Christianity*, Part 3, Chapter 3.5.

1101 3 Nephi 3:24. See "A Primary Reason for Not Gathering in the Land Northward" in this book (Part 3, Chapter 3.7).

1102 3 Nephi 3:21

1103 Helaman 1:18

1104 Helaman 1:23

1105 Helaman 1:24–27; The term "center of the land" is used four times in this passage.

1106 Helaman 1:27

1107 Alma 2:15–27—As indicated in these verses, the Sidon River flowed northward from its headwaters at Manti, passing Zarahemla on the east side of the city.

1108 Mosiah 27:6

1109 See Alma 3–15.

1110 Alma 8:3–5

1111 Alma 16:2–4; 49:12, 25

1112 Referring to the small plates of Nephi.

1113 Referring to Mormon's abridgment.

1114 The loss of the 116 pages is painful for those who would find value in knowing in greater detail the history and geography of the land of Nephi during the initial 470-year period, as written by Mormon, the historian.

1115 See page 143 in the Book of Mormon.

1116 Alma 43:4

1117 Helaman 11:24–26

1118 3 Nephi 1:29

1119 Gadianton had organized the robbers 38 years previously in 50 BC—see Helaman 2.

1120 Helaman 11:26

1121 3 Nephi 3:9

1122 Helaman 6:37

1123 Helaman 6:37

1124 Helaman 11:10

1125 Alma Chapter 16; Lamanite eastward expansion began with the turn of events that followed the destruction of Ammonihah. See *The War Against Christianity*, Chapter 3.3, "The Expanding Political Dimensions of Nephi" (p. 160).

1126 Alma 50

1127 Helaman 11:25, 28, 31; 3 Nephi 3:20 and 4:1

1128 Alma 59:5–11

1129 3 Nephi 3:23

1130 Alma 27:22

1131 This is likely a reference to Lamanite lands of habitation in Nephi, as well as Nephite lands in Zarahemla, because after 13 AD, the Lamanites were numbered among the Nephites. See 3 Nephi 2:16.

1132 Alma 22:1; 24:3

1133 Alma 25:1–5

1134 Alma 24:3–4.

1135 Alma 4–16

1136 Alma 17–26

1137 See *The War Against Christianity*, endnote 430 on page 269.

1138 Alma 28:1–2

1139 Alma 23:8–15

1140 Alma 21:1–2 and 23:14–15

1141 See Chapter 5.1: Map 7.0.

1142 Alma 2:37

1143 Omni 1:12

1144 Alma Chapter 50

1145 Alma 22:27

1146 Alma 22:32

1147 Alma 22:27

1148 See *The War Against Christianity*, Part 3, Chapter 3.3, "Migration of the People of Alma from Nephi to Zarahemla along the Narrow Strip of Wilderness (p. 165).

1149 Mosiah 23:36–38

1150 Alma 17

1151 Alma 2:37

1152 Rhett Butler, "The Forest River—River Types," Mongabay.com, July 2012.

1153 See also Part 2, Chapter 2.1.

1154 No other rivers in the world bear the names Maroni and Courantyne, whether in combination, or individually.

1155 See Alma 31–35, 43–44, and 46–63.

1156 Alma 31:7; 43:16–17

1157 See *The War Against Christianity*, Appendix C, p. 211.

1158 The eastern Lamanite lands of habitation lay to the south of the Nephite cities of Aaron, Nephihah, and Moroni.

1159 Alma 31:7

# ABOUT THE AUTHOR

Troy J. Smith is an LDS author and researcher. Throughout the last forty-four years, he has studied the archaeology of the Americas, in correlation with Book of Mormon history and geography. His studies have been founded upon the belief that all of the major cultures of the Western Hemisphere were either biblical or Book of Mormon cultures, and that there were no pre-Adamic cultures.

Troy and his wife, Debbie, are empty nesters and live in Utah. They have two sons, six daughters, and twenty-six—soon to be twenty-nine—awesome grandchildren.

Scan to visit

troyjsmith.wordpress.com